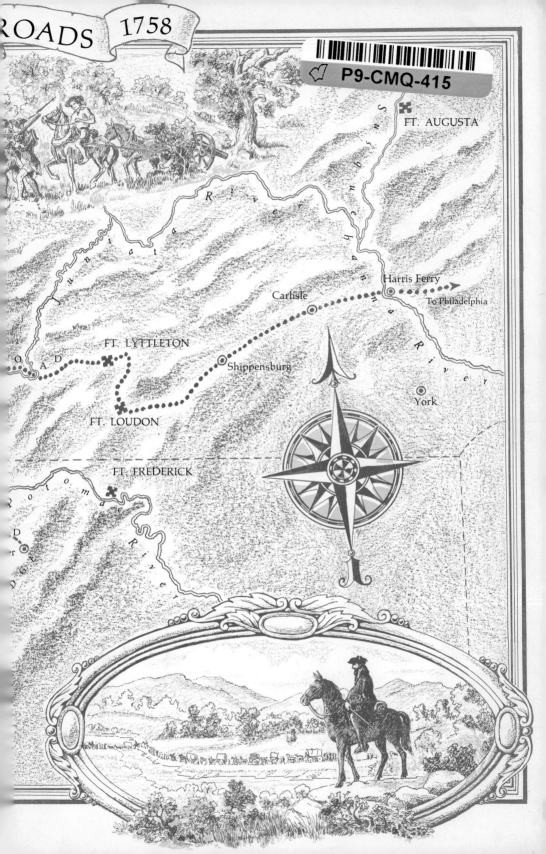

ROADS 1758

P9-CMQ-415

FT. AUGUSTA

River

Juniata

Susquehanna River

Harris Ferry

To Philadelphia

Carlisle

FT. LYTTLETON

Shippensburg

R O A D

FT. LOUDON

York

FT. FREDERICK

Potomac River

GUNS AT THE FORKS

[

THE AMERICAN FORTS SERIES
edited by Stewart H. Holbrook

Other Subjects in Preparation

FORTRESS LOUISBOURG
by Fairfax Downey

SUTTER'S FORT
by Oscar Lewis

FORT LARAMIE
by Remi Nadeau

VINCENNES
by August Derleth

FORT NIAGARA
by Robert West Howard

THE FORTS OF MACKINAC
by Walter Havighurst

FORTS OF THE UPPER MISSOURI
by Robert G. Athearn

GUNS AT

THE FORKS

Walter O'Meara

PRENTICE-HALL INC.   *Englewood Cliffs, N. J.*

Guns at the Forks
by Walter O'Meara

Library of Congress Catalog Card Number: 65-12921

Printed in the United States of America

T   37168

PRENTICE-HALL INTERNATIONAL, INC., *London*
PRENTICE-HALL OF AUSTRALIA, PTY., LTD., *Sydney*
PRENTICE-HALL OF CANADA, LTD., *Toronto*
PRENTICE-HALL OF INDIA (PRIVATE), LTD., *New Delhi*
PRENTICE-HALL OF JAPAN, INC., *Tokyo*

PREFACE

This book tells the story of two frontier forts and their part in a vast struggle between England and France for ownership of a continent. All of the action takes place in North America, chiefly at the Forks of the Ohio, where the city of Pittsburgh now stands; and most of it in a short span of about ten years.

What happened in this remote wedge of wilderness between the years 1750 and 1760 affected profoundly the course of world events. It sparked a terrible global war. It helped to decide the fate of empires. And because things turned out as they did, Americans are speaking English today—instead of French.

Our story opens on a December night in 1753 at a lonely, forest-bound outpost of the French forces on the Ohio. To understand the situation there, it is necessary to review, if only briefly, events in Europe during the preceding half century.

For many years trouble between the world's two greatest powers had proliferated from roots deep in the soil of colonial ambition and dynastic rivalry. In 1688, Louis XIV of France, having already fought two wars, detonated a third by raiding his neighbors' lands. England, backed by Spain, Holland, the Empire, and other states, promptly intervened; and the great War of the League of Augsburg was on.

This war was fought mainly on the battlefields of Europe; but in America, the colonies of England and France soon became engaged in their own *petite guerre*. Canada's great governor, the Comte de Frontenac, loosed his ferocious scalping parties on New England. Sir William Phips captured Port Royal, then almost took Quebec. In the closing years, the incomparable Pierre

Le Moyne, Sieur d'Iberville devastated the New England coast, chased the English out of Hudson Bay, and dealt a grievous blow to British power in Newfoundland.

On the continent, the fight ended in a draw. The Treaty of Ryswijk (1697) marked the end of hostilities, but neither side was really ready to quit; and only five years later England and France were again at each other's throats in the War of the Spanish Succession.

Once more it was the *Grand Monarque* who led off, this time by attempting to place his grandson Philip on the throne of Spain. England countered with her own claimant, the archduke Charles; and the armies began to march and countermarch.

The War of the Spanish Succession drew most of the nations of Europe into its vortex. It was an even bigger and more destructive war than its predecessor; and a grimmer one. This time England's objective was no longer the classic one of capturing forts and out-manoeuvering the enemy; it was the total destruction of Louis XIV's power. And this, of course, included the obliteration of French interests in the Western Hemisphere.

Hence, although the main action took place in the Rhine Delta, North Italy, and Spain, a bloody phase of the conflict—known as Queen Anne's War—was fought in North America. New France, deprived of aid from the Motherland, resorted to the only kind of fighting she was equipped to wage. She sent her raiders against the North Atlantic seaboard, hurling mixed parties of French regulars, Canadian militia, and Indians at the New England villages. And to this day, Deerfield and Haverhill are bywords for French and Indian savagery.

When the English finally launched a great land-and-sea counterattack, it came to an unimpressive end. Sir Hovenden Walker, sailing against Quebec, lost eight ships and near a thousand men in the stormy St. Lawrence. Colonel Francis Nicholson, advancing by the Hudson River-Lake Champlain route, got no farther than Lake George. There, shouting treason and jumping on his wig in rage, he turned and marched back to Albany. Of all the British attempts against New France, only a thrust against Port Royal succeeded.

On the continent and high seas, however, it was the British who were everywhere victorious; and when, in 1713, the war finally ended in a complex series of treaties known collectively as the Treaty of Utrecht, France received the short end of the stick. She ceded Newfoundland, Nova Scotia (Acadia), the Island of St. Kitts, and the Hudson Bay territory to England. She also relinquished all claims to sovereignty over the Iroquois, and suzerainty over that powerful confederation of nations passed to England. Thus, increasingly, the aftermath of European wars was felt in the American colonies of England and France.

The Peace of Utrecht lasted for almost thirty years. Then, in 1740, the male Hapsburg line became extinct on the death of Charles VI, and the succession of his daughter Maria Theresa to certain Hapsburg territories was disputed by Bavaria, Saxony, and Spain. Frederick II of Prussia, claiming part of Silesia, declared war. England and France promptly got into the struggle; and the War of the Austrian Succession took up where the War of the Spanish Succession had left off.

This time the conflict assumed a truly global character, with heavy land and sea engagements in India and the West Indies. In America—where it became known as King George's War— the fighting was on a broader scale than ever before. Canada at once sent her privateers and guerrilla bands southward. New England responded by organizing a strangely assorted army of patriots and religious bigots to march against Louisbourg, the elaborate fortress the French had built between wars on Cape Breton. Col. William Pepperrell and his unruly farms lads not only marched, but actually captured the great stronghold. And France's maritime power in America was shattered.

Desperate to recover Louisbourg, the French sent a great fleet of warships and transports, carrying 3500 men, to rendezvous with 700 militia in Acadia for an attack on the fortress. Storms and pestilence drove it back to France, however, with 3000 soldiers and sailors dead of the plague. Next spring, La Jonquière, the new governor of Canada, had no better luck: half of his fleet was lost in a sea battle with an English squadron, and the other half limped to Quebec with no further thought of giving fight to the British seadogs. And so, in frustration and humiliation, ended the French dream of retaking Louisbourg and Annapolis Royal—and after that, Boston.

On the continent, however, France's magnificent armies had come so close to victory that when, in 1748, the Treaty of Aix-la-Chapelle finally ended the war, she fared much better than at the close of the previous round. Everything she had lost in North America was, in fact, restored to her; and once again the *fleur-de-lis* floated above the massive stone ramparts of Louisbourg.

But neither France nor England regarded the Peace of Aix-la-Chapelle as anything more than a truce—a pause before the next, and probably decisive, phase of the struggle. Both sides scrupulously observed the forms of peace; but both prepared for the showdown, the final test of armed might seeking territorial supremacy.

For inevitably the naked struggle for power in Europe had broadened to a global rivalry for world markets and colonial possessions in distant corners of the earth—India, Africa, the West Indies. And of all colonial prizes, of course, the most dazzling was ownership of that vast and as yet little known domain, the continent of North America. Squabbles over successions and scraps of European territory had triggered the first two rounds of eighteenth century Anglo-French conflict; but nobody doubted what the ultimate objective of the contending powers had come to be: it was nothing less than possession of half of the Western Hemisphere.[1]

Now, quite suddenly, the focus of this titanic struggle had shifted to the heart of the North American wilderness—to the headwaters of the Beautiful River, as the French called the Ohio. And it is here that we pick up the thread of obscure but momentous happenings.

Walter O'Meara
West Redding, Connecticut
October, 1964

[1] Spain too, it should be noted, was deeply involved in what was actually a three-cornered struggle. Since earliest times, the Anglo-Spanish frontier on the Atlantic Coast had been the scene of harassment and contention. On the Gulf Coast, the French, having occupied Louisiana, were thrusting into Texas. Farther north, they were menacing New Mexico from the direction of the Missouri. Spanish claims were not, however, affected directly by the contest shaping up in the Valley of the Ohio.

CONTENTS

BOOK ONE

"Drive from the Beautiful River..."

Just as Capt. Philippe-Thomas de Joncaire, the French commander at Venango, sat down to dinner on the evening of December 4, 1753, word was brought to him that a party of Englishmen had arrived. The leader was demanding to see the commandant.

What, Captain Joncaire might have wondered, could have fetched these idiots over the mountains in the dead of winter? Into the heart of hostile country, to boot, for France and England were on terms little short of war on the Ohio River. Curious, perhaps, to learn what could be back of such insanity, he ordered the leader of the party brought in to him.

The leader turned out to be a powerfully-built young man, well over six feet tall, and not much more than twenty years of age. He introduced himself as Maj. George Washington, of the Virginia Militia. He was accompanied by half a dozen white men: Christopher Gist, a famous scout, who had guided the party to Venango; Jacob van Braam, a Dutchman who knew some French, and had come along as interpreter; and four frontiersmen, two of whom were well-known fur traders. With him, also, was a band of Indians, led by the famous Seneca chief, Half King.

After presenting himself and his companions, young Washington asked where he could find the commander of the French forces on the Ohio. He carried an important letter for the commander from His Excellency, Robert Dinwiddie, Governor of the Province of Virginia.

As Captain Joncaire sized up Governor Dinwiddie's envoy, standing stiffly in his blue-and-buff regimentals, he must have wondered at the English governor's having sent so youthful a man on such an important mission. For who could doubt that a message brought more than three hundred miles, through the most difficult kind of country, contained something of great weight? Joncaire, indeed, could almost guess what it was. A protest, no doubt, against the presence of himself and all other Frenchmen on the Beautiful River;[1] for the English had some-how got hold of the absurd idea that the whole Ohio country belonged exclusively to them. Possibly it was something stronger than a protest: a warning, or even a threat of force.

He, Joncaire, was not the proper person, at any rate, to accept such a letter. He explained that the ranking officer in those parts was Captain Legardeur de Saint-Pierre. The major would have to take his letter to M. Saint-Pierre, whose headquarters were at Fort Le Boeuf, almost a hundred miles upriver. And now, wouldn't the major and his friends join him and his fellow officers at dinner—such as it was?

Captain Joncaire had little, indeed, to offer his unexpected guests. He had been on short rations for a long time, subsisting on little else than Indian corn and meat without salt. And the brandy supply was so low at Venango that the neighborhood Indians were boiling the old casks and inhaling the vapor. But of wine, at least, there seems to have been an ample supply; and a few bottles served to break down the reserve that naturally marked the opening exchanges of two such essentially antagonistic parties. In his journal of the expedition, Washington wrote:

> The wine, as they dosed themselves plentifully with it, soon banished the restraint which at first appeared in their conver-sation; and gave a license to their tongues to reveal their senti-ments more freely.

It may be doubted, however, that so experienced a backwoods diplomat as Captain Joncaire said any more than he intended to the purposeful young Virginian. The Joncaires—father and three

[1] La Belle Rivière was the usual French name for the Ohio, including the Allegheny.

sons—were all famous for their skill in dealing with the Indians; and Washington's host at the moment had scored some especially fine successes for the French side. Just that same year, indeed, he had won over the powerful Miami—a great blow to the English in the contest for Indian allies. Wine or no wine, therefore, it is highly unlikely that Captain Joncaire failed to say precisely what he wished to say—and with calculated effect on his Indian listeners—when he genially assured Washington:

"It is our absolute design to take possession of the Ohio—and, by God, we will do it!"

He even explained just how they would do it. The English, he said, were too slow-moving for the French. They could never agree among themselves on anything, every colony at odds with all the others. They had twice as many men in the field as the French, to be sure; but the French, with only one master to obey, could act swiftly, hit hard.

The Ohio country, Joncaire informed his guests over the *vin ordinaire*, was French by right of discovery and occupation. Two thousand Frenchmen—troops with artillery and fort-building equipment—had entered the country the previous summer and would return in the spring. The Beautiful River was French, and it was going to remain French.

These forthright remarks aside, Captain Joncaire treated his visitors "with the greatest complaisance." But his Gallic courtesy did not deter him from trying hard to subvert Washington's Indians. Half King, a staunch friend of the English, had come to Venango for the express purpose of returning a French "speech belt"—sign of an open diplomatic break. Joncaire skillfully evaded accepting it. He went to work on Half King and his followers with gifts, liquor, and persuasive promises. And such was his skill that, when Washington was ready to leave Venango, the Indians were not at all sure they wanted to go with him.

It was eleven o'clock before a start was finally made—very late for wilderness travelers, who were usually on the road by three in the morning. And then it was with an unwelcome escort of four French Indians headed by a mysterious M. La Force. Four days later, having been hampered all the way by snow, rain, and heavy going through swamps and mud, the little party rode wearily into the headquarters of the French forces on the Ohio.

Fort Le Boeuf gave Washington his first glimpse of just how serious the French were about seizing and holding the Ohio country. Venango, after all, had been nothing but a stockaded cabin—the former house of John Fraser, a Scotch gunsmith and trader. Joncaire, a friend of Fraser's had good-naturedly ousted him, run up the French flag, and moved in with a few half-starved troops. Washington had not been much impressed by the place.

But Le Boeuf was something quite different. Here was a proper fort, designed by military engineers, built of stout materials, and —the ultimate symbol of territorial possession in the wilderness—armed with brass cannon. It was hard, tangible evidence of military occupation; and Washington made some notes that—who could tell?—might have a future usefulness:

> Four houses compose the sides. The bastions are made of piles driven into the ground, standing more than 12 feet above it, and sharp at the top: with portholes cut for cannon and loopholes for small arms to fire through. There are eight 6-pound pieces mounted, two in each bastion; and one piece of 4-pound before the gate. In the bastions are the guardhouse, chapel, doctor's lodging, and the commandant's private store: around which are laid platforms for the cannon and men to stand on.

In a clearing around the stockade huddled some log barracks, stables, and the usual dog-ridden Indian village of bark huts. On every side rose the forest—dark, restless, interminable, silently awaiting the turn of great events.

The weary Virginians were cordially welcomed to Fort Le Boeuf by its commander. With a faint hint of youthful condescension, Washington described him as "an elderly gentleman with much the air of a soldier." Legardeur de Saint-Pierre was that—and much more. An able, resourceful, courageous man, he had traveled far and suffered much in the service of France. Only the previous year he had wintered on the Canadian prairie, a good two thousand miles from Montreal. In search of the Western Sea, he had ascended the Assiniboine and sent his canoes up the Saskatchewan to within sight of the Rockies. And now, having just completed a hard, fast journey from Montreal, it was Legardeur de Saint-Pierre who faced George Washington in perhaps the most fateful confrontation yet to take place on the North American continent.

Washington was twenty-one years old at this time, full of personal ambition, determination, and lofty moral sentiments. That he was a youth of unusual qualities must have been plain to Saint-Pierre; but he was a youth, nevertheless, and a rather emotional and unpredictable one, at that. Saint-Pierre might have forgiven a dry comment on British effrontery in sending so raw and inexperienced an envoy to treat with His Majesty Louis XV's Commandant on the Ohio. But if he had any reservations, he was too much "the elderly gentleman" to express them for history.

The meeting was conducted in an atmosphere of impeccable courtesy. Washington presented his credentials and was graciously received. After the preliminary amenities, a translator was sent for. Saint-Pierre then asked to be excused, and retired with his interpreter to study Governor Dinwiddie's letter.

It is not recorded what his private reactions to this document were, but they might well have been apoplectic. For this, word for word, is what his translator spelled out to him:

> Sir:
>
> The lands upon the Ohio in the western parts of the colony of Virginia are so notoriously known to be the property of the Crown of Great Britain that it is a matter of equal concern and surprise to me to hear that a body of French forces are erecting a fortress and making settlements upon that river in H.M.'s Dominions . . .
>
> If these facts are true and you shall think fit to justify your proceedings, I must desire you to acquaint me by whose authority and instructions you have lately marched from Canada with an armed force and invaded the King of Great Britain's territories . . . that according to the purport and resolution of your answer I may act agreeably to the commission I am honored with from the King my Master . . .

Following these vague threats, Governor Dinwiddie came to the point with a direct demand for the "peaceful departure" of all the French from the Ohio. Legardeur de Saint-Pierre listened impassively; and as he listened, the cold war that had been waged between the empires of France and Great Britain ever since the sham treaty of Aix-la-Chapelle, suddenly reached the ignition point. This was no longer the pseudo-friendly language of diplomacy. This was nothing less than a rude and insolent ultimatum.

• 2 •

At this time, both France and England were asserting title to vast stretches of the continent; exactly how vast neither could define, for territorial claims were based on an ignorance of North American geography that was truly colossal. Thus an English map in 1738 showed Lakes Huron, Ontario and Erie stacked one on top of another, skipped the Ohio River altogether, and depicted the Mississippi emptying into the Gulf of Mexico after a brief run of sixty miles. Mercator's error in placing the source of the St. Lawrence River in what is known today as Arizona was prolonged into the late seventeenth century. Early English maps actually ignored the Atlantic Coast range, but showed a chain of mountains running due east and west, with the Mississippi Valley extending in the same direction!

The French, who went everywhere and saw everything, had a somewhat better idea of how the land lay; but even they could be guilty of gross errors in cartography. Thus the geographer, Jalliot, drew a map of the Great Lakes which ignored Lake Michigan and showed Green Bay on Lake Huron. And this despite the fact that the French had long been using both the Chicago and St. Joseph portages!

Such ignorance, however, did not stop either power from laying claim to huge slices of the North American land mass. With the British, it seems to have been a matter of simply seeing it first—even though the view might be from the pitching deck of a ship at sea. Actually setting foot on land was not considered necessary to prove occupation, and the coasting voyages of the Cabots were considered sufficient to confer title to everything west of the Atlantic seaboard.

Later on, royal charters carved up the continent and awarded the pieces to individual colonies. Thus in 1750, Virginia, citing her charter of 1609, claimed to be bounded on the north by

Maryland and Pennsylvania, on the south by Carolina, and on the west "by the South Sea, including California."[2]

The French, taking natural exception to this light-hearted parcelling out of God's acres, stated their own position in the flattest of terms: "England has no rightful titles to North America except those which may be granted her by France." Disregarding the aboriginal inhabitants, she rested her own claims to vast stretches of wilderness on the old legal maxim, "What belongs to nobody is given to him who possesses it." And she could support her stand with a history of exploration and military occupation extending back to earliest times.

Not long after Columbus dropped anchor off a West Indian island, French ships were searching for cod along the eastern coast of America. In 1524, Giovanni da Verrazano made the first voyage of discovery for Francis I, examining the Atlantic coast from North Carolina to Maine. Ten years later, Jacques Cartier entered the Gulf of St. Lawrence. The following year Cartier sailed upriver as far as the site of Montreal, where he wintered after erecting a cross with the King's arms affixed to it, and taking possession for France.

In the French view, this was certainly *bona fide* occupation; and a long line of explorers followed Cartier, to clinch their nation's territorial claims. In 1603, Samuel de Champlain founded the colony of Montreal and mapped the Atlantic Coast as far south as the Charles River. After him came an endless cavalcade of intrepid explorers, traders, and missionaries: Nicolet, Radisson and Groseilliers, Jolliet, Jogues, Marquette, Vérendrye, Duluth, Menard, Allouez, and many more, including Washington's host at the moment, Legardeur de Saint-Pierre.

Before the century's end, Robert Cavelier, Sieur de La Salle, descended the Mississippi and met his tragic death in what is now Texas—having established France's principal claim to ownership of the Ohio country. After La Salle, the tide of exploration swelled and spread to every corner of the continent.

[2] England also based her claims on a somewhat involved line of legal reasoning. The Iroquois, it was pointed out, had subdued all other tribes as far west as the Mississippi. By the Treaty of Utrecht, England had assumed "sovereignty" over the Iroquois. Therefore her jurisdiction extended to all tribes subject to the Iroquois, and included all lands west of the mountains.

By 1743, the commandants had sighted the Big Horn Mountains, a hundred miles east of present Yellowstone Park. Their canoes and bateaux were everywhere on the Great Lakes, and on the Mississippi, Illinois, Wabash and Maumee Rivers. Their relentless search for a Northwest Passage had carried them far into the modern provinces of Manitoba and Saskatchewan.[3]

While the French were thus ranging the continent, the British remained rooted to the coastal strip. Governor Byrd of Virginia complained, "Our country has now been inhabited for more than 130 years, and still we hardly know anything of the Appalachian mountains, which are nowhere more than 250 miles from the sea." As for what lay beyond, only a few long hunters and fur traders had ever ventured so far, and they were notoriously close-mouthed about what they had seen. Another Virginia governor, Alexander Spotswood, was quite unaware in 1720 of any French settlements south of the Great Lakes.

It could be said for Governor Spotswood, however, that he at least had curiosity. He wondered what lay on the other side of the Blue Ridge, and he organized an expedition of fifty men and a great many pack horses to find out. But the expedition got no farther than the Shenandoah River, where the King's health was drunk in champagne and a large variety of liquors. After a leisurely return, the Governor reported to the Lords of Trade that he had reached a point only five days' march from Lake Erie!

Except for an earlier probe by Abraham Wood, in search of the South Sea, this was the only organized British attempt before 1750 to explore the mysteries beyond the "never-ending mountains."[4] Then, as the middle of the century neared, and the big push of settlers pressed against the "fall line" and toward the passes of the Alleghenies, a sudden interest dawned in the dis-

[3] Between 1732 and 1734, the French trader and explorer Pierre Gaultier de La Vérendrye had established important trading posts—Fort St. Pierre, Fort St. Charles, Fort Maurepas, and Fort La Reine—between Lake Superior and Lake Winnipeg. In 1720 the French had a post at the Forks of the Platte.

[4] On the Great Lakes, however, English traders had penetrated the West as far as Lake Huron. In 1686 Governor Thomas Dongan of New York sent a strong expedition in their support. It was captured by the French near Detroit.

tant Valley of the Ohio. A fever of land speculation gripped the colonies. Rich and powerful citizens, foreign promoters, even fur traders and trappers, began to talk only of land titles, surveys, purchases, and Indian treaties for the acquisition of great tracts of wilderness. Simultaneously, there developed a sudden official interest in tramontane territory—and a vast concern about what the French were up to in those mysterious regions.

In this, however, traders from Virginia, Carolina, and Pennsylvania were far ahead of the Provincial authorities. For a long time, they had carried on their own strenuous, and sometimes bloody, war for a foothold on the Ohio. Hundreds of them, including the Irishman George Croghan, "King of the Traders," were in competition to the knife with the French *coureurs de bois*. The Indians, frequently split into tribal factions, took sides. Violence was common. Frenchman were massacred and their furs confiscated. English traders were seized and sent to the French mines in the West.

But the French, locked in a grim European war with the British, were fighting a losing battle in the Ohio Valley. With their ports blockaded, they were unable to import Indian trade goods, and had to charge exhorbitant prices for what little they could offer. It was inevitable that British guns and ammunition, blankets, gew-gaws, and rum should win. One after another, the Indians defected to the English side. By mid-century the Pennsylvania and Virginia traders definitely had the upper hand.

All this backwoods turmoil received little official attention, however, from the Colonial governments. Aside from a few negotiations to protect their trade in peltries and some bribes in the form of "presents" and rum, the Provincial authorities did little to consolidate the British hold on the broad, empty Valley of the Ohio. It took the sudden rise of the land companies to bring that about.

Of these, the most famous and most important historically was the Ohio Company, formed in 1747 by London and Virginia speculators, and granted 500,000 acres of land by the British Crown. In return for this grant, the Company promised to seat a hundred families on the Upper Ohio within seven years. It also contracted to build a fort and maintain a garrison for the protection of the settlers. For the first settlement, a tract of 200,000 acres between the Monongahela and Kanawha Rivers was chosen.

No sooner had George II signed the grant, than the Ohio Company went into action. Two large cargoes of Indian trade goods were ordered from London. At Logstown[5] deals were made with the Indians—who were naturally not uninterested in this wholesale give-away of their ancestral hunting grounds. And Christopher Gist was dispatched on two explorations of the country north and south of the Ohio.

On his first trip Gist went as far as the falls of the Ohio, where Louisville now stands, and visited Indian towns, including one near Muskingum. Here he met a white woman, Mary Harris, captured at the age of ten, who "wondered how the white men can be so wicked as she has seen them in these woods." When Gist returned to his own house on the Yadkin River, he found that the Indians had killed five people on a nearby farm and frightened his own family away to Roanoke. Along with a good deal of fresh information about the Ohio country, he brought back a mammoth's tooth weighing four pounds.

Gist's second trip took him down the south side of the Ohio as far as the Kanawha, where he chisled on a rock:

The Ohio Company
FEBy 1751
By Christopher Gist

Gist's reports determined the location of the Ohio Company's fort and settlement. A site was chosen near the Forks of the Ohio. A road was started from Wills Creek, head of navigation on the Potomac. Trade goods for the Indians began to arrive from England. Everything was going very well, indeed, when the bad news from the North reached Williamsburg.

• 3 •

Paris had not been watching British activity on the Ohio placidly. While the English colonists were puttering about the coastal plain with their farming, trading, shipping, and town-

---

[5] Logstown, or Chiningué, was an old Indian trading village and council town, about fifteen miles below the Forks of the Ohio.

building, the agents of New France were ranging the interior of
the continent and scattering their forts and settlements from
Quebec to New Orleans. As early as 1726, the Jesuits in Louisiana were planting oranges, figs, sugar cane, and indigo; and
regular shipments of "casket girls" were arriving from France
to provide the settlers with wives. On the Mississippi, near
present St. Louis, Fort Chartres with a garrison of two companies
of infantry protected the settlements along the river, among
them Kaskaskia, a thriving village of farmers. Detroit was a
palisaded town of 500 inhabitants. In the lead mines at Galena,
200 miners and 500 slaves labored for the French Crown. Around
Vincennes on the Wabash, St. Joseph's, Peoria, La Pointe, and
many other outposts, missions were beginning to thrive, and settlements springing up. Slowly, the commandants and habitants
were building the vast inland empire that had been the dream of
LaSalle. And now, with the British in virtual control of the Ohio,
the dream was in mortal peril.

For whoever commanded the Ohio, it had become clear,
held the key, not only to the Ohio Valley itself, but to the
basin of the Mississippi and the watersheds of the Illinois,
Wabash, and Maumee Rivers as well. There were other roads to
the interior, to be sure; the much-traveled one, for instance,
by way of Detroit and the Miami portage. But with the Ohio in
their possession, the British could interdict these routes and cut
Canada's lifeline with Louisiana. Command of the Beautiful
River, indeed, was vital to the very existence of New France.

Oddly enough, France was slow in coming to a realization
of this terribly important fact. Partly, perhaps, because the
Iroquois stood in the way, few French soldiers, settlers, or even
traders had filtered into the Upper Ohio country. But the influx
of English fur hunters—combined with an advancing tide of
British settlers toward the passes of the Alleghenies—could no
longer be ignored. Both nations were plainly on a collision course,
and it became every day more apparent that the final crash
would take place on the Ohio, perhaps near its headwaters.

Against this background of impending crisis, the abiding
policy of the French in North America became the defense of the
Beautiful River. La Salle had long ago laid down the hard outlines of this policy; by 1720 Iberville had given it substance

with his plan for key forts at the mouths of the Missouri, Ohio, and Arkansas; and now the Comte de Galissonnière, Governor General of New France, enunciated it clearly in a *mémoire* of 1750: "A free and certain passage from Canada to the Mississippi is an absolute necessity." Having settled on this line, the French acted swiftly.

The first thing Galissonnière did was to send a military expedition under Capt. Céloron de Blainville[6] to take formal possession of the Ohio country for France. It was a rather formidable force, comprising 20 regular troops, 180 Canadian militia, some cadets, and 30 Indians. Second in command was the same Philippe Joncaire who was to receive Washington at Venango. Céloron launched his canoes on the Allegheny after a difficult portage from Lake Erie, buried a lead plate claiming the country for France, and proceeded to the Forks of the Allegheny and Monongahela. At the Indian village of Logstown, just below the Forks, he encountered a party of six English traders with fifty horses and 150 packs of furs. Céloron took a polite but tough line with them. He packed them off with a letter to the Governor of Pennsylvania that clearly gave notice of French territorial claims. The letter read:

> We, Céloron, Captain, Knight of the Military Order of St. Louis commanding a detachment sent by the Marquis de la Galissonnière, Governor-in-Chief of New France, have on the banks of the Beautiful River summoned the Englishmen whom we found in an Indian town situate on the banks of the Beautiful River, to retire with all their effects and baggage to New England on pain of being treated as interlopers and rebels in case of refusal; to which summons they have answered that they are going to start for Philadelphia, their country, with all their effects.

Céloron then proceeded down the Ohio, burying lead plates at intervals (one of which was dug up by the Indians and sent to William Johnson[7] at Albany), and nailing the King's arms to trees. To the Indians he read long speeches prepared by Galissonnière,

[6] Sometimes called Céloron de Bienville.
[7] Sir William Johnson, famous Commissary of Indian Affairs, long exerted a powerful influence among the Six Nations and other tribes in behalf of the British.

and passed out brandy and wampum. The Indians responded none too cordially with speeches and salutes of musketry—in one case, Céloron notes somewhat ruefully in his journal, from guns loaded with ball.

The last lead plate was buried at the mouth of the Miami River. Céloron ascended this river as far as he could, then burned his canoes and started across country on horseback to Detroit. After a journey of 1200 miles, he was finally back in Montreal with anything but an encouraging report on his trip. He summed up his dim view of the situation on the Ohio in a single paragraph:

> All I can say is that the nations of these places are very ill disposed against the French and entirely devoted to the English. I do not know by what means they may be reclaimed . . . Our traders can never give our merchandise at the price the English do.

The British traders had, indeed, done their work well on the Ohio; and the Marquis de Jonquière, who had now succeeded Galissonnière as Governor, decided to act on instructions from Paris. These instructions were simple and to the point: *"Drive from the Beautiful River any European foreigners, and in a manner of expulsion which should make them lose all taste for trying to return."*

Jonquière asked for regular troops from France with which to carry out this stern order, but he died suddenly, without having expelled a single British trader from the Ohio country. A hard blow, nevertheless, was struck at English pretensions in that region—although from an unexpected quarter.

At a town on the Miami River with the mellifluous name of Pickawillany, scores of Pennsylvania and Virginia traders were now meeting and trading with the Ohio Indians. Heavily fortified, and flying the British colors, Pickawillany had become a center of English power and the focus of Indian rebellion against the French. So galling was its presence to Quebec, indeed, that Jonquière had made plans to wipe it out with a force of a thousand Canadian militiamen. These plans fell through, but Pickawillany was not to escape its evil day.

The job of destruction was carried out by a band of tough

Ottawa and Chippewa from around Michilimackinac. Led by the Frenchman, Charles Langlade, they attacked the town when most of the traders and Indians were away hunting. A handful of defenders including five white men, put up a brief fight, then surrendered with a loss of fifteen Miami and a white trader. After pausing long enough to boil and eat the Miami chief Old Britain (the French called him La Demoiselle), the raiders burned the traders' cabins, hoisted two French flags above the fort, and made off with five white prisoners.

So matters stood on the Beautiful River in the summer of 1752. After Jonquière's death a new Governor General of Canada was appointed. His instructions were to reverse his predecessor's policy of exterminating the Indian rebels. The new line was: treat the savages as friends, forgive past offenses, bring the western tribes back into the French fold. There was to be no reversal, however, of the policy of driving out the English. "We are not opposed to our Indians trading with the English," Paris observed dryly, "but we are opposed to the English trading on our lands."

At this time, France and England were still at peace, to be sure; but it was a peace that deceived nobody. The world was rushing toward war, and the most explosive spot on the globe now happened to be the Forks of the Ohio. Here would start the conflict between the world's two greatest powers. And here, under the walls of a wilderness stronghold called Fort Duquesne, would be enacted some of the most dramatic episodes in that colossal Anglo-French struggle for the ownership of a continent.

• 4 •

In the Marquis Duquesne, Sieur de Menneville—for whom the future fortress at the Forks would be named—Louis XV had an able and energetic leader of his North American forces. Duquesne was an experienced naval officer who had seen action in a great sea battle and had commanded the large naval base at Toulon. He was a man accustomed to making swift decisions and carrying them out with every resource at his disposal. The easy-going Canadians resented his haughty bearing and strict discipline, but when he issued orders they snapped to attention. Duquesne had a way of getting things done. France could hardly have asked for a better man to defend her claims in America.

When he arrived at Quebec in July, 1752, Duquesne sized up the situation and saw that events of incalculable importance were in the making. The time for aimless skirmishing in the bush had passed. If the slow, steady tide of British power were to be halted short of the mountains, if French forts and settlements from the St. Lawrence Valley to the mouth of the Mississippi were to be made secure, a blow of the first magnitude would have to be struck. What Duquesne decided on was nothing less than a systematic, full-scale military occupation of the Ohio country.

But first it was necessary to mobilize Canada's slender resources, organize an army, and win Indian allies. In any all-out struggle with the English, the odds were indeed heavily against the French. The whole of Canada could muster no more than 55,000 souls—as against more than a million for the British colonies, 40,000 for tiny Rhode Island alone. Not only did the colonies outnumber New France twenty to one, but they were incomparably richer in food supplies, manufactures, transport, credit, everything needful to a country in a state of war—including overwhelming sea power. To make matters worse, Duquesne arrived in Canada to find the government reeking with graft, the army's morale depressed to a point of near-mutiny, and the whole country on the verge of starvation.

From such a beginning, how did one go about attacking the strongest nation on earth? Duquesne started with the army. He beat it into shape so relentlessly that by autumn he had in hand a reasonably dependable force of regulars, militia, and reserves. To this force he could add the fighting men of powerful Canadian Indian tribes—and, he could hope, the strength of new Indian allies in the West. On one front he could rest easy: his communications were well protected by such formidable strong points as Quebec, Montreal, Fort Niagara, and far out on the sea road to France, the great fortress of Louisbourg.

Before the first snow fell in Canada, Duquesne had settled on his plan of invasion. A vast yet simple plan, deriving from the earlier grand strategy of La Salle, Talon, and Frontenac, it

envisioned the building of a chain of forts down the Ohio and
Mississippi Rivers to the Gulf of Mexico. The key to such a system would be an impregnable stronghold at the Forks of the
Ohio. Such a fort, planted where the Allegheny and Monongahela
joined to form the Ohio, would shield the center of the French
position against the advance of the English frontier. At the same
time, it would deny the English colonists access to the West by
the principal routes from the Atlantic coastal strip. And, of
course, it would dominate the entire country eastward to the
mountains and westward to the Mississippi.

As early as 1750, Paris had suggested to Vaudreuil, then
Governor of Louisiana, that a post be built on the Ohio, "before
the English do," to secure the communication to Canada. Now
Duquesne received specific instructions to establish such a stronghold. The North American specialists in Paris even chose the
exact site on which he was to build it: at the old Indian trading
village of Logstown, about fifteen miles below the confluence.
Once this key fortress had been constructed, another at the
mouth of the Scioto was to be added. But first it would be necessary to build several smaller forts to guard the invasion route
between Lake Erie and the Forks. And all this would have to be
accomplished in one summer; for lightning rapidity was im-
perative.

Such were the Marquis Duquesne's orders, as he landed in
poor, corrupt, starving, near-mutinous Canada and prepared
for the invasion of the Ohio Valley.

· 5 ·

As commander of the expeditionary force, Duquesne called
in the veteran Pierre-Paul de la Malgue, Sieur de Marin, from his
post at distant Green Bay.[8] For his second in command he chose

[8] Pierre-Paul de la Malgue, Sieur de Marin, had spent many years at French
posts in the West. In 1727 he was at the Sioux post at La Baye (Green
Baye); in 1730 among the Folies Avoines in Wisconsin; in 1739–40 at
Rock River and La Baye; in 1745 he commanded an expedition against
Saratoga; in 1747 he was in command at St. Joseph River. Marin had
reoccupied his old Sioux post at La Baye when, in 1752, he was called to
the Ohio.

young, brilliant, immensely rich Michel-Jean-Hugues Péan—a selection that was not uninfluenced, the gossipy Capt. Francois Pouchot's memoirs suggest, by the Governor's admiration for Péan's attractive wife. To Marin he entrusted over-all direction of the field operations, to Péan the difficult business of supply and transport. In Quebec, he himself wrestled with the problems and frustrations of a large-scale offensive.

Besides the usual ones, these included a few of a special nature. There was the tireless cupidity of all ranks of Canadian officers and officials, from the Intendant François Bigot down to the most obscure clerk. There was Bigot's jealousy and double-dealing. There was a woeful lack of supplies and arms—in the whole colony, Duquesne could round up no more than a couple of 6-pounders and seven 4-pound guns. There was an equal shortage of food for his troops.

But Duquesne was a hard-driving man. In spite of graft, famine, and Bigot's under-cutting, he succeeded in accumulating arms, ammunition and equipment for an invasion army; and "a prodigious number of canoes and bateaux" in which to send men and supplies down the lakes. Food he wrested by force from recalcitrant farmers or bought from English traders who, no less rapacious than the Canadians, were quite willing to sell provisions to their enemy. By early spring he had gathered a reasonably well-equipped striking force of 400 regulars, 5000 militia, and 600 Indians.

Now time was of the essence. With France and England still technically at peace, Duquesne's army could enter the Ohio Valley without expecting to meet any opposition from British forces. But once war was declared, he would have the overwhelming military resources of the thirteen English colonies arrayed against him, not to mention the power of the British fleet. His only hope was to move with lightning speed, build his forts, and install his garrisons on the Ohio before the British even suspected what was happening.

He planned his campaign accordingly. His timetable called for occupation of the Ohio Valley by the end of the year 1753.

Duquesne did not even wait until spring to launch the first wave of the invasion. On February 1, an advance party of 250 men left Montreal under Lieut. Charles Dechamps de

Boishébert. This detachment made a landing on the south shore
of Lake Erie, near present Westfield, New York. Here a back-
breaking portage—it rose a thousand feet in eight miles—led
to Lake Chautauqua. The route was then down Conewango
Creek and the Allegheny River to the Ohio. It was the same route
that Céloron had taken in 1749.

Duquesne's plan was to establish a beachhead here, build
a fortified supply depot, and provide a base for 2000 invasion
troops. Boishébert's pioneers were well along with barracks and
storehouses when word came from Montreal to halt all work.
Duquesne had learned of a better way to enter the Ohio country.
The new route left Lake Erie about 35 miles farther west, from
the harbor of Presqu' Isle, where the city of Erie, Pa., now stands.
From Presqu' Isle, a level portage brought one to Rivière-aux-
Boeufs (French Creek). Then the way was open by canoe and
pirogue down the Allegheny to the Ohio. This would be the invasion route.

Boishébert accordingly broke camp and embarked his men
for Presqu' Isle, where he landed May 3. A little later, a detachment of 70 specialists under the engineer of the expedition,
the Chevalier François Le Mercier, arrived and began to lay
out the fort. They were followed early in June by the main
invasion force under Captain Marin.

Marin appears to have been a difficult man. Nobody under-
stood the Indians better; Duquesne remarked that he had been
born with a hatchet in his hand and with a flour sack as a diaper.
And nobody questioned the hard-boiled old campaigner's ability
as a soldier. But Marin, alas, had a talent for rubbing people—
especially his own officers—the wrong way. He was hot-tempered,
suspicious, tactless, and—Duquesne again—"half-ferocious" in
his dealings with friend and foe alike. Nor did the fact that
he was now old and sick do anything to sweeten his disposition.

Yet, Marin had his own ways of getting things done, and
his men were still fresh. They worked hard, even "with gaiety,"
Péan reported. The country around Presqu' Isle was pleasant and
full of game, the bay teeming with fish. The Indians—especially
their women—were friendly. And for once there was enough to
eat and drink. To the incessant crash of falling trees, the walls

of the little stronghold on the high bank overlooking Lake Erie went up rapidly. On August 3, Marin was able to write Duquesne that Le Mercier had made splendid progress, and "the fort at Presqu' Isle is finished."

Like most French forts on the frontier, Presqu' Isle was built according to the principles laid down by the great military engineer Vauban, adapted to wilderness needs and conditions. For Presqu' Isle, however, Le Mercier employed a style somewhat more elaborate than usual. Instead of the regulation picketed wall or stockade, adequate defense against Indian attack, he laid up horizontal log walls about ten feet apart, and filled the space between with earth. The resulting work was strong enough to resist not only small arms, but the portable cannon of a frontier army.

We have a number of on-the-spot descriptions of Fort Presqu' Isle, not always in full agreement with one another. Perhaps the most concise is that of Stephen Coffen, a New Englander who, taken prisoner by the French, joined Duquesne's forces, and later deserted:

> They fell to work and built a square fort of chestnut logs, squared and lapped over each other to the height of fifteen feet. It is about one hundred and twenty feet square, a log house in each square [corner], a gate to the southward and another to the northward, not one porthole cut in any part of it; when finished, they called it *Fort La Briske Isle*.

• 6 •

While Fort Presqu' Isle was building, Péan was sweating at the truly Herculean task of moving 2000 men, with equipment, supplies, and armament, over 500 miles of water and rough country. Erie, the shallowest of the lakes, was sometimes the most turbulent, and the long haul from Niagara was a very unpleasant, if not downright dangerous, experience. But nothing on the whole trip could compare with the staggering toil and hardship of the portage around the great falls of the Niagara. Péan described it thus to Duquesne:

The effects to be transported form a total of at least 10,000 to 12,000 pieces . . . I swear to you, Monsieur, I am in a quandry difficult to express. There are almost no Indians. The horses are worn out. The French carry little and pretend all sorts of indispositions. It is necessary always to have officers at them. They lie down to sleep on the portage, and they cry that they are sick. The irons are always filled with them.

Many an exhausted, half-starved soldier deserted, preferring the perils of the howling wilderness to a slow and weary death on the terrible Niagara portage. Not a few were caught, shackled, and sent overseas to the galleys. At last, Péan seems to have solved his difficulties by the simple expedient of paying the Canadian militia for their work. By early September, everything was over the portage and on its way to Presqu' Isle.

So far, Duquesne's timetable was holding up; but he was beginning to worry. When he learned how Fort Presqu' Isle had been built, he sent word to stop such nonsense. In the case of future forts, would Marin "please conform to the usual way of building them in the Upper Country." There was no time for fancy construction. Intelligence from the south was disturbing. The British were moving up from Virginia, perhaps in force; and what had started out as a one-sided invasion, now promised to become a race for the Forks.

But Marin was wasting no time. Even before Fort Presqu' Isle was finished, he sent a crew to the south end of the portage and started a fort on French Creek. Fort Le Boeuf it would be called, and it would serve as a support base for the key fort at the Forks. At the same time, he sent Captain Joncaire to establish a fortified post at Venango, where French Creek emptied into the Allegheny. And simultaneously, he pushed the portage road from Presqu' Isle southward through unbroken forest.

Meantime, despite the difficulties Péan was having at Niagara, a steady flow of invasion supplies was pouring into Presqu' Isle. It piled up in the warehouses and on the landings: barrels of flour, biscuits, salt pork, dried peas, lyed corn, brandy and wine; powder, bullets, spare flints, cannon and ammunition; tree-felling, road-making, fort-building equipment and tools; bake ovens and smithies, tents, clothing, medical supplies, and all the other gear of a wilderness campaign—not excepting a portable altar for the priest who accompanied every French military expedition and said Mass each morning, even when the army was in retreat.

It is possible, as Pouchot tells us, that the Ohio Expeditionary Force also "took into that region goods of every kind, even to velvets, damask, shoes for women, silk hose, etc., and plenty of Spanish wines." Graft took many, and sometimes odd, forms in New France!

So, day after day, the bateaux and canoes—at Quebec alone, Bigot had built a hundred bateaux and 120 canoes for transport— came up from Niagara. The bateaux were big, flat-bottomed boats with flaring sides and long, slanting bows and sterns, and capable of carrying as much as twelve tons of cargo. The famous Grand River canoes of the fur trade were thirty-six feet long and six feet wide amidships, and good for five tons of lading besides their crews of ten. And the great, flat-bottomed barges were weighted with heavy cannon and horses. Péan watched them all arrive and wrote to Duquesne enthusiastically:

> Nothing has pleased me more than the management of provisions and stores . . . I can assure the General that there is not a king's warehouse in any country in the world which is better ordered and arranged. As soon as the stores arrive, they break open the barrels of pork, put it in new brine and store them in marked places; they mend the flour sacks and repair other goods which have got damaged. The storehouses are superb and well-managed. The fort is a jewel; our wish is that the General could see it; I am sure he would be unable to give enough praise to Messieurs Marin and Le Mercier.

The picture was not quite as rosy, however, as Péan painted it. The summer months were running out. There was still the job of transporting the vast accumulation of supplies through twenty miles of dense forest. And first, a road had to be made.

Marin cleared out and widened an old Indian trail, bridged the streams that crossed it, corduroyed the low spots, and built a storehouse at the halfway point. Although the summer was a dry one, patches of swamp held their moisture and soon became deep mudholes under the continuous coming and going of the road crews and their horses.

Marin spared neither himself nor his men. "The Sieur Marin joins everything," Péan wrote, "does not stop an instant . . . He is perpetually at work, in the storehouses and on the portage." At last the indefatigable old martinet was able to write Duquesne —who was now complaining that he never heard from his commander and did not even know where he was—that the portage would be finished at the beginning of August. The timetable was still intact.

• 7 •

The real trouble began with the transfer of the huge supply dump to Fort Le Boeuf, at the south end of the portage. Bureaucratic red tape was now hampering Marin at every step. Disputes over authority and priorities. Stupid directives from Montreal, even from Paris. And graft: salt pork—the indispensable ingredient of the soup, without which no French soldier could march—arrived short-weight and not enough. Later on, after the war, high officials would stand trial for corruption—among them the Intendant Bigot, who took more than 600,000 livres in "profit" from his office in one year alone. Heads would roll, but this was no help to Sieur Marin in the month of August, 1753, with 12,000 pieces of baggage and 2,000 men to get across a twenty-mile portage.

Without such troubles, indeed, his task was a staggering one. Marin's Canadians were superb packers. They were the only people in the world, Duquesne commented, capable of enduring the immense labor of the portages. In the fur trade, they regularly tossed two ninety-pound packs on their backs and trotted over the most difficult kind of trail. At times they carried three packs, 270 pounds in all.[9] But such men broke down and even died on the road to Fort Le Boeuf.

To ease the work of transporting cannon and such heavy equipment as bake ovens and smithies, Duquesne had requisitioned about fifty horses; but most of them had died on the way

---

[9] The great Negro voyageur Bonga is reputed to have managed five packs, weighing 450 pounds, on the most punishing of portages.

to Presqu' Isle, and the survivors were too worn out by the Niagara portage to be of much use. In the end, it was a job of manhandling everything across—a job for exhausted, hungry, fly-tormented men floundering through mud to their knees and broken down, at last, by toil and dysentery. Péan—who himself slept no more than two hours a night during the portaging—wrote to Duquesne: "Conceive, Monsieur, that all the carts which you see pass your windows pass over the bodies of men already half dead." "The portage road," he added, "is covered with the sweat of our militia."

But Marin was plagued by anxieties other than the physical problems of transport. Duquesne was writing him that 2,000 British troops were rumored on their way to block the invasion. His officers were openly expressing a dissatisfaction that was near to mutiny. When one of his captains, Jean-Daniel Dumas, brought this to his attention, he exploded: "If there are any who are not pleased to continue the campaign, you can assure them, Sir, that upon any request they make me I shall not hesitate to send them back immediately." Dumas—who would one day bring Gen. Edward Braddock to defeat and death—dismayed Marin by asking to be among those sent home.

It took all of Péan's diplomacy to patch up that break; and when the dust had settled, even Marin could see that the situation had become so serious that a drastic revision of the invasion plan would have to be made. He called Péan and Le Mercier in for consultation, and together they drafted a report for Duquesne. It held nothing back: "M. Marin, with the advice of MM. Péan and Mercier, finds himself compelled by lack of provisions to enter the Belle Rivière with only 1,350 men, including Indians."

Péan set off with this report for Niagara. When he returned early in September, he found fever raging through the army, and large stores of supplies still heaped up at Presqu' Isle. It was near the end of the month before everything was over the portage. The invasion was now seriously behind schedule. But the difficulties that Marin had so far encountered were as nothing, compared with what lay ahead for the sick, over-burdened old commander of the French forces on the Ohio.

• 8 •

To all his troubles was now added a new one—the threat of Indian attack.

In the white man's struggle for land and power, the Indians were always a factor to be reckoned with, and both sides competed feverishly for their backing. On the whole, France had been more successful than England in seducing the tribes. "Her agents," Francis Parkman noted, "were busy in every village, studying the language of the inmates, complying with their usages, caressing them, cajoling them, and whispering friendly warnings in their ears against the wicked English." French soldiers, traders, and even officers married Indian women, raised families of half-breed children, dressed, talked, acted, and finally thought as Indians. Besides, the French were not intent on turning Indian hunting grounds into farms and town sites. They wished merely to trade for furs. They did not drive the game away.

The English, on the other hand, had a spectacular record of inept dealings with the aborigines. Excepting a few men like William Johnson, George Croghan, Christian Frederick Post, and Conrad Weiser (none of them actually English), they exhibited little understanding of the Indian nature and scant respect for Indian dignity. Despite a certain lip service in the form of treaties and ceremonial gift-giving, they were arrogant, grasping, debased, and contemptuous of tribal rights and usages. Nor were they noted for standing by their Indian allies after inciting them to war with the French.

Their traders—"a set of abandoned wretches," Dinwiddie called them—did little indeed to make the Indians love them. Yet, they were able to offer better guns and blankets than the French, and at lower prices; and there was never a shortage of English rum. So, all things considered, the situation was not entirely one-sided.

Indeed, it was highly complex, with French and Indians, English and Indians, and Indians and Indians lined up in ever-changing and incredibly complicated combinations with or against one another. If there was any simple and enduring aspect of the

Indian-European relationship, it was probably the warrior's abiding belief that all whites were cowardly, servile money-grubbers, without honor or dignity, and with only one thought in mind: to debase and corrupt the Indian and cheat him out of all his land.

At this time, as we have seen, the English had succeeded in subverting most of the Ohio Indians from an ancient loyalty to the French. Joncaire and other French agents were hard at work to correct this situation, and had brought the powerful Miami back into line. Now they were plying their diplomatic skills along the Allegheny, where the situation was still highly fluid.

To the east, the Iroquois were keeping carefully neutral. At one time they had been violent enemies of the French, unforgiving of Champlain's massacre of some Mohawks in 1609. But after settling that score with the sack of the French settlement of Lachine—a butchery that Canada still remembered with a shudder—they had adopted their historic role of neutrals and middlemen. French and English were both careful of treading on Iroquois toes.

In the summer of 1753, the Iroquois were playing it cozy. Having subjugated every other tribe as far west as the Mississippi, they were by far the most powerful Indian force in North America. But they refused to commit this power in the Ohio Valley showdown. Siding with neither France nor England, they watched both parties with narrowed eyes. When Marin landed at Presqu' Isle, they sent a delegation of their women to inquire about his intentions; but that was all—for the time being.

The Ohio Indians, on the other hand, observed with deep concern the intrusions of white soldiers and settlers into their forests and game preserves along the Allegheny. For the most part, they were new-comers to the region—bands of Delaware, Shawnee, and other tribes—who occupied the land by sufferance of their Iroquois conquerors. The Iroquois denied most of them independent status, regarding them as mere "hunters" on territory actually belonging to the Six Nations. These Ohio Indians, however, did not share their masters' lofty equanimity when 2,000 French soldiers began to swarm down from Presqu' Isle. And least of all, the Seneca chief, Half King.

Half King—whose Indian name was Tanaghrisson—had been

appointed by the League of the Iroquois as a sort of viceroy and spokesman for the vassal tribes. His own attitude toward the whites was at first a simple distaste of being drawn into their quarrels. But as the English settlers began to breach the mountain barrier, and French troops interdicted the waterways with their forts, Half King sensed that his people were being caught between the advances of two irreconcilable forces. The time had come to take a stand. Establishing a council fire at Logstown, he had invited the agents of both sides to present their cases to the head men of the Ohio tribes. Then, with the launching of the French invasion, Half King's sympathies quickly swung toward the British.

Marin, it must be admitted, had done little to win him to the French view. At first he was polite, even placating, in his answers to the Indian's anxious inquiries. When they asked him if he came with his hatchet uplifted, he replied reassuringly that he did, indeed—but only for his enemies. To a second delegation from Half King his answer was a little firmer. He had been commanded to build four forts along the river, *and that he would do.* When, on a third and final visit, Half King himself warned Marin to leave the Ohio, the old commandant lost his temper completely.

At this time, Marin was frantic with the troubles and frustrations of getting his men and supplies over the Presqu' Isle-Le Boeuf portage. The spectre of low water in French Creek had arisen. His men were dropping dead on the portage road, and he himself was down with a sickness that would soon relieve him of all his cares. Half King's intervention at this precise moment must have hit him as an intolerable impudence.

Marin's reply to Half King's long and rather pompous speech was, at any rate, a violent outburst of his famous temper. "I am not afraid of flies or mosquitoes," he roared, "for the Indians are such as those. I tell you, down that river I will go. If the river is blocked up, I have the forces to burst it open and tread under my feet all that oppose me. I despise all the stupid things you have said."

He threw at Half King a string of good-will wampum. "Here is your wampum!" he shouted. "I fling it at you." Then, he kicked it around in the customary gesture of contempt.

After that, of course, war was to be expected from the Ohio tribes. Scarroyady, an Oneida chief, said almost sadly, "Now we have nothing to do but strike the French." Yet there was no immediate sign of hostility along the invasion route. The Indians still hung around Marin's camps, providing horses and carriers in exchange for brandy and trade goods, and offering their women for the divertissement of his soldiers.

But Marin had violated an old maxim of French Indian diplomacy: "It is better to risk being embroiled with the Iroquois than with the other nations, who hate them." He was now at odds with both the Six Nations and their natural enemies. However brave a face he might put on it, he could not shrug off this new Indian threat to his timetable.

* 9 *

In October, with the portage trail ankle-deep in the drift of fallen leaves and shell ice crackling in the wagon ruts, Marin's men began to feel the full impact of that twin scourge of field armies, scurvy and dysentery. No day passed, now, without its toll of dead. At Le Boeuf, the victims were being buried four at a time. Finally, Marin himself began to hemorrhage, and Péan wrote to Duquesne, requesting the Governor to have a replacement ready.

In the midst of his misery, however, Marin went doggedly ahead with his plan to descend the Allegheny before the freeze-up and establish a fort at the Forks of the Ohio. Péan even prepared to start down the river in October, with a force of about 900 men, in 180 dugout canoes. This was only half of the original force; but it would be enough, Marin estimated, to build the fort and garrison it with a hundred men, while the remaining 800 proceeded farther down the Belle Rivière.

In this, too, he was to be thwarted. Ensign Drouillon, who had been sent down French Creek to check on its navigability, sent back his report: impassable. The long, hot summer had failed to dry up the mud holes on the portage, but it had lowered the water in rocky, twisting French Creek to a point where not even a canoe could make its way to the Ohio.

In the face of this disastrous news, Marin made one more desperate attempt to move his troops down river and start work on the fort he had been ordered to build at the Forks. He contracted with a band of Mohicans for a hundred pack-horses to carry supplies and guns to the Allegheny; but the Indians, after loading up their animals, departed and were never heard from again.

Now there was nothing for the stubborn but fast-failing old commandant to do but abandon his plan for 1753. He prepared to winter his effective troops at Le Boeuf, Presqu' Isle, and Niagara, and send his sick back to Montreal. There were few, indeed, who remained behind. The terrible three-months ordeal of portaging without sufficient food or adequate shelter had reduced most of his army to haggard ghosts who fell easy victims to the epidemic now raging along the whole route of invasion. Duquesne was shocked at the pitiable state in which his soldiers straggled back to Canada. He wrote:

> It is not to be doubted that if these exhausted men had been put in route to follow their destination, the Ohio River would have been filled with the dead by fevers and consumption which began to get hold of his troops, and the evil-intentioned Indians would not fail to attack them, being composed of spectres.

This cleared Marin of any suspicion that he had called off the campaign in order to rest his decimated army. But the old campaigner found it less easy to excuse failure to himself. Too weak to exercise command, Stephen Coffen tells us, he begged his officers to place him in Fort Le Boeuf, set the post on fire, and return with the surviving troops to Montreal. His officers, Coffen remarks, coldly refused.

Marin died on October 29 and was buried in the fort cemetery. It is unlikely that he was deeply mourned by any of his officers or men. He died in the midst of ruin; yet it could not be said of him that he ever gave less than his best in the performance of his orders.

With Marin's death, the primary objective of the Ohio Expedition—the establishment of a French stronghold at the Forks—must be put off for another year. But Marin had not, after all, failed completely. He had made secure the approaches to the

Ohio. He had taken the first giant step toward the establishment of French supremacy on the North American continent. In Montreal, Duquesne wrote of him:

> I regard the loss of Sieur Marin as irreparable. This officer combined the spirit and excellent head with the appearance and manners of the savages . . . With regard to zeal, never has a man shown more. Besides, he preferred death in battle rather than health at home.

• 10 •

Thus matters stood on the Ohio shortly before Major Washington arrived at Fort Le Boeuf. Marin's place had just been filled by Saint-Pierre. And it was fortunate, perhaps, that it was to this courtly officer, rather than the terrible-tempered Marin, that Washington delivered Governor Dinwiddie's pompous ultimatum.

Saint-Pierre read the letter in private, then suggested that Washington take it to Quebec. A communication of such importance obviously required the personal attention of the Governor General. When Washington firmly rejected this proposal, Saint-Pierre shrugged and asked for a little time in which to compose his own reply.

This required three days, during which interval Saint-Pierre and his staff did their best—with the help of liquor, presents, and promises—to win over Half King. At the same time, Washington was making good use of his idle hours. Besides noting down the main features of the fort itself, he made other observations, all carefully recorded in his journal:

> I could get no certain account of the number of men here; but according to the best judgment I could form, there are an hundred exclusive of officers, of which there are many. I also gave orders to the people who are with me, to take an exact account of the canoes which were hauled up to convey their forces down in the spring. This they did, and told 50 birch bark, and 170 of pine; besides many others which were blocked out, in readiness to make.

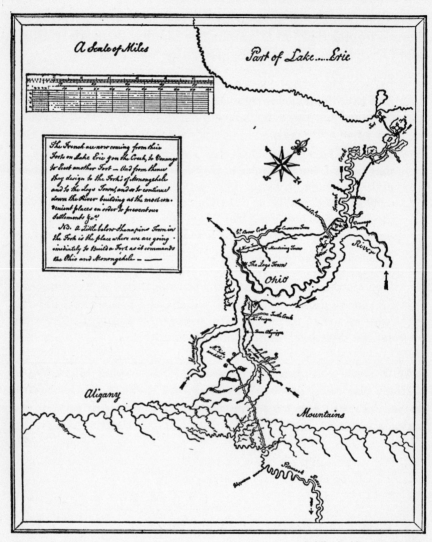

After his return from Fort Le Boeuf, Washington drew this map of the Forks of the Ohio and the French forts and trading posts in the vicinity. It was published in his *Journal* of the trip.

On the evening of December 14 Washington received Saint-Pierre's formal reply to Governor Dinwiddie's demands. Nothing could have been phrased more gracefully—or firmly:

> Sir:
>
> As I have the honor of commanding here in chief, Mr. Washington delivered me the letter which you wrote to the commandant of the French forces.
>
> I should have been glad that you had given him orders, or that he had been inclined to proceed to Canada, to see our General; to whom it better belongs than to me to set forth the evidence and reality of the rights of the King my Master, upon the lands situated along the River Ohio, and to contest the pretensions of the King of Great Britain thereto . . .
>
> As to the summons you sent me to retire, I do not think myself obliged to obey it. Whatever may be your instructions, I am here by virtue of the orders of my General; and I entreat you, Sir, not to doubt one moment but that I am determined to conform myself to them with all the exactness and resolution which can be expected from the best of officers.

With some complimentary remarks about young Major Washington's charming personal qualities and great merit, Legardeur de Saint-Pierre closed his letter. For all its courteous tone, it was a declaration of open war—if the English desired it—on the Ohio.

• 11 •

With this letter in his pocket, Washington could not get away from Fort Le Boeuf fast enough. But Saint-Pierre was in no hurry to provide his visitors with the means to depart. He was making progress with the Indians; and Washington saw clearly that to leave Half King and his followers would be to abandon them to the French. He was in a tight spot, and he wrote about it later with no relish:

> I can't say that ever in my life I suffered so much anxiety as I did in this affair: I saw that every stratagem which the most

fruitful brain could invent, was practiced to win Half King to their interest, and that leaving him here was giving them the opportunity they aimed at.

It is possible, as some scholars suggest, that Washington under-rated Half King's capacity for loyalty; but only after a face-to-face confrontation with Saint-Pierre, nevertheless, and Washington's blunt demand to know why the Indians were not allowed to leave, did the French commandant drop his delaying tactics. Apologetically, he disclaimed any knowledge of why the Indians lingered; and he certainly had no idea of detaining his English visitors.

Next morning, however, just as the canoes were ready to push off, Half King and his followers were subjected to the supreme test of will—an offer of all the liquor they could drink *on the spot*. It was nip and tuck for a while, with Washington holding his breath; but finally Half King turned his back on temptation and eased himself down into a canoe. As soon as the Indians' craft was well away, Washington and his party launched their own.

He must have felt great relief—and some elation. He had come off better than he had any right to expect, really. Yet, his victory was a sobering one. For what was this little battle of the rum kegs compared to the great struggle that now loomed ahead? A struggle, young Major Washington must have sensed uneasily, that might well spread fire and death along the whole frontier . . . a conflagration, indeed, into which half the civilized world could easily be drawn. And in his pocket the spark that could ignite the flames.

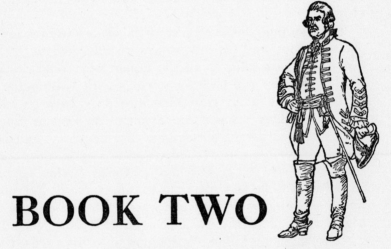

BOOK TWO

The Race to the Forks

In his pink brick palace at Williamsburg, Governor Robert Dinwiddie, listening to Washington tell about Fort Le Boeuf, staring at Saint-Pierre's letter, might well have marveled at the headlong velocity of fatal events.

Only a year ago, in the spring of 1753, he had still clung to the hope that "these people are only French traders and they have no other view but trade." There was, he told himself, "no great army of French among the lakes." He had tried to discount the mounting evidence of aggression beyond the mountains: Céleron's expedition, the attack on Pickawillany, the defecting of the Miami, Joncaire's brazen efforts to intimidate the Indians on the Allegheny, the capture and deportation of English traders to Canada and even to France . . .

Then, suddenly, had come reports of a large body of troops moving down from Canada—of what appeared indeed to be "a great army of French among the lakes." And now—to end all doubt of what was happening on the Ohio—Legardeur de Saint-Pierre's letter in his own hands.

Word of Duquesne's invasion thrust had reached Dinwiddie early in the spring—not long after the English garrison at Fort Oswego was astonished at the sight of Boishébert's advance force sailing gaily down Lake Ontario on its way to Niagara. The French canoes had made it a point to pass so close to Oswego's guns that their crews could hurl insults and ribald jests at the English. They left no doubt about French intentions.

Immediately, there was a great posting of messengers. Dispatch

riders took off from New York for Pennsylvania, Virginia, and
Maryland. Word of the invasion was hurried to England. Expresses crossed the mountains to warn the Ohio traders. A vast
excitement, mixed with apprehension of bloody French-Indian
strikes along the frontier, swept through the colonies.

The reports, of course, were generally exaggerated. The overawed Indians along the invasion route described the earth as
shaking under the march of the French forces. The commander
at Oswego notified William Johnson that an army of 6000 men
was on its way to the Ohio. A French deserter confirmed this
figure, and added that the troops were all gigantic grenadiers
from Old France. English spies were sent to follow the march of
the French. At Presqu' Isle, an officer and five men lurked in
the woods for four months at constant risk of losing their scalps,
watching Marin erect his forts and cut his roads to the Ohio.
They sent back reports of a great build-up of troops, supplies,
and armament. The over-all picture was one of a massive military
movement of stunning rapidity—which indeed it was.

After the first wave of excitement and alarm had subsided,
however, the reaction of the Colonies was anything but energetic.
Except for frantic efforts to line up the Indians on their side,
the English did little to meet the French threat. Of all the
Colonial governors, indeed, Robert Dinwiddie alone seems to
have grasped the far-reaching implications of that challenge.
Even before Duquesne launched his drive, Dinwiddie had been
waging a one-man campaign to enlist Virginia's lethargic neighbors in a Stop-the-French movement. When word of Marin's
march reached Williamsburg, he decided to take unilateral
action. His authority was a directive from the British ministry
instructing the Colonial governors to demand withdrawal of the
French; and, if it came to that, "to repel force by force." Dinwiddie had also been authorized by the Crown to build forts on
the Ohio at Virginia's expense. He lost no time in calling the
General Assembly into session. By November 1, Williamsburg
was thronged with Burgesses, Ohio Company stockholders, and
other speculators clamoring for action in the North.

Among the early arrivals was a tall young man in a beautifully-
tailored uniform of the Virginia Militia, Maj. George Washington,
Adjutant of the Southern District. Having heard of Dinwiddie's

plan to send a formal protest to the French commander, Washington had hurried down from the Northern Neck to offer his services as the Governor's messenger. His qualifications for this delicate and arduous, even dangerous, mission were impressive: he was young, strong, a superb horseman, an experienced surveyor, a natural leader, and he knew his way around in the woods. He was also a gentleman; and this especially recommended him to Dinwiddie. It was appropriate that the bearer of so important a communication should be an officer and a man accustomed to the best social usages, rather than an illiterate frontiersman. Washington's offer was quickly accepted; and, as we have seen, Dinwiddie's preemptory letter was duly delivered to Legardeur Saint-Pierre at Fort Le Boeuf.

It was only by grace of a watchful Providence, it would seem, that Washington got safely back to Williamsburg with the French commandant's reply. Twice he had the narrowest escapes from death, once when shot at by his Indian guide, once when swept off a raft into the icy Allegheny. At last, however, having firmly planted a charmed-life legend that would proliferate through the years, the future Father of his Country reached home safely and delivered Saint-Pierre's rejection of Dinwiddie's ultimatum.

The Governor's immediate decision was to "repel force by force." Specifically, he made up his mind to raise troops, march to the Forks, and occupy that strategic location before the French could seize it.

• 2 •

Even before sending Washington to Fort Le Boeuf, indeed, Dinwiddie had moved in that direction. As early as 1752, he had asked the Lords of Trade for money with which to build forts on the Ohio—particularly one at the Forks. An Indian road already ran from the Potomac to the Monongahela, he informed the Lords, over which guns—20 or 30 would do—could be transported. A regiment of regulars, he estimated, could build the forts; 50 soldiers in each would suffice to garrison them.

The French, as we have seen, had failed to complete their long, difficult, 500-mile dash from Montreal in the autumn of

1753 only because of sickness and low water. Their misfortune, of course, was Britain's gain. It gave the English time to make their own bid for supremacy on the Ohio. In July, 1753, the Province of Virginia—or, more accurately, the Ohio Company— set the machinery of occupation in motion. The race to the Ohio was on.

Three veteran frontiersmen, William Trent, Thomas Cresap, and Christopher Gist, were commissioned to start work on a fortified post at the Forks. It was to enclose a space 90 feet square, with bastions at each corner, and a 12-foot wall around houses, stores, and magazines. Twenty swivel guns would defend it.

This proposed stronghold was not, however, to stand at the precise confluence of the Allegheny and Monongahela, but at the mouth of Chartier's Creek, some four miles down river. Here a Gibraltar-like height (known today as McKees Rocks) rose abruptly from the flat valley floor. It had the appearance of a natural citadel; and, in fact, it had served as a famous Indian fortress in ancient times. But Washington, on his way to Le Boeuf, passed the spot, took particular note of it, and in his journal recorded a dim view of its possibilities:

> Nature has well contrived this lower place for water defense; but the hill whereon it must stand being about a quarter of a mile in length, and then descending gradually on the land side, will render it difficult and very expensive, to make a sufficient fortification there. The whole flat upon the hill must be taken in, the side next the descent made extremely high, or else the hill itself cut away: otherwise the enemy may raise batteries within the distance without being exposed to a single shot from the fort.

With an assurance rather awesome in one so young, he then set forth the advantages of a site at the actual juncture,

> which I think extremely well situated for a fort, as it has absolute command of both rivers. The land at the Point is 20 or 25 feet above the common surface of the water; and a considerable bottom of flat, well-timbered land all around it, very convenient for building.

In the end, the Ohio Company agreed with Washington's judgment, and decided to build at the Point. In June, John Fraser wrote from the Forks:

> Capt. Trent was here the night before last and viewed the ground the fort is to be built upon . . . The money has been laid out for the building of it already, and the great guns are lying at Williamsburg, ready to bring up.

Trent was commissioned a captain in the Virginia militia and ordered to raise a company of frontiersmen with which to build and garrison the fort. In January, 1754, he put up a storehouse on the Monongahela, as an operational base. In February he and forty of his militiamen loaded some rafts with tools and poled down the river to its juncture with the Allegheny. There they began a fortified stronghouse.

Half King was on hand to give the project his blessing, and to pledge his warriors' guns, should the French dare to interfere with the work. No sign of resistance was visible, however; and, as the first log was laid and the King's health drunk by Trent's axmen, it seemed certain that the race to the Forks had been won by the British.

But neither Robert Dinwiddie, back in Williamsburg, nor William Trent, on the actual ground, had any idea that the French would give up so easily. In the autumn, with Marin's fever-ridden troops limping back to Montreal, some such hope had indeed flared up; but it had long since been smothered by alarming reports of preparations for a new spring offensive.

Dinwiddie—surely one of the most prolific letter writers of all time—sent impassioned pleas for help to the other colonial governors. "We must act together," he warned them, and quickly, quickly! But his appeals for concerted action against the French threat still yielded nothing but moral support—and much of that grudgingly given.

At the Forks, however, nobody was dragging his heels. The imminence of danger was in the air, and construction was pushed by every means available to Trent's small force. George Croghan again visited the site and found the men putting their backs into the work. The exertions of Trent's sweating militiamen, he reported, "seemed to give the Indians great pleasure and put them in high spirits."

No stockade had yet been built—although Half King urged one—but the stronghouse was stoutly constructed of squared logs and provided with loopholes for musketry. With a little imagination, it could be called a fort; and Trent decided to christen it Fort Prince George, in honor of the future George III.

By the middle of April, just as Fort Prince George was completed, reports reached the Forks of a French army on its way down the Allegheny.

• 3 •

The reports were quite true. Once more, Duquesne had thrown away the rules book and launched his second campaign in midwinter. Hardly had his wretched veterans of 1753 got back on their feet before they were again on their way to the Ohio. Duquesne's scouts on the Monongahela were sending back alarming reports of English preparations to move on the Forks; emphatically, there was no time to be lost.[1]

On a bitter January 15, the expeditionary force began to march westward in blanket coats and sealskin shoes. Five hundred regulars and militia left Quebec, picked up 300 troops at Montreal, and set out on February 2 along the frozen St. Lawrence and the north shore of Lake Ontario. Provisions for two months were dragged along on sledges. The troops marched on snowshoes.

This time, the invasion army was led by Capt. Claude-Pierre Pécaudy, Sieur de Contrecoeur, who had been chosen by Duquesne to replace the ailing Capt. Legardeur de Saint-Pierre. Unwell himself with a trying skin affliction, Contrecoeur did not relish the idea of leaving his family and comfortable quarters at Fort Niagara, where he was commander. He was, however, the one man for the job—a nobleman of marked ability and great

---

[1] La Chauvignerie, in a letter from Chiningué, February 26, 1754, to Saint-Pierre, reported that his Indians looked for a thousand English troops to arrive on the Ohio in three days. Chauvignerie added that he placed little credence in the report.

experience; and there was no refusing the Governor General's orders.

The orders directed Contrecoeur to "take possession of the Belle Rivière, where you will have Fort de Chiningué built." Later, when he learned of Trent's activities at the Forks, Duquesne added a postscript to these orders, urging his commander-in-chief to "hasten to interrupt *and even destroy their work from the start.*"[2]

The march westward was no holiday jaunt. Both the St. Lawrence and Lake Ontario were frozen solid, so that the troops must slog their way on foot along the bleak, wind-swept shores. At times, long stretches of smooth ice opened ahead; and then the men skated in single file, drawing as many as seven or eight sledges, laden with men and provisions, behind them. But often huge, jagged blocks of ice piled up in their path, to cut and maim them. Or the road gave way beneath the weight of sleds piled high with bags of flour and barrels of pork, plunging the soldiers into near-freezing water. And not infrequently the march was into the teeth of a stinging blizzard of powder snow, sweeping on sub-zero gales down the dazzling reaches of ice.

Thus, sometimes covering as much as 20 leagues a day, sometimes barely progressing beyond sight of their previous camp, Contrecoeur's army of some 800 men pushed on to Toronto Bay, where it crossed over to Fort Niagara. Scarcely pausing to gape at the famous falls, the troops hurried everything over the portage, and set sail for Presqu' Isle. By March 8, most of them had completed the long, cold march from Canada.

At Presqu' Isle the going was somewhat easier than it had been on the previous expedition. This time there was no fort to build, no portage to cut. But the road to Fort Le Boeuf was in such execrable shape that it took twelve days to drag the guns over it; and French Creek presented even greater difficulties and delay. There was plenty of water now, but a hurricane had choked the stream with such a tangle of fallen trees and debris that it was more the work of axmen than of paddlers to bring the canoes and pirogues to Venango.

[2] In his instructions to Contrecoeur, January 27, 1754, Duquesne reveals that he expected the fort at the Forks to be named in his honor. He refers to it as "the fort which has my name."

Before leaving Fort Le Boeuf, Contrecoeur relieved Captain Saint-Pierre of his command. Then, in the ancient usage of soldiers, he wrote a farewell letter to his wife: "Good-bye, my dear. Please do not worry and be sure that I shall take care of myself in every way. I hug you and my dear children a thousand times."[3]

At Venango—where Washington had met with Joncaire—Contrecoeur received important reinforcements. He was joined by Le Mercier and 350 picked men. With Le Mercier came new instructions from Duquesne. Only 18 men were to be left at Presqu' Isle, 12 at Le Boeuf. All the rest—a full 600, Duquesne hoped—were to push on to the Ohio with all possible speed.

These orders—as well as the reinforcements—revealed that Duquesne's only worry was not that the English should reach the Forks first. He was also greatly concerned about the size of their force. Just as the colonies had received highly colored reports on the French advance, so his own scouts were making alarming estimates of the English strength. Trent's party of forty, for example, was said to number a thousand men!

The Governor General's anxiety is also shown by the instructions sent to Captain Péan—Marin's second in command during the 1753 expedition:

> In case the Sieur Péan, on reaching Niagara, learns that the Sieur de Contrecoeur has met superior forces which obliged him to fall back, he will hasten to join that officer, if in his judgment an increase of forces will enable him to drive the English from places where they have established themselves. At such times, make the most determined attempt to repel force by force; but if the Sieur de Contrecoeur foresees that even with the unified force it is impossible to drive the English from the Ohio, he will notify the Sieur Péan, who will than continue his route to Detroit.

As it turned out, Péan's help was not required; but Contrecoeur welcomed the arrival of Le Mercier and his 350 picked men. He, too, had been receiving disquieting reports from down river.

---

[3] Contrecoeur, in his quaint French—which he spelled phonetically—added a postscript that he had received all his children's letters: *"jay receu tout les letre demes anfans."*

After having gathered his whole force at Venango, he lost no time in launching the final push to the Forks of the Ohio. About April 1, 1754, he set out on his historic descent of the Allegheny. With him, in 60 bateaux and 300 canoes, went 500 men and 18 cannon.

• 4 •

While the French, with the singleness of purpose and concentration of means peculiar to a completely authoritarian power, were thus driving to the heart of the continent, the attitude of the English colonies seems to have been: if we don't notice them, maybe they'll go away.

From Williamsburg, to be sure, Dinwiddie's expresses were racing up and down the coast, carrying warnings of the French peril. To underscore the imminence of a take-over at the Forks, the Governor had Washington's Fort Le Boeuf journal published and distributed throughout the colonies. He also sent it by fast sloop to England, thus bestowing an overnight international literary reputation on the somewhat astonished young Virginian.

Dinwiddie himself loosed a barrage of correspondence on the other Colonial governors, his own House of Burgesses, and even distant Indian chiefs. He used every means—logic, fear, pathos, appeals to patriotism—to move them to concerted action. He invented the modern form-letter to broaden his range. He poured it on with descriptions of border atrocities that would have been pure bathos, had they not been so true: "savage barbarity" . . . "poor, unhappy family" . . . "cries of the tender infant" . . . "parents' entreaties" . . . "you see the infant torn from the unavailing struggles of the distracted mother, the daughters ravished before the eyes of their distracted parents, and then with cruelty and insult butchered and scalped."

All this was bad enough, Dinwiddie reminded his fellow governors, but the French were even worse than the savages. They were the "abettors of these villainies." And "such are the people whose neighborhood you must now prevent."

The response to Dinwiddie's frantic appeals was somewhat less than electric. It was, in fact, a vast and puzzling apathy. New

England, perhaps, might have been excused: she had much to do in defending herself elsewhere. But New York's interest in the Ohio Valley was at least as immediate as Virginia's. Yet all that Dinwiddie could get from Governor Clinton was a promise to double the garrison at Oswego. Some New York politicos even expressed doubts that the French occupation of the Forks would be an encroachment on English territory. Why look for trouble? Besides, Albany traders were making a fast buck by selling supplies and ammunition to the French forces.[4]

The reaction of Pennsylvania—the colony that, above all others, should have been concerned about French guns pointing at her back door—was even more discouraging. The Quakers were, of course, opposed to the shedding of blood—including that of Frenchmen. The large German population was slow in awakening to a danger that did not threaten it directly. The Assembly voted no funds. The Proprietary was somewhat more responsive, but wanted to make sure that the French forts were actually within Pennsylvania territory. Why kill men and spend money to defend Virginia's claims? In the end, Governor Hamilton stalled by dispatching a surveyor, John Pattin, to determine the actual western boundary of the Province.

The other colonies were even less helpful. Connecticut and New Jersey had more urgent matters to attend to. Maryland refused to appropriate funds for military operations: what was the hurry? The weather would soon tie down the French. Governor Glen of South Carolina was irked by Dinwiddie's pleas. Only North Carolina, poorest of the colonies, voted a little money and a few men.

In this welter of indifference and disunity, a few private citizens evinced an awareness of impending disaster that was completely lacking in the Colonial assemblies, and in most of the people. Among these was Benjamin Franklin, whose famous "Join or Die" cartoon of a snake cut into thirteen pieces expressed his own feeling of urgency about uniting against the French. Franklin's was naturally a strong voice when, at the bidding of

---

[4] The buck—like the beaver in Canada—was the standard unit of frontier currency. Thus one fall buckskin was the equivalent of 4 foxes, 2 fishers, etc. Prices in the British area in 1761 were: blankets 4 bucks, match coats 3 bucks, 100 wampum 1 buck, a ruffled shirt 4 bucks, etc.

the Crown, a Colonial convention was finally called to consider
defensive measures, and to persuade the Six Nations to take up
the hatchet against the French. Commissioners of seven Colonies
met at Albany in the spring of 1754, almost two months after the
French had struck their blow on the Ohio. The meeting was
poorly attended by about 150 Indians, among them the famous
Mohawk chief Hendrick. From Hendrick the commissioners
heard a few blunt truths. War was surely on the way, he told
them. The French were preparing for it, while the English acted
like women. The French, he said, were subtle and vigilant; the
English stupid and asleep.

The Albany Convention, under Franklin's prodding, agreed on
a remarkable Plan of Union which, among other things, provided
for the entire Atlantic seaboard acting in concert against French
aggression. The commissioners then returned home and sub-
mitted the plan to the various assemblies—who unanimously
rejected it. The proposed union, they felt was not strong enough;
the King was accorded too much power. The King also rejected
the plan; he thought it too "republican" and a threat to royal
authority. Thus, as it turned out, the French alone benefited
from the Albany Convention.

The end result of the lethargy and shortsightedness on the part
of the other Colonies was to dump responsibility for stopping the
French on the Province of Virginia. Or, more properly perhaps,
on Governor Robert Dinwiddie. For even on his home grounds,
Dinwiddie was having trouble with the lawgivers.

On December 19, 1753—while Washington was hurrying back
with the bad news from Fort Le Boeuf—the General Assembly
had adjourned without voting the Governor a penny for defense
against the French. All his letter writing had netted him less
than nothing. The Burgesses had refused even to grant him permission to send a delegate to the Albany Convention.

Why this obdurate opposition to Dinwiddie's plans? The
Province of Virginia considered the territory around the Forks
her legal domain. By royal grant, and by treaty with the Iroquois, it belonged to her. Why, then, was that proud Province
so backward about defending her borders?

The personality of Robert Dinwiddie—blunt, testy, insistent
on the prerogatives of royal authority—may have had something

to do with it. As a major stockholder in the Ohio Company he was also open to the suspicion that his motives were more personal than patriotic—as, indeed, was Washington himself. And the French, quite naturally, were not backward in exploiting this suspicion. "Your schemes," Contrecoeur reminded the Virginians, "are contrived only by a company which has the interests of trade more in view than to maintain the union and harmony existing between the Crowns of Great Britain and France."

Despite his formidable power as Governor, at any rate, Dinwiddie's pleas for action went unheeded by the Assembly at the very time Duquesne was setting his second invasion force in motion.

The Governor, however, had one card left to play. As Commander-in-chief of the Province, he had authority to use the militia in repelling invasion. He now decided to exercise this authority, and to raise 200 men. These he would rush to the Forks to protect Captain Trent's little party of fort builders. In the spring, the Burgesses willing, he would raise and equip another 400 militia and march them to the Ohio. With 600 men on the ground, perhaps the French could be stood off long enough to enable Virginia and the other colonies to gather their forces.

Thus it happened that when Maj. George Washington had been back from Fort Le Boeuf only five days, he received orders to raise 100 militia in his district. Captain Trent was already collecting a company of frontiersmen and Indian traders. "Repel force by force," Whitehall had instructed Dinwiddie. He had little with which to carry out those instructions, but he would do what he could. He would reinforce the little party at the Forks with what he had—and hope for something better in the spring.

• 5 •

Captain Trent accomplished prodigies in the short time allowed him after receiving Governor Dinwiddie's orders. Those orders instructed him "to keep possession of His Majesty's lands on the Ohio and the waters thereof, and to dislodge and drive away, and in case of refusal and resistance, to kill and destroy and take prisoners all and every persons not subjects to the King of Great Britain." And, of course, to raise troops and build a fort with which to enforce the orders.

So, in three months of midwinter, Trent built a storehouse at Redstone on the Monongahela, as a base of operations; brought in supplies and provisions for the fort at the Forks; delivered fourteen horse loads of presents from Virginia to the Ohio Indians; raised a company of militia; and laid out the site for his fort and got the work started.

Yet by April, the situation at the Forks was not far from desperate.

The backwoodsmen Trent had hoped to recruit were, for one thing, less than eager to join his militia company. Instead of the 100 he had expected to sign up, only 70 answered his call; and of these, only 33 could be spared for the work at the Forks. The Indians who gathered around the site were not of much help to the builders; but they did consume a lot of food. Vain appeals were sent to Washington to hurry reinforcements and supplies. At last, when nothing was left to eat but a little Indian corn, Captain Trent turned the command over to his subordinate, Ensign Edward Ward, and set out for Wills Creek in quest of men and food.

While he was away, rumors of a great French advance down the Allegheny spurred the half-starved fort builders to frantic efforts. At Half King's suggestion, a stockade was begun to protect the already-completed storehouse. Even the Indians— whose anger had been rising at the puny defensive measures of the English—now lent a hand, and the crash of falling trees echoed from the forest.

Ward made a fast trip for help to Turtle Creek, where John Fraser had set up a trading post after being ejected from Venango by Joncaire. Fraser had been made a lieutenant in Trent's militia company, and was Ward's superior officer. Ward begged him to come to the Forks, but Fraser's attitude was, "What can we do?" Besides, he was too occupied with business to lend any help as a soldier.

Disgusted and angry, Ward returned to the Forks, swearing he would complete the stockade with whatever force he had—no more than 40 men, perhaps, including 33 armed recruits. What was more, he would stand off the whole French army as long as he could. He would, he declared, "hold out to the last extremity before it should be said that the English retreated like cowards before the French forces appeared." What, he demanded, would the Indians think?

On April 13 Ward received the most specific word that had yet come to him on the French movements. Contrecoeur, he was told, would arrive with a thousand men on April 17. That left only four days in which to complete the poor defenses of Fort Prince George, but somehow the work was finished. On April 16 the last of the gates was hung.

On the same day Contrecoeur arrived with 500 troops and Indian auxiliaries.

• 6 •

The French commander—in contrast to the amateurish tactics usually employed by the English Colonials—acted with professional skill and precision. On his way down the Allegheny, he had sent his scouts ahead to reconnoiter the English position. As early as March 6, indeed, French spies had Fort Prince George under close observation, and the state of its defenses was well known. Less accurate, however, was information on the strength of the English forces; so Contrecoeur prudently landed his troops a short distance above the fort, at Shannopin's Town, an Indian village inside the present limits of the city of Pittsburgh.

On the following day, April 17, the French moved down the river toward the Point and disembarked on the south side of a stream near the fort. Here they got four of their cannon ashore and mounted on gun carriages. Under cover of this artillery they formed up and marched in the best military style to within 150 yards of Ward's rude stockade.

Captain Le Mercier then advanced with drums, colors, and a strong guard, and was met by Ensign Ward. Le Mercier politely handed Ward a written demand for immediate surrender of Fort Prince George. This summons, composed by Contrecoeur at his camp on the preceding day, was a document remarkable for its graceful Gallic obliquity. It expressed shocked surprise that the

English should have thus intruded on King Louis's lands, to rudely disturb the peace and amity which, it was well known, existed between Their Gracious Majesties. Ensign Ward, indeed, might have listened with a degree of wry amusement as Le Mercier's interpreter read:

> Sir: Nothing can surprise me more than to see you attempt a settlement upon the lands of the King, my master, which obliges me now, sir, to send you this gentleman, Chevalier Le Mercier, Captain of the Artillery of Canada, to know of you, sir, by virtue of what authority you are come to fortify yourself within the dominions of the King, my master. This action seems so contrary to the last treaty of peace, at Aix la Chapelle, between His Most Christian Majesty and the King of Great Britain, that I do not know to whom to impute such an usurpation, as it is incontestable that the land situated along the Beautiful River belongs to His Most Christian Majesty.

Contrecoeur threw in a paragraph placing the blame for everything on the Ohio Company, acting without regard for "the peace and harmony which subsists between the two crowns of France and Great Britain." Then he got down to business:

> Let it be as it will, sir, if you come into this place, charged with orders, I summon you in the name of the King, my master, by virtue of orders which I have got from my General, to retreat peaceably with your troops from off the lands of the King, and not to return, or else I will find myself obliged to fulfill my duty, and compel you to it. I hope, sir, you will not deter an instant, and that you will nor force me to the last extremity. In that case, sir, you may be persuaded that I will give orders that there shall be no damage done by my detachment.
>
> CONTRECOEUR

Done at camp, April 16, 1754

With 36 armed men against Contrecoeur's 500, there was not much that Ensign Ward could oppose to this summons. He made a half-hearted attempt to stall for time. He himself had no authority to surrender Fort Prince George, he explained; the summons should be given to Lieutenant Fraser, his superior officer. If he were allowed to go to Turtle Creek and bring Fraser back . . .

Le Mercier looked at his watch. It was twelve o'clock, he said. He would give Ward exactly one hour to make up his mind. What was the Ensign's answer? Ward, recognizing the futility of further attempts at negotiation, surrendered. He agreed to evacuate the fort by noon the next day.

That night Contrecoeur, always the officer and gentleman, invited Ward to dinner—without, however, allowing the Englishman and his men to sleep inside the stockade walls. His conditions of surrender were generous. Ward was permitted to march away with all his personnel, arms, provisions, and working tools—everything except four cannon, which could hardly have been carted off in any event. Contrecoeur even issued three days' rations to Ward's hungry troops.

Thus, completely without bloodshed—and to the raging indignation of Half King—the little point of land between the Allegheny and the Monongahela, an arrow pointing straight down the broad and fertile Ohio Valley and into the heart of the continent, passed to French hands.

At daybreak next morning, the fleur-de-lis was hoisted, and 50 men went into the woods with felling axes, to bring out logs and timbers with which to build Fort Duquesne.

BOOK THREE

*Fort Duquesne of the Blessed Virgin at
the Beautiful River*

• 1 •

If you were to look at a map of North America for the 1750's, you would find it dotted—except for the Atlantic Coast and Lower Canada—with the names, not of towns and cities, but of forts. From Louisbourg far out on Cape Breton Island, to La Jonquière on the Upper Saskatchewan, and down to Mobile on the Gulf, the flags of France—and, farther west, of Spain— flew almost solely above military posts.

A second glance at the map would tell you why each of these wilderness strongholds had been built. Aside from the forts, what would you find? Rivers . . . lakes . . . inland seas . . . an interminable maze of waterways binding together the two great mountain chains of the continent, and giving access to the oceans surrounding it. In Europe the rivers all flow away from one another. Here, in North America, they interlock to tie the remotest corners of the land together.

When you went anywhere in the 1750's, you traveled the water routes. There were no roads.[1] In all the vast expanse of forest beyond the Atlantic coastal range, there was nothing but a few dim Indian traces and game trails. So, wherever you went, it was by canoe, or pirogue, or bateau. If you were a trader in the Illinois country, you paddled up or down the Ohio, the Wabash, the Mississippi, the Illinois, even the Missouri. East, west, north or south, you could go a thousand miles or more in

[1] This statement applies, of course, only to the interior of the continent. East of the coastal range, there was a good deal of travel by coach and horseback; and even in the mountains, horses were used on the Indian trails.

55

any of these directions without once leaving your canoe. If you were a French bush ranger, you would go west by the much-used St. Lawrence River route, then through the Great Lakes, then by an intricate system of waterways to any place you fancied in what was called the *pays d'en haut*. If you lived in Albany or New York and had business in Montreal or Quebec, the Hudson River-Lake Champlain highway was always open—unless the Iroquois decided otherwise. Indeed, everyone—traders, explorers, missionaries, soldiers, settlers, and Indians—could and did move freely and quickly in any direction they wished over the endless highways of navigable water.

Except, of course, when a fort blocked the way.

If it was easy to get about the continent by water, it was equally easy to prohibit water travel. A few cannon at the Niagara portage, for example, could interdict all traffic westward from Lake Ontario through Lake Erie. A fort at the southern end of Lake Champlain or Lake George would take care of the great New York-Montreal road. Detroit obviously commanded the Illinois country, as well as the Upper Lakes. Oswego dominated the Mohawk River route from Albany—the Atlantic seaboard's only means of access to the West. Michilimackinac stood squarely across the entrance to Lake Michigan. Chartres held the key to the Lower Mississippi. Whoever controlled these vital water communications was master of the thousands of square miles of territory they drained.

And so, at strategic narrows, on important portages, at the mouths of great rivers, forts sprang up. Not all of them, to be sure, were purely, or even primarily, military establishments. Often, as at Oswego and Michilimackinac, they were trading posts and supply depots, combining business with defense against the Indians. Sometimes, as at Chartres and Detroit, they were centers of agricultural communities. Later on, as roads were opened, forts provided protection for troops and travelers. And, as the frontier moved westward, a different kind of fort—the private "station," frequently no more than a stockaded cabin—served as a refuge in times of scalping raids. Occasionally, indeed, forts were built by white men to shelter the wives and children of Indian warriors on the warpath against other white men!

But at mid-century most of the important North American forts had been designed for defense of water communications. And of all these, perhaps none occupied a site of such enormous strategic consequence as the one Contrecoeur's soldiers were now building at the Forks of the Ohio.

Even today, as one stands at "the Point," it is impossible not to experience something of what Contrecoeur must have felt when he stood there in the spring of 1754 and looked down the broad Ohio . . . a sense of the tremendous geographical, and hence military and political, significance of this quiet meeting of two great wilderness rivers.

From his right flowed the Allegheny—viewed by the French as merely a continuation of the Ohio, and called by them the Belle Rivière. It was the road to Lake Erie—already guarded by Forts Presqu' Isle and Le Boeuf—and to Canada. From his left glided the Monongahela, reaching back toward the Valley of the Potomac and tidewater. And dead ahead, the Beautiful River itself—broad, quiet, winding with hardly a riffle through more than 200,000 square miles of fertile watershed to the Mississippi, a thousand miles away.[2]

It was for nothing less than the mastery of these three vital routes of travel, and the vast domain they controlled, that the Marquis de Duquesne had been instructed to build an impregnable fort on the Ohio. For this—and defense of New France's long lifeline to Louisiana—his men were now sweating in the summer sun at the building of Fort Duquesne of the Blessed Virgin at the Beautiful River.

• 2 •

Like the English, the French had not at first recognized the Forks as the logical site for a key fortress on the Belle Rivière. Originally, they had planned to build Fort Duquesne at the trading village of Logstown. Saint-Pierre, in fact, had sent an advance party there under Sieur de la Chauvignerie to cut trees and square timbers for the work. But la Chauvignerie immediately

[2] The only serious obstacle to navigation was at modern Louisville, where there was a fall of some twelve to fifteen feet, called the Rapids.

encountered all sorts of difficulties—chief of which was a complete lack of logs at Logstown. He ran short of provisions too, and the Shawnee in the vicinity gave him trouble. Then one of his scouting parties discovered that the English were already building at the Forks, and word was hurried back to Saint-Pierre at Fort Le Boeuf. This was alarming news: a fort *above* Logstown would obviously cut communications between that point and Canada. It would also sever Canada's link with Louisiana.

Contrecoeur, coming up from Niagara, had as yet learned nothing of these developments. His orders from Duquesne were "to enter the Belle Rivière with the detachment which he commands, in order to march toward Chiningué [Logstown] where he will have a fort built, of which he will take command." Duquesne, however, having been informed of Trent's descent of the Monongahela, wisely added: "If it is true that there is a river [the Monongahela] six leagues this side of Chiningué which they say is the usual route of the English who come from Philadelphia, you will place the fort at the spot to bar their passage and stand in the way of their trade." Dim though Duquesne's geographical knowledge may have been, this was enough to authorize Contrecoeur to oust Ward and begin work at the Forks.

It was a delightful bit of ground on which to build a fort, and long a favorite resort of the Indians, who called the Point—as it was already known—Chonderoga. "The finest place on the river," Céloron called it, and many years later Parkman described it as "charming to the eye of an artist." From a military standpoint, however, the Point was rather less than might have been desired.

For one thing, it was not on high ground. Although some 30 feet above the rivers—both about musket-shot wide—the flats at the Point were commanded by lofty hills. John McKinney, a prisoner at Fort Duquesne in 1756, noted its vulnerability to artillery: "Opposite the Fort, on the west side of the Monongahela is a long, high mountain, about a quarter of a mile from the fort [today's Mount Washington], from which the Fort might easily be bombarded and the bombarder be quite safe." The French engineer, de Léry, also pointed out the ease with which the fort could be shelled from either Mount Washington or the hills north of the Allegheny. Later on, Sir John St. Clair was to urge General Braddock to occupy "a small eminence" and set the fort afire with red-hot cannon balls—a piece of advice which, if taken, might have averted one of the most famous disasters in military history.

Aside from its vulnerability to cannon fire, the Point had other inadequacies. To the east, it was cut by a stream and coulee in which an enemy could find protection from the fort's artillery. It was to be hoped, de Léry remarked dryly, that the French would have enough men to route any attackers in the open, before they had time to organize a siege!

Yet, despite all these shortcomings and more—including the annual threat of devastating floods—the Point was, as Washington had noted, "extremely well situated for a fort, since it has absolute control of both rivers." It was protected on two sides by the Allegheny and Monongahela. And to the eastward, its rear was secured by dense forests and the wavelike ridges of the Alleghenies.[3]

As to the actual building plot, it was flat, well-drained, already cleared of trees, and so fertile that in less than a year's time it would produce 2000 bushels of corn for the garrison. Just as important, an abundance of timber was near at hand.

In any event, the choice of the Point had now been imposed on Contrecoeur by the English; and he wasted no time in putting it into a posture of defense. There was, indeed, no time to be wasted. Scouts were bringing back reports of an English force of 3000 troops assembling at "the nearest settlement." The vanguard of 700 men under Col. George Washington, it was said, had already arrived. Fear of a counter attack by overwhelming numbers increased daily—and Fort Duquesne prepared feverishly to meet it.

* 3 *

Buried deep in the wilderness, the forts of the frontier were built of wilderness materials—trees, earth, perhaps a little native

[3] Army engineers and military men were almost unanimous in condemning the Point as a fort site; yet even the great works of Fort Pitt were, in the long run, built on approximately the same ground chosen by Contrecoeur and approved by Washington.

stone. Often they were thrown together hurriedly by anxious men. Frequently they were neglected after their first desperate need had passed, and allowed to fall into disrepair. But occasionally they were the work of professional military engineers, skillfully planned, solidly built, and proof against almost anything but starvation, treachery, or superior fire-power.

Of such forts there were two main varieties: those defended by a wooden stockade (called *forts de bois* by the French), and those with earth-and-timber defenses (*forts de terre*). Fort Duquesne was a combination of both.

The stockaded fort—by far the most common—was a square or rectangular enclosure of stout posts or pickets. These pickets were a foot or more in diameter, from twelve to fifteen feet long, and immensely difficult to cut and transport—as Contrecoeur's men were finding out.

Even a small redoubt could demand an exhausting toll of labor. La Chauvignerie made this clear to Contrecoeur while working on Fort Le Boeuf:

> I would also have great need of horses to cart the wood to the place, because everything being oak, it is very heavy; the posts are big, a long way off, and 16 feet each; and my men are having a hard time bringing wood for these little redoubts I am having built here, although these pieces are not nearly so large nor long nor so far away, being only 10 feet and mostly split in two. Even then five or six men can hardly carry one and can scarcely make one trip a day . . .

The pickets, sunk four or five feet into the ground, were almost always sharpened with an ax to discourage scaling and retard rotting. On the inside, they were bound together near the top by means of split saplings secured with strips of elm bark or vines. Gates were hung, portholes cut at intervals, and a firing platform of earth or halved-logs installed at a convenient height. Blockhouses were added at diagonally opposite corners of the enclosure to provide flanking fire along the walls. After a powder magazine and other necessary structures had been built—often as part of the palisade walls—the fort was ready to receive friendly Indians in trading or enemy ones with musket fire. A resolute garrison, well-supplied with food, water, and a reasonable reserve of rum, could stand off almost any attack by hostile natives.

Quite another matter, however, was a planned attack by disciplined troops supported by field guns and mortars; and frontier forts designed to withstand this kind of assault differed in both plan and construction from the simple stockade.

• 4 •

Such forts called for the skills of a military engineer who, with the help of a handbook, adapted the principles worked out by the great fort-builders Vauban and Coehorn to wilderness conditions. Whether French or English, they exhibited a striking similarity in their distinctive ground pattern—often miscalled a "star" pattern—and in their dirt-and-timber construction. Essentially, they consisted of artillery positions connected by flanks to the main walls of the fort. The bastion was the dominant element.

In laying out a fort of this type, the engineer first selected his site, then cleared and leveled the ground, and proceeded to stake off a "great square" representing the outside dimensions of the fort. Next, according to well-defined rules, he marked off one side of the square to outline the bastions and curtain walls connecting them. At this stage, one side of his plan, or trace, would look something like this:

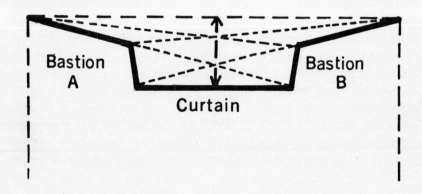

The process was repeated on each of the other sides of the square, thus completing the ground plan of the fort:

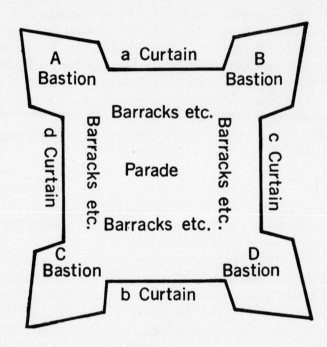

What the engineer now had was the outlines of four bastions (A,B,C,D), connected by curtain walls (a,b,c,d), along the four faces of the fort. If he were in a desperate hurry, he could construct both the bastions and the curtain walls of pickets, with large ports for cannon. Otherwise, as was almost always the case, he built his walls of horizontal logs, binding together two tiers of squared timbers with crossbeams, and filling the intervening space with earth. These criblike walls were usually from 10 to 12 feet thick, and well able to absorb the fire of any guns that might be brought against them in wilderness warfare. Often, as at Fort Duquesne, only the exposed sides of the fort were given this sturdy construction, while less-vulnerable sections were merely stockaded.

In profile, too, the engineer's fort conformed to a conventional pattern. A most important feature was a good ditch—about 10 feet deep and 15 wide—in front of the wall. The earth taken from this ditch was used to form a cannon-proof parapet on one side, and a slope, called the glacis, on the other.

The various parts of the fort were given impressive names in the handbooks—parade, terre plein, banquette, superior slope, scarp and counter scarp, etc.—but the essential features were: (1) a wall and dirt parapet with firing platforms for cannon and musketry, (2) a wide, dry ditch in front of the wall, (3) the glacis on the far side of the ditch, exposing attackers to fire from the fort, (4) a space cleared of stumps and brush, within cannon range on all sides of the fort.

In somewhat simplified form, the profile of an engineer-designed frontier fort would look like this:

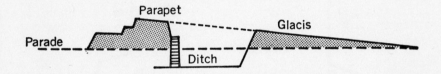

Inside the fort, cannon were mounted on elevated platforms in the bastions, and sometimes at the curtain walls. At ground level, the parade occupied the center of the fort, usually surrounded by ranges of log buildings. In some cases, as at Fort Duquesne, the bastions also contained buildings or powder magazines. Access to the fort was given by heavy plank gates, and these were sometimes approached by drawbridges.

Many elaborations of the basic four-bastioned square fort were, of course, to be found along the frontiers. In some instances, outworks called ravelins and redoubts gave shelter to advanced detachments of defenders during an attack. An outer stockade, completely surrounding the fort, was often added to protect barracks and other buildings outside the walls. Or a hornwork was thrust out from the fort proper for the same purpose. And super-forts with dirt walls 60 feet thick, masonry revetments, five bastions, and a complex system of ravelins, redoubts, forward batteries, and other outworks were to come later.

But elaborate fortifications were not encouraged by either the French or British authorities. In England it was suspected that the Americans were rather too fond of building forts; and we have already noted Duquesne's impatience with the time and labor lavished by Marin on Presqu' Isle. The conventional bastioned square of pickets or horizontal log walls was considered quite good enough for most frontier needs; and with few exceptions, wilderness forts conformed to this basic pattern.

In many ways, however, Fort Duquesne, now building at the Forks, was one of these exceptions. It was being thrown together hurriedly, in desperate haste, almost in the presence of the enemy. Compared to such great French strongholds as Chartres on the Mississippi, it would be but a small fort. Yet, a skilled engineer was in charge of the work, and he was directing it in accordance with sound principles of design and construction. When finished, Fort Duquesne would be one of the strongest forts in the West—the most formidable bastion of French resistance, indeed, yet to be planted in the path of British power between the mountains and the Mississippi.

• 5 •

The architect of Fort Duquesne was the same Captain Le Mercier who, with so much energy, had directed the construction of Marin's invasion base at Presqu' Isle. With equal vigor, he now set to work on headquarters for the French forces on the Ohio. At daybreak, following Ward's capitulation, his men were in the woods, felling trees for timbers, and his demolition crews were tearing down the English buildings.

Le Mercier did not content himself with enlarging and strengthening the structures already completed by Ward's militiamen. His orders were to build a strong fort, capable of housing a garrison of 300 men. A fort such as Duquesne desired, and urged in his letters to Contrecoeur:

> Very far from disapproving of the strength of the fort which you are having built, I highly commend the wisdom of your decision in view of the importance of this establishment and the unfortunate circumstances which would result if we could not hold out there . . .

So Le Mercier, discarding everything the British had started, followed a plan that had probably been put on paper before the invasion force had even left Canada. He proceeded to build a formal military work "by the book." Ward's storehouse he may have kept; but the stockade, so hastily set up by the English, he pulled down.

With all the implements of fort building—axes, pickaxes, spades, shovels, wheelbarrows, handbarrows, and other "intrenching tools"—his men now began the enormous labor of rooting out stumps, cutting brush, digging ditches, and moving earth. As near as possible to the tip of the Point—which was considerably smaller than it is today—a square was measured off, with bastions thrusting out at each corner. The overall dimensions were about 154 feet by 160 feet—a very compact layout compared to Fort Chartres, for instance, with its 460-foot walls.

Because the Allegheny and Monongahela offered some protection against artillery—and because time was so desperately short —Le Mercier decided to build the walls facing those rivers of pickets, and let it go at that. The northwest bastion and half of the southwest and northeast bastions were similarly constructed. The pickets, however, were massive—more than a foot in diameter and from 11 to 12 feet high, with joints covered by split logs. A firing platform of planks was provided at a height that enabled defenders to shoot downward through slanting portholes.

The remaining curtain and bastion walls were constructed of the criblike timberwork, filled with earth, already described. These walls, about 12-feet thick and 14-feet high on the outside, were designed to resist cannon fire from the landward side. But so urgent was the need for speed, that only the southeast bastion —the one least protected by water—was built entirely in this manner.

The walls of Fort Duquesne were, like those of most forts, pierced by two gates. The main gate, made of squared logs, was in the east wall, and was approached by a drawbridge across the wide, dry ditch surrounding the entire fort. Beneath the drawbridge, a pit was dug down to water as further protection to the entrance. The postern gate in the north curtain wall, also made of squared logs, contained a wicket through which one could pass while the gate itself remained closed.

After seizure of the Point, it probably took Le Mercier's work crews at least a month to complete these essential features of Fort Duquesne; for as late as June 29, nobody except Contrecoeur and the guard of 40 men had yet moved into the fort. But with the enemy near at hand, strong walls and gun emplacements must come before comfortable living quarters and bake ovens. And every day, now, the danger of attack became more imminent, the reports from the South more alarming.

· 6 ·

We have a number of on-the-spot descriptions and several drawings which give us a good idea of Fort Duquesne's appearance when finished. Of the drawings, the most famous is the plan made by Maj. Robert Stobo, while a prisoner of the French, and smuggled out to General Braddock—from whom the French ultimately recovered it, much to Stobo's embarrassment. The most important contemporary French drawing of the fort, however, is one discovered by Charles Morse Stotz in the Bibliotheque Nationale in Paris. In its preparation, Mr. Stotz assumes, Le Mercier probably had an important part. Aside from these two plans, no important contemporary drawing of the fort, while still in French hands, is known to exist.

The earliest description of the physical details of Fort Duquesne were supplied in 1754 by Thomas Forbes, a soldier of fortune who served with the French forces on the Ohio:

At our arrival at Fort Du Quisne we found the garrison busily employed in compleating that fort, & stockadoeing it round at some distance for the security of the soldiers barracks (against any surprize) which was built between the stockadoes & the glacis of the fort. Fort Du Quisne is built of square logs transversely placed as is frequent in mill dams, & the interstices filled up with earth. The length of the logs is about 16 feet which is the thickness of the rampart. There is a parapet raised on the rampart of logs, & the length of the curtain is about 30 feet [50 feet?] & the demigorge of the bastions about 80. The fort is surrounded on the two sides that do not front the water, with a ditch, about 12 feet wide & very deep, because there being no covert way the musqueteers fire from thence having a glacis before them.

By far the most complete picture of Fort Duquesne, however, is the verbal account of John McKinney, an American who was captured by Indians and taken to the Forks in February, 1756. McKinney's description was reported as follows:

Fort Du Quesne is situated on the east side of the Monongahela, in the fork between that and the Ohio. It is four square, has bastions at each corner; it is about fifty yards long and about forty yards wide—has a well in the middle of the fort, but the water bad—about half the fort is made of square logs, and the other half next the water of stockadoes; there are entrenchments cast up all around the fort about 7 feet high, which consists of stockadoes driven into the ground near to each other, and wattled with poles like basket work, against which earth is thrown up, in a gradual ascent, the steep part is next the fort, and has three steps all along the entrenchment for the men to go up and down, to fire at the enemy—these entrenchments are about four rods from the fort and go all around, as well the side next the water as the land, the outside of the entrenchments next the water, joins to the water.

The fort has two gates, one of which opens to the land side, and the other to the water side, where the magazine is built, that to the land side is, in fact, a draw-bridge, which in daytime serves as a bridge for the people, and in the night is drawn up by iron chains and levers.

Under the draw-bridge is a pit or well the width of the gate, dug down deep to water, the pit is about eight or ten feet broad, the gate is made of square logs, the back gate is made of logs also, and goes upon hinges and has a wicket in it for the people to pass through in common—there is no ditch or pit at this gate. It is through this gate they go to the magazine and bake house, which are built a little below the gate within the entrenchments—the magazine is made almost underground and of large logs, and covered four feet thick with clay over it. It is about 10 feet wide and about thirty five feet long; the bake house is opposite the magazine, the waters at some time rise so high as that the whole fort is surrounded with it so that canoes may go around it, he imagines he saw it rise at one time near thirty feet.

The stockadoes are round logs better than a foot over, and
about eleven or twelve feet high, the joints are secured by split
logs; in the stockadoes are loop holes made so as to fire slanting
towards the ground. The bastions are filled with earth solid
about eight feet high, each bastion has four carriage guns about
four pounds, no swivels, nor any mortars that he knows of, they
have no cannon but on the bastions.

The back of the barracks and buildings in the fort are of logs
placed about three feet distance from the logs of the fort; between the buildings and the logs of the fort, it is filled in
with earth about eight feet high and the logs of the fort extend
about four feet higher, so that the whole height of the fort
is about 12 feet. There is no picketts nor pallisadoes on the
top of the fort to defend it against scaleing; the eaves of the
houses in the fort are about even with the top of the logs
or wall of the fort, the houses are all covered with boards,
as well the roof as the side that look inside the fort, which
they saw there by hand—there is no bogs nor morasses near
the fort but good dry ground, which is cleared for some distance
from the fort, and the stumps cut close to the ground; a little
without musket shot of the fort in the fork is a thick wood
of some bigness full of large timber.[4]

From these and other contemporary descriptions, it is possible
for one to imagine the interior of Fort Duquesne as it was in the
summer of 1754: a compact jigsaw of low log buildings jammed
into the narrow space around a parade only 34 feet square—half
the size of a tennis court!—and overflowing into some of the
bastions.

After entering through the main gate, a visitor to Fort
Duquesne would have fought his way through a mob of soldiers,
militiamen, Indians and backwoodsmen toward the central parade, where the fleur-de-lis fluttered from a tall flagpole. He
would have passed Contrecoeur's quarters and the officers' lodg-
ings on his right, the troops' barracks and the guardhouse on his
left. Perhaps, as he shouldered his way through the milling
crowd toward the general store on the far side of the square, his

[4] From an extract of McKinney's description ("taken from his own mouth")
in *The Olden Time*, Neville B. Craig, ed., and in *Papiers Contrecoeur*.

nose would have apprised him of still other buildings, jammed into the bastions. The aroma of freshly-baked bread might have drifted to him from the kitchen and bake oven in the northeast bastion. The acrid smell of burning charcoal and white-hot iron would have come from the blacksmith shop in the southwest angle. And, as he drew nearer to the store, he would have sniffed the unmistakable odor of raw hides and pelts—for Fort Duquesne was a trading post as well as a military establishment. The northeast angle, our visitor might have noticed, was occupied by other buildings, the cadets' barracks, and back of them the fort prison. Only the southeast angle, he would have observed with some surprise, was filled with earth to a height and width sufficient for gun emplacements, and uncluttered by buildings.[5]

Crowded quarters, coupled with a salt meat diet, soon brought on crippling epidemics of sickness at Fort Duquesne; and, next to defense against the ever-threatening arrival of the English, more room became the most pressing need. "There are about 250 Frenchmen in this fort," McKinney wrote, "besides Indians, which at one time amounted to 500." According to Duquesne, the number of men wintering at Fort Duquesne in 1754–1755 totalled 258 officers and soldiers, besides about a hundred Indians. Whatever the precise figure might have been, the crowding was intolerable; and to relieve it, a "second fort," comprising a group of buildings, defended by outworks, was built along the Allegheny shore. In this "second fort" 200 men, out of a total garrison of 300, were later quartered.

• 7 •

Like almost all eighteenth century forts, large or small, Fort Duquesne was designed for a defense in depth, in accordance with the system developed by the celebrated Sebastian le

[5] Most of the structures at Fort Duquesne do not seem to have been built in the post-in-sill style common in New France—horizontal logs, often squared, tongued at each end and dropped into grooves cut into vertical corner posts. According to Captain Pouchot, they were "huts made of round logs of oak notched into each other at the corners."

Prestre de Vauban. A simplified ground plan, or trace, of the fort and its outworks would have looked something like this:

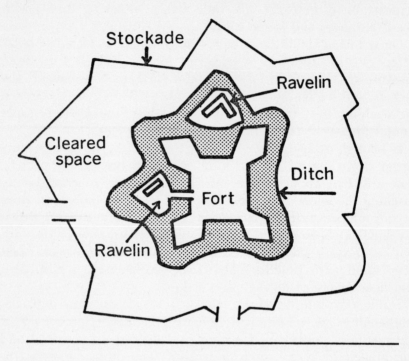

River

An attacking force approaching the fort from landward was confronted, first of all, by a stockaded entrenchment completely surrounding the main work at a distance of about 65 feet, and coming down to the water at the river sides. To reach this stockade of stout seven-foot pickets, the attackers must first cross about half a mile of ground which offered little or no cover from cannon or musket fire.[6]

As they launched their assault from cover of the timber beyond this clearing, they could expect to meet fire from the fort's artillery. Fort Duquesne probably mounted 15 cannon in three of her bastions (the fourth contained only buildings). Half a dozen of these were 6-pounders, i.e., guns firing castiron shot

[6] Except, perhaps, that offered by the coulee or dry ditch mentioned by de Léry with so much disapproval.

weighing six pounds. The remainder were 2-pound or 3-pound pieces, possibly swivel guns. In addition to hurling solid shot against enemy batteries, all could sweep attacking troops with deadly canister and grape shot.

Once within small arms range—60 to 80 yards from the outer defences—the attackers would run into a hail of lead from musketeers, ranged two-deep on the earthen steps behind the pickets, and loading and firing alternately. Those who succeeded in reaching the stockade walls, and thus found safety from frontal fire, were raked from the flanking angles.

If enough attackers got through to scale the outer stockade, batter down one of the gates, or otherwise breach the pickets, they still had about 65 feet of difficult terrain to cross before reaching the walls of the fort proper. To add to their difficulties in this phase of the attack, two bastion-like outworks, called ravelins had been constructed on the landward side of the fort. But so pressing was the need for housing that these works had been filled with buildings—barracks, storehouses, a hospital— and hence were of no defensive value.

Inside the outer stockade, the attackers must deal with the mathematics of a bastioned defense—the deadly geometry of four artillery positions connected by flanks to a main wall and surrounded by a dry ditch and glacis. The ditch, according to Forbes, was "about 12 feet wide and very deep." This, in effect, increased the height of the walls of the fort to about 14 feet. Some of the dirt dug out of the ditch was used in the earth-and-timber defenses, no doubt, and for the bastion fills. The rest was heaped up at the outer edge of the trench and sloped gently away, to form the glacis.

Attackers swarming up the glacis would be silhouetted against the sky at the outer edge of the ditch, easy targets for fire from the fort. Those who survived this fire must then jump down into the ditch and clamber up the opposite side, where they would be confronted by the 14-foot walls or the equally high stockades with their down-slanting loopholes. It might now be possible to scale the walls; Fort Duquesne lacked the protection of the pro-jecting stakes, called *fraises*.[7] Or fireballs might be lobbed over

[7] *Fraises* were short, pointed pickets inserted in the ramparts, below the parapet, at a down-sloping angle.

the walls—although the roofs of houses adjoining the parapets were removable, so as to lessen the danger from that kind of attack.

Or, of course, an entirely different set of perils might beset this lonely fort, deep in the heart of the forest. What has been described is an attack by troops equipped only with small arms— militiamen and Indians, perhaps—and unsupported by artillery. It was quite possible, however, that an army of trained and disciplined troops, hauling siege guns with it over hundreds of miles of wilderness roads, might appear before Fort Duquesne.

Such an army, officered by professionals, would know how to get close under the walls of the fort by means of parallel trenches. It would also find high ground from which to bombard the fort with shell and red-hot balls—today's Mount Washington, for instance, across the Monongahela, or a certain island near the opposite shore of the Allegheny. And, once the walls had been breached by cannon fire, there would be little that Contrecoeur could do except capitulate—or, if he chose to continue resistance, expect a general slaughter of all his men, according to the prevailing rules of warfare.

And there was always the possibility, of course, of treachery, surprise, stratagem, or—in a fort that must draw its supplies and munitions all the way from Canada or even the Illinois country—starvation.

• 8 •

Captain Contrecoeur, feverishly throwing up his stockades and entrenchments on the Point, was naturally not unaware of these dire possibilities. Nor of the even more immediate likelihood that a strong British force was already on its way to attack his position before he was fairly dug in.

Yet, as the wild cherry began to blossom along the Ohio, he could see his situation growing steadily better.

In April he had arrived with 600 men to take possession of the Forks. Shortly afterwards, he had been reinforced by 200 troops under Lieutenant de Carqueville. Then by 130 Indians and 20 Frenchmen under Captain de Villiers. And finally by another

150 men commanded by Lieutenant Dubuisson. This brought his whole force up to 1100 regulars, militia, and Indian auxiliaries— 100 more than the 1000 men that Governor Duquesne had intended for his initial garrison.

The Point, already cluttered with Indian cabins, was hardly large enough to accommodate so many troops—let alone its original inhabitants; and it is doubtful that the crowding and confusion did much to expedite work on the fort. Yet, that too progressed. It would be a whole year before Fort Duquesne could be considered finished—if ever. But on May 15 the post was deemed ready for defense; and the commandant of Fort Duquesne of the Blessed Virgin at the Beautiful River could await, with a little more confidence, the expected counter attack.

He would not, it seemed, have long to wait. Only a few days later, scouts reported that a British force under Col. George Washington had already crossed the mountains. This party, the scouts concluded, was the advance guard of 5000 English, coming to recapture the Point.

"I am certain," Contrecoeur wrote to Duquesne, "the English are on their march."

BOOK FOUR

Round One: Washington

• 1 •

On almost the same January day that Contrecoeur started from Quebec for the Ohio, Washington and Trent received their orders to enlist a hundred men each and march them with all speed to the same spot. Thus the race to the Forks began, as it were, at the crack of a starter's gun. But from the very first, the English were left far behind.

The Colonials, as it turned out, were not eager to risk their scalps in the Indian country for a militiaman's paltry pay of fifteen pounds of tobacco a day. Trent, it was thought, would have no trouble raising his quota from among the 300 frontiersmen who every year went to the Ohio country to trap and trade —self-interest, defense of their trading rights, all that. But at the first whiff of a recruiting officer, the hardy backwoodsmen faded into the bush.

In the Old Dominion, Washington fared no better. "You might as easily raise the dead," he decided, as a company of Virginians. Washington, in fact, faced near-mutiny among the militia officers of Fairfax County. It was very discouraging.

Then the House of Burgesses finally voted £10,000 for the Ohio expedition, and Dinwiddie, optimistically launching a drive to recruit six fresh companies of 50 men each, posted a proclamation on courthouse and church doors promising to distribute 200,000 acres of tax-free Ohio land among volunteers.

But when Washington, in his smart new uniform, opened headquarters at City Tavern in Alexandria, things immediately became very dull in that formerly popular gathering place. En-

77

listments were few, and the quality of recruits wretched. In one of the many despairing letters he was to write during his lifetime, Washington told the Governor: "We daily experience the great necessity of cloathing the men, as we find the generality of those who are to be enlisted are those loose, idle persons that are quite destitute of house or home." Many, he added, were without shoes, stockings, shirts, coats, or "even a waistcoat to their backs."

In the north, Trent's luck was no better. It is doubtful that he ever succeeded in raising more than 70 of the 100 frontiersmen he was expected to enlist. He sent back nothing but discouraging news—accompanied by alarming reports of a great French force coming up the lakes.

At Williamsburg, in the meantime, Governor Dinwiddie was having his own private frustrations. Aware of the importance of Indian auxiliaries, he formed a grand plan for enlisting a thousand Cherokee, Catawba, and Chickasaw allies, and called a great Indian council at Winchester. But when he arrived at Winchester with his kegs of rum and bales of presents, very few Indians were there to receive them. After waiting sixteen days, Dinwiddie went home in disgust—wondering, perhaps, what he had done wrong.

The stubborn old Scot, however, was not one to give up easily. He went ahead with his campaign plans and tables of organization. At one point, although not himself a military man, he seems to have toyed with the idea of assuming personal command of the Ohio troops. He even ordered a suit of regimentals from England. "I do not care much for lace on the coat," he wrote his tailor, "but a neat buttonhole." On reflection, he must have thought better of this, however; for as colonel and leader of the troops, he commissioned Joshua Fry, a former teacher of mathematics at the College of William and Mary. Young Maj. George Washington was advanced to a lieutenant-colonelcy and named second in command.

Recruiting, meanwhile, continued to be backward. Virginia— and, even more, the other colonies—persisted in what Dinwiddie could only call their "lethargic stupidity." Along the coastal strip, there was little apparent concern about what was happening to people in the back country. England, indeed, showed more awareness of the danger to the colonies than did the colonies themselves—and more willingness to do something about it. Encouraging word came from the home government that a company of Independent troops—financed by Crown funds—soon would arrive from South Carolina, and two from New York. In addition, 30 cannon came from England, and 10 of these were immediately started on their way to Wills Creek.

Washington, for his part, was at last making some headway. Despite miserable weather, he succeeded in enrolling about 75 volunteers at Alexandria, and was hopeful of rounding out his quota, when a messenger from Dinwiddie cantered into town with urgent orders. Washington was to cease recruiting activities and, with whatever men he had, march with all possible speed to Captain Trent's assistance at the Forks of the Ohio. Colonel Fry, with the artillery and the remainder of the men, would follow. There was no time to put the men in uniforms. There was not even time to provide pikes, cutlasses, or halberts for the officers—they must lead their companies with small arms.

A day later, Col. George Washington, then twenty-two years of age, formed up his little band of raw recruits, mounted his best horse, and gave the order to march. He recorded this somewhat ludicrous beginning of fateful events in his diary:

> Every thing being ready, we began our march according to orders, the 2nd of April, with two companies on foot, commanded by Captain Peter Hog, Lieutenant Jacob Vanbraam, five subalterns, two sergeants, six corporals, one drummer, and one hundred and twenty soldiers, one surgeon, one Swedish gentleman, who was a volunteer, two wagons guarded by one lieutenant, sergeant, corporal, and twenty five soldiers.

> We left Alexandria on Tuesday noon and pitched our tents about four miles from Cameron, having marched six miles.

There is no record of any cheering crowd of townspeople having gathered to see this rather forlorn little force set off to oppose the might of the world's most formidable military power.

• 2 •

It was Washington's idea to cover the first stage of the journey to Winchester—about 90 miles northwest of Alexandria—

in the lightest possible marching order. The entire baggage train, therefore, was limited to a couple of farm wagons loaded with tents, food, ammunition, and medical supplies. At Winchester, it was confidently expected, additional wagons and horses would be waiting for the second leg of 50 miles to Wills Creek. From Wills Creek it was 110 miles to the Forks of the Ohio, and the only road westward was an Indian war trail known as Nemacolin's Path.[1] Pack horses would be used until Nemacolin's Path could be made into a proper road for the transport of supplies and artillery.

It seemed a feasible enough plan. Maj. John Carlyle, Governor Dinwiddie's Commissary, had promised to procure flour, bread, salt beef and pork for the subsistence of Washington's troops; and what was lacking could be obtained en route. "I am told that provisions are very plenty in the back country," the Governor wrote Carlyle. And John Fraser, he added, could provide "large quantities of venison, bear, etc."

But at Winchester, young Colonel Washington learned the real meaning of the ugliest word in the vocabulary of frontier warfare. The word was wagon. There were many ways in which wagons could frustrate, enrage, and drive a commander of troops to despair. They could break down on impossible mountain grades. They could be mired in swamps, swept away in rivers. They could collapse under the weight of cannon and ammunition they were never built to carry. Worst of all, they could be lacking.

War on the frontier was a business of moving men, supplies, and guns over great distances to the battlefield; of cutting roads through dense forests and over precipitous mountains; of transporting every pound of food, equipment, and fodder the army required on its march—for not even a horse could live off the country that frontier armies traversed. And so, wagons—plenty of sound, strong wagons, and stout horses to draw them.

Washington arrived at Winchester to find neither.

Something had gone wrong in Williamsburg, no doubt; but the young commander had no time to check back through channels.

[1] The original Nemacolin's Path ran from Wills Creek westward to Washington Spring in present Fayette County, Pa., then through present Uniontown to Nemacolin's village (Brownsville) on the Monongahela River. One branch of it eventually reached the Forks of the Ohio.

He began impressing vehicles and horses from unwilling farmers, and not too successfully. Seven wagons must be impressed for every one that was brought into camp—most of them wrecks. And the horses no better.

A precious week was wasted at this—a week during which the French, no doubt, were racing down from Canada to attack Trent at the Forks. Indeed, the column was hardly on the march again when an express rider lathered up with a desperate note from Captain Trent himself: 800 French troops, he wrote, were descending the Allegheny, and expected at any hour.

Washington pushed on with all dispatch to Wills Creek, where he received more bad news. No supplies. The flour, bread, beef and pork promised by Carlyle had not arrived. Worse yet, not a single one of the pack horses that Trent had guaranteed to deliver was on hand; and, as far as Washington could ascertain, none was on the way.

This meant, of course, that plans for a quick march to the Forks with pack animals would have to be abandoned. But bad news sometimes cancels out bad news. Two days later, who should ride into camp but Ensign Ward himself—living proof that the Forks were already in French hands! He was soon followed by his starving carpenters and militiamen, each an abject symbol of defeat. Then by fugitive traders and settlers, with tales of murder and rapine, and the whole Ohio country in a state of terror.

Washington bivouaced his dispirited little force of 159 "loose, idle persons," and considered what to do next.

• 3 •

Governor Dinwiddie's instructions, ordering him so abruptly out of Alexandria, were:

> You are to use all expedition in proceeding to the Forks of the Ohio . . . and there you are to finish and complete in the best manner and as soon as you possibly can the fort which I expect is already begun by the Ohio Company. You are to act on the defensive, but in case any attempts are made to obstruct the work or interrupt our settlements by any persons

whatsoever, you are to restrain all such offenders, and in the case of resistance to make prisoners of or kill and destroy them. For the rest you are to conduct yourself as the circumstances of the service shall require.

All this was a grim jest now, of course; but there was still that final sentence: *"For the rest you are to conduct yourself as the circumstances of the service shall require."*

Washington decided that the exceedingly dismal circumstances of the service now required him to push on as far as he could, set up a forward base, and wait for the promised reinforcements—100 Virginians under Colonel Fry, 350 Independents from North Carolina, another 200 from Maryland, and two companies from New York: almost 800 men in all. With such a force, the objective of the campaign—which had suddenly become not just the occupation of the Forks of the Ohio, but the capture of a strong French fort at that strategic point—could still be attained.

This may have been a rash decision; but it was a very young and inexperienced commander's best judgment—and, he reasoned, according to orders. After holding a council of war, Washington gave the command to march. The best location for a base from which to launch an attack on Fort Duquesne, he decided, was at the mouth of Redstone Creek, on the Monongahela. Captain Trent had already finished his storehouse there. Redstone, then, was the goal.

Between Wills Creek and Redstone rose the jeering heights of the Allegheny Mountains, Laurel Hill, Chestnut Ridge—each one a gigantic thicket of great trees and laurel "slick" so dense that not even the sun could penetrate them.[2] It rained incessantly from the start of the march, and rampaging streams frustrated and infuriated the axmen as they sweated at widening a dim Indian trail into a road broad enough for wagons and artillery. They never advanced more than four miles a day, often only two.

Other troubles besides mountain roads and foul weather beset Washington on this march. Trent's unruly backwoodsmen became rebellious, and he had to get rid of them. He was threatened

[2] All early travelers in the Appalachians commented on the extreme difficulty in penetrating the thickets of laurel that covered the mountains—so dense as to constitute a serious barrier to the westward movement of settlers.

with mutiny by his Virginia officers, too; and he wrote a 2000-word letter to Dinwiddie setting forth their complaints about low pay. To add to his worries, traders from the Ohio country brought alarming reports of French reconnoitering parties just over Chestnut Hill, and of a large force marching down from Fort Duquesne to attack him. These fugitives also told of the progress the French were making with their new fort, and he recorded their reports in his journal:

> The French continue to erect their fort. What is on the land side is very well enclosed, but the side toward the water is much neglected, at least it is undefended. They have only nine pieces of cannon, and some of them very small, and none of them are mounted. There are two on the point, and the others some distance from the fort on the land side.

Pondering these reports, Washington chafed impatiently at the Great Crossing of the Youghiogheny, where high water tied his column down. Then, at last, came a spell of good weather and he pushed on, almost elatedly, toward the Monongahela. On May 24 he camped in a broad valley between Laurel Hill and Chestnut Ridge called the Great Meadows.

Here he received word from his scouts that the French were marching out to meet him, were only a few miles away.

• 4 •

From Fort Duquesne, the movements of Washington's little army had been constantly and, on the whole, accurately observed —although the actual strength of the main British force, not yet on the march, was much over-estimated at 5,000 men.

England and France were still at peace, but both countries operated an elaborate system of espionage, with agents skulking about Whitehall and Versailles, as well as in the wilds of America. One French agent, indeed—an Irish physician named Hennessey—had access to the very top secrets of the British ministry. He was caught, and saved from the gallows only by George II's intercession as a personal favor to the French monarch. Six British spies, with less helpful connections, were hung at Quebec.

In the vast forests of the New World, the importance of military intelligence was underscored by the opportunities for ambush and surprise. To march blind through the woods was to meet with almost certain disaster so pains were spared in gathering reliable information on the enemy's movements and intentions.

As scouts, the Indians were naturally superior to almost any white man; Braddock was to discover tragically that not even the most powerful force could operate successfully without a good Indian intelligence corps. And it was here that the French, with their numerous Indian allies, held an important advantage over the English.

"The French may be pretty well informed of our proceedings," a British colonel wrote. "I am ashamed that they have succeeded in all their scouting parties and that we never have any success in ours." There was, of course, a little question about the reliability of the Indians: Washington once had reason to suspect that one of his red scouts was a double agent—working for both sides! Indian "ears" needed watching.

Next to a trustworthy Indian—like Half King, who served as Washington's intelligence chief—an experienced frontiersman was to be valued. Unfortunately, however, the woods were not full of them. A few, such as Christopher Gist, Andrew Lewis, and George Croghan—on whose scalp Contrecoeur had put a price of $1,000—were as good as their Indian counterparts. But most, it would seem, were far from Hawkeyes. Reconnaisance parties sometimes did not go to their destination—as one commander proved by following his scouts' trail in the weeds. Or they lost themselves in the woods: one of General Forbes' scouts did for eight days. Even Major Rogers' vaunted Rangers were sometimes careless on scouting expeditions. On one occasion a Lieut. Thomas Barnsley was forced to report:

> The French Indians are not so forward in scouting as they us'd to be, before Major Rogers had the last skirmish with them; it is remarkable in that attack of Rogers' that he was surprised by about 600 of the French who lay in ambush watching Rogers' party, which consisted of about the same number, shooting of

pidgeons as they went along the woods for their diversion, that all the provincials, commanded by Major Putnam, and most of Rogers' own Rangers ran away.

In fairness to Rogers, it must be added that he rallied his men, killed a hundred of the attackers, and "made them very backward in their scouting ever since."

Another good source of intelligence was prisoners—called "living letters" by the Indians. Parties were sent out for the express purpose of bringing back captives; and there is plenty of evidence that the art of prisoner interrogation was practiced on a sophisticated level. "I examined the Englishman a second time," a French captain reported, "sometimes terrifying him, and at other times giving him hopes of reward."

Still another source—not always very credible—was deserters. A soldier who left his outfit beyond the frontier had no place to go, really, but to the enemy; and naturally he told his captors what he sensed they wanted to hear. It was because every deserter was a potential informer, perhaps, that the penalty for the act was so severe—usually a thousand lashes, but sometimes hanging.[3]

At Fort Duquesne, of course, Contrecoeur was using every means at his disposal—scouts, deserters, prisoners—to keep an eye on Washington's progress toward the Forks. On the basis of his intelligence, he would soon have to make an important decision: should he sit tight in Fort Duquesne, or should he send a force out to engage the English in the field? Should he stand a siege or fight a battle?

But there was still another alternative. His country and England had not yet broken openly. Neither side was anxious to start a shooting war: indeed, he had been ordered specifically by Duquesne *not to fire first*. Perhaps the proper course would be to send the English fair warning that they were entering French lands—just such a warning as Governor Dinwiddie of Virginia had once sent Captain Saint-Pierre at Fort Le Boeuf.

Colonel Washington, Contrecoeur learned, was now at the Great Meadows, just beyond the last mountain ridge, with an

[3] Often—if they were not scalped—deserters, and occasionally their wives with them, were rounded up and brought to forts or army headquarters by Indians.

advance party of 150 or more English. He decided to send one
of his young officers, Ensign Coulon de Jumonville, with a small
detachment to the Great Meadows.

Was it to carry a warning, and summon the English to leave
French lands? Or was it to gather information? Was Coulon de
Jumonville an envoy, or was he a spy?

In Europe as well as America, this was to become the most
furiously debated question of the day; and one that has never
been answered.

The record clearly shows that Jumonville did indeed carry
with him a "summons" to the English commander to depart from
the territory of France; or—much as the French loved peace—
forcible ejection would become necessary. It also shows that
Jumonville's instructions were: to find a road to the English
position; to hand the commander the summons, and report back
his reply; but not to harass the English column if it were still
east of "the Great Mountain."

Were these documents *bona fide,* or were they really "cover"
—grist for the French propaganda mill in case Jumonville and his
scouts were killed or captured? Nobody has yet found the answer
to that question, either.

The hard facts are that on the morning of May 23 Jumonville,
with 28 picked men, an interpreter, some cadets, and two officers,
marched out of the postern gate of Fort Duquesne and down to
the dock, where canoes were waiting to carry them up the
Monongahela.

Coulon de Jumonville was the young son of a patriotic and
illustrious French family of seven brothers, six of whom, together with their father, were to die in the service of their country in Canada. He was, no doubt, proud of the responsibility
Contrecoeur had placed in him, and excited by the prospect of
danger that obviously attended such a mission. He could hardly
know, on that soft May morning, that it was a mission from which
he would not return.

Still less could he guess that he was marching out to begin
one of the greatest wars of all time—a conflagration that, flick-
ering up in the forests of North America, would ultimately sweep
across most of Europe and the Far East for seven catastrophic
years, and decide the fate of a continent.

• 5 •

Washington was having less success than Contrecoeur in obtaining "hard" intelligence about enemy movements. But all reports brought in by traders and friendly Indians strongly suggested the advisability of preparing for a fight. He therefore pitched his tents and grouped his few wagons in the fork of two small creeks flowing through the Great Meadow, cut down the surrounding brush and weeds so as to provide a clear field of fire, and awaited developments.

It was not a long wait. Early in the morning of May 27, Christopher Gist rode into camp with the news that 50 French soldiers had appeared just beyond Chestnut Ridge. That same evening, Half King sent word that he had found the trail of the French party only six miles away. Day had faded into a black, rainy night, but Washington immediately set off with 40 men to join Half King and his Mingoes.[4] If anyone was going to attack, he wanted to be the one. He resolved to jump Jumonville's party at dawn.

At the break of a sodden day, Washington's men and Half King's warriors fanned out and advanced through the dripping woods. They found the French soldiers in bark shelters they had put up against the rain, huddled in "a low, obscure place" among the rocks. Some were still asleep, others eating breakfast.

What happened next is anybody's guess. We have two versions of "the Jumonville affair," and they could not possibly be farther apart. First, Washington's own, as he reported it to Governor Dinwiddie in an exultant dispatch:

> I set out with 40 men before 10, and it was from that time till near sun rise before we reached the Indian's camp, hav'g marched in small paths, a heavy rain, and night as dark as it is possible to conceive; we were frequently tumbling over one another, and often so lost that 15 or 20 minutes search would not find the path again.
>
> When we came to the Half-King, I council'd with him, and got his assent to go hand in hand and strike the French. Ac-

---

[4] Mingo was a name applied to the Iroquois (properly the Six Nations) by the English. In the Delaware tongue it meant "stealthy" or "treacherous."

cordingly, himself, Monacatoocha, and a few other Indians set
out with us, and when we came to the place where the tracts
[tracks] were, the Half-King sent two Indians to follow their
tract and discover their lodgment, which they did ab't half
a mile from the road, in a very obscure place surrounded by
rocks. I thereupon, in conjunction with the Half-King and
Monacatoocha, form'd a disposition to attack y'm on all sides,
which we accordingly did, and after an engagement of ab't
15 minutes, we killed 10, wounded one, and took 21
prisoners . . . Among those that were killed was Monsieur De
Jumonville, the Commander.

The English loss was one killed and a few wounded. The only
Frenchman to escape was a soldier named Mouceau. When Con-
trecoeur heard the story of this wild-eyed, half-naked survivor, he
sat down and wrote Governor Duquesne an account of what, in
French usage, became known as "the assassination of Coulon de
Jumonville."

The English gave them two volleys, but the Indians did not
fire. Jumonville, through his interpreter, told them to desist,
that he had something to tell them. Upon which they ceased
firing. Then M. de Jumonville ordered the summons which I
had sent them to retire to be read . . . The aforesaid Mouceau
saw all the Frenchmen coming up close to M. de Jumonville
whilst they were reading the summons, so that they were all
in platoons between the English and the Indians, during which
time said Mouceau made the best of his way to us . . . The
Indians who were present when the thing was done say that
M. de Jumonville was killed by a musket shot in the head,
whilst they were reading the summons.

The French view was more fully set forth in a *Mémoire*
based on Washington's own journal (later captured by the
French), published in Paris, and sent to every court in Europe.
The *Mémoire*—which noted that Jumonville's head had been
scalped—produced world-wide indignation and made an international *cause célèbre* of the Jumonville skirmish.

There can be no doubt that the French reaction was deep
and sincere, and not just something whipped up for propaganda
purposes. Yet, to the cries of assassination! *"le cruel Wasinghton
(sic)"* could ask: "If Jumonville came as an envoy, and not as a

spy, why did he bring so many men with him? Why did he not come directly to me with his summons? Why did he lurk for several days in hiding about my camp?"

From any point of view it was a catastrophically unfortunate affair. Perhaps, older, more experienced leaders on both sides would have handled it differently. It is doubtful that Washington grasped, at the time, the terrible gravity of what had happened. He had fought his first fight, and won his first victory; and with the heartless exuberance of youth, he wrote his brother Jack: "I heard the bullets whistle, and, believe me, there is something charming in the sound."

• 6 •

Of one thing Washington could now be reasonably sure: the French would not let Jumonville's death go unavenged. He could expect retaliation, and he had but 159 raw recruits against perhaps 2,000 French, many of them professional soldiers from Europe. Where were Colonel Fry and the rest of the Virginians? Where were the New York and South Carolina companies? Where were the 1,000 Cherokee that Dinwiddie had promised? He sent off an urgent, anxious express to Colonel Fry, supposedly at Winchester, begging him to hurry reinforcements.

Reinforcements and supplies. "We have been six days without flour," he wrote Dinwiddie, "and there is none upon the road for our relief that I know of . . . We have not provisions of any sort enough in camp to serve us two days."

To worsen matters, Half King herded about eighty Indians into the Great Meadows, including squaws, children, and the famous Queen Aliquippa;[5] and they demanded equal rations with the soldiers. The whole command might have starved, indeed, had not a passing trader showed up with a store of flour—"for which," Washington protested, "I was obliged to give twenty-one shillings and eight pence per hundred."

In the midst of these troubles, constantly expecting Jumonville's avengers, Washington did what he could to keep things

[5] Queen Aliquippa, an influential Seneca woman, was chief of an Indian community near the Forks of the Ohio. She is said to have met William Penn in 1701, and Washington visited her in 1753.

going. He sent Gist off with a long letter to Dinwiddie about the shameful failure of supplies. He started the French prisoners, taken in the Jumonville skirmish, to Winchester. He made speeches to the Indians, sent out scouting parties in every direction, set his men to building a small stockade, and "had prayers in the fort."

On June 6, Gist returned with shocking news. Colonel Fry had been killed by a fall from his horse. And so, at the age of twenty-two, George Washington received his commission as a full colonel and commander of the expedition to the Ohio. Everything was now on his shoulders.

A few days later the three remaining companies of the Virginia regiment—about 180 men—arrived under Maj. George Muse. They dragged nine swivel guns with them, but nothing much in the way of supplies. On June 14, Capt. James Mackay showed up with his company of South Carolina Independents. They were accompanied by about sixty head of lean cattle, but nothing else to eat.

Washington now had around 400 men and nine small guns. And very little to live on. A more cautious commander might have dug in at this point, and waited for more men, guns, wagons, food. Or he might even have retreated to the security of Wills Creek. But Washington's instincts told him that to show weakness, or even indecision, would result in demoralization of his green, half-frightened troops—and, just as bad, loss of the Indian allies he still hoped to gain.

Besides, he had his orders; and his orders were to march to the Ohio, attack Fort Duquesne, and drive the French from the Forks. So he did what was, no doubt, a brave but rash and foolhardy thing. On June 16 he started for Redstone and the Ohio.

• 7 •

Captain Mackay and the South Carolina company did not go with him. Mackay had arrived in a carriage, very much the gentleman and King's officer—and not at all disposed to take orders from a "buckskin colonel." He set up his own camp, refused even to accept the parole and countersign from Washington. Nor would he hear of his red-coated regulars lending a hand at the road work or other menial labor.

With infinite patience, Washington tried to make the best of this sticky situation, confining himself to a dry comment in a letter to Dinwiddie: "I can very confidentally say that his [Mackay's] absence would tend to the public advantage." But Mackay remained aloof and adamant in his laced regimentals; and there is reason to believe that Washington decided to march away with his Virginians as the best way to break the impasse.

Washington described the march-off in one of his finest under-statements: "*June 16th.* Set out for Red Stone Creek, and were extremely embarrassed, our wagons breaking very often." Actually, the march was a nightmare from the start. It was the old story of hacking a road through a dense forest of oak, black walnut, cherry and other hard woods, with trees—often five feet in diameter—laced together by an impenetrable tangle of branches, vines, and laurel thickets. Horses dropped dead and wagons shattered on the heart-breaking grades. The men, half-starved, could hardly lift the axes, picks, and shovels with which they were supposed to work. On June 28, after two weeks of killing labor, the column had progressed less than 13 miles.

But on that date, at least, Gist's "new settlement"—about 16 miles from Redstone—had been reached. Here Gist had brought out eleven settlers in the spring and had begun a stockaded post. Washington decided it was a good place to stop—cleared fields, stout cabins, a well of good water, even some cattle. Reports of the French force on its way from Fort Duquesne were becoming more frequent now; it would not do to be caught in a long, strung-out column of road workers. So a halt was called and the wagons sent back to Great Meadows for provisions. Gist's fences were torn down for pickets and his house fortified; a proper stockaded fort was begun. Captain Lewis, however, was spared sixty men to push the road a little closer to Redstone: young Colonel Washington never lost sight of the main objective of the expedition.

At Gist's, Washington called a council of the Ohio Indians. The Delaware, Shawnee, and Mingo were rumored to have abandoned the English and taken up the hatchet on the French side, and Washington wanted assurance of their loyalty. The council was a resounding failure. The Indians came to it—then

went away. Even Half King and his Mingoes found some excuse
for fading away. Not more than three Indians were left to
Washington as scouts.

This in itself was disquieting enough: either the Indians were
for you or against you. At this point, they most emphatically
were not with Washington; he even suspected, indeed, that they
had come to the council only as spies! But even more alarming
was the news now sent by Scarroyady, an Iroquois chief who
could be trusted. Two days previously, Scarroyady said, he
had been at Fort Duquesne; he had seen strong reinforcements
arriving there; he had learned that the French were about to send
800 soldiers and 400 Indians against Washington's column.

It was time, Washington decided, to pull his scattered forces
together; and the best place would be Gist's settlement. He
ordered a general rendezvous there. This time Mackay, perhaps
smelling battle, responded with alacrity to the "buckskin
colonel's" orders. Lewis hastened back from his road building.
On the morning of June 29, the whole command of 400 men was
together again, in a ramshackle stockade defended by a few
swivel guns[6]—and with nothing to eat but 24 emaciated milk
cows.

Washington called a council of war. Over it lowered the
spectre of starvation, severed supply lines, Indian defection to the
French, and—not by any means the least probable—destruction
at the hands of an overwhelming enemy force. The decision of
the council was swift and unanimous: the column must immediately retreat to Great Meadows.

⋆ 8 ⋆

At Fort Duquesne, Captain Contrecoeur was grimly preparing vengeance for Jumonville's "assassination"—a mean return, he felt, for the courtesy that Joncaire, Saint-Pierre, and he
himself had invariably shown in their dealings with the English
on the Ohio.

[6] Swivel guns were light pieces that could readily be carried by packhorse.
The larger sizes were about 3 feet long, with a breech diameter of between
5 and 6 inches. They were mounted, by means of a swivel and socket, in a
solid base, so that they could be rotated horizontally.

"I believe, sir," he wrote Governor Duquesne, "it will surprise you to hear how basely the English have acted; it is what was never seen, even amongst nations who are the least civilized, to fall thus upon ambassadors and murder them." And he asked Minister of Marine de Machault if he did not think it time, at last, to break openly with England.

Meanwhile, he was getting ready to deal out retribution in his own fashion.

He was in good shape to strike a counter-blow. Ever since taking possession of the Point, he had driven his men hard; and now Fort Duquesne was almost finished, her artillery in place, her supply lines secure, her garrison 1000 strong, her Indian contingent swelled by bands of savage warriors from the Western tribes. Without risk, he could throw 500 seasoned troops against Washington's exhausted little army; and this he now prepared to do. Chevalier Le Mercier would command them.

But while these steps were being taken, news of Jumonville's death reached his brother, Capt. Coulon de Villiers. Coulon, perhaps the most distinguished of all the valiant sons of Nicolas Antoine Coulon de Villiers, was commonly called, "le Grand Villiers," to distinguish him from his almost equally famous brother François, styled, "Le Chevalier." Coulon was at the old Chautauqua portage, on his way to Fort Duquesne, when word of his brother's death reached him. He had with him 130 Indians and 20 French soldiers, and with these he hastened by forced marches to the Forks. On June 26 he reached Fort Duquesne: this was the reinforcement that Scarroyady had correctly reported to Washington at Gist's settlement.

"The Great Villiers," burning for personal revenge, demanded to lead the French force against Washington; and, since he outranked Le Mercier in any case, this was granted. He also requested that his 150 Indians and French regulars be added to the force already organized, thus bringing its total strength up to 650—almost twice the number of Washington's effectives.

Before this army of avengers could march, however, certain preliminaries must be disposed of. First, Contrecoeur called his Indian allies together and harangued them in the style they were accustomed to: "The English have murdered my children, my heart is sick; tomorrow I shall send my French soldiers to take revenge. And now, men of the Sault St. Louis, men of the Lake of Two Mountains, Hurons, Abenakis, Iroquois of La Presentation, Nipissings, Algonquins, and Ottawas—I invite you all by this belt of wampum to join your French father and help him to crush the assassins. Take this hatchet, and with it two barrels of wine for a feast."

The hatchet and, with even greater enthusiasm, the wine were accepted; after which Contrecoeur succeeded in enlisting the more difficult Delaware, traditional friends of the English.

The matter of Indian loyalty having been taken care of, the principal officers of the fort—Contrecoeur, Villiers, Le Mercier, and Longueuil—sat down to write out a statement of their position for history. The fiery Villiers urged a very tough course, but Le Mercier, with an eye out for world opinion, pleaded for more moderate action. What resulted was a sort of compromise manifesto. It affirmed the justice of marching against the English "with the greatest possible number of French and savages, in order to avenge ourselves and chastise them for having violated the most sacred laws of civilized nations." At the same time, it promised that if the English, after taking their medicine, withdrew to their own side of the mountains, they would be treated by the French as friends. If, however, the English should retreat without giving battle, "they should be followed to their settlements to destroy them as enemies, till that nation should give ample satisfaction and completely change its conduct."

This document out of the way, Villiers' war canoes pushed off next morning for Redstone.

Two days later, on June 30—the same day that Washington's council of war was voting for a retreat to the Great Meadows—the French arrived at the mouth of Redstone Creek. They camped on high ground, about two musket shots from Trent's storehouse, and prepared for the march inland. After Mass next morning, a guard was placed over the canoes and heavy supplies, and the main body of troops plunged into the forest.

The going was easier for the French soldiers than it had been for Washington's men; they were traveling light, unencumbered by artillery, with no necessity for cutting a road. Yet, it was rough enough to discourage the chaplain of the expedition, who, after absolving the whole detachment of its sins, sensibly returned to Redstone.

On information that the English were entrenching themselves
at Gist's settlement, Villiers made a forced night march, which
brought him to Washington's half-finished stockade at dawn of
July 2. A few volleys loosed from the surrounding woods were
unreturned, proving that the place had been abandoned.

From a well-terrorized deserter, Villiers now learned that the
English had pulled out of Gist's only two days before. The
deserter also volunteered the information that Washington had
retreated to the Great Meadows and was fortifying his position
there. Villiers promised to reward this wretch if his story was
true, to hang him if it was false. After resting his footsore troops,
he started off at dawn next day, hoping to reach the Great
Meadows before the English could entrench themselves. As his
journal of the expedition tells us:

> At break of day I prepared to depart from the camp abandoned
> by the English . . . The weather was inclining to rain, but I
> saw the necessity of anticipating the enemy in the works he
> might construct. I even flattered myself that he would be less
> on his guard in such bad weather.

Thus, hoping to effect a surprise attack, Villiers marched his
men in the rain, sending out "scouts after scouts" to screen his
approach. He came to the spot where his brother had been
killed, and lying in the downpour he "saw some dead bodies there
yet." Now within a few miles of the Great Meadows, he proceeded with extreme caution through the dripping forest.

When less than a mile from Washington's camp, Villiers sent
out scouts, with twenty men to cover them, for close reconnaissance. He formed his troops into columns, "in a manner
suited to bush fighting," and advanced to the edge of the wood
surrounding the Great Meadows.

In the center of the clearing, less than a musket shot away, the
blurred outlines of a wretched little fort were visible through the
rain.

• 9 •

"Fort Necessity," its hungry, bedraggled builders had
christened it; and by the most meager of frontier standards, it
was indeed not much of a fort.

Perhaps a better-fed, less-weary lot of men might have put up a better one, even in the scant five days allowed them. But the dreadful march back from Gist's had left the English with little strength for hewing logs or digging ditches. It could hardly be called an army at all that finally dragged itself into the Great Meadows: it was 400 sick, half-starved totally-spent farmers and village boys—who had never had any stomach for soldiering in the first place.

Washington had fondly hoped to find provisions from Wills Creek waiting for him on his return to the Great Meadows; but nothing had come except a few bags of chopped flour. So it was a choice between starving here or pushing on to Wills Creek. But there was no choice, really. The men could not possibly march another mile. There was nothing for it but to dig in here and wait. Wait for what? For food, perhaps, from below. For the New York and Carolina companies—with the 4-pounders from England that had never, for some reason, reached Wills Creek. For news, perhaps, that the French had gone back to Fort Duquesne, unwilling to risk an attack on his fortified position without artillery.

Hoping thus forlornly, Washington's hungry and demoralized little army prepared to fight. Military pundits have expressed the opinion that its leader could hardly have chosen a worse place for a battle. The ground was low and commanded on three sides by wooded hills, one of them only 60 yards from the edge of the Meadow. The interior of the stockade could be raked by fire from the timber on these hills.

But it was by necessity, not by choice, that young Colonel Washington found himself pinned down to this unlikely spot; so he prepared to strengthen his defenses, deploy his forces, and make the most of a difficult situation.

In one respect, at least, the Great Meadows offered a defensive advantage. Two small streams—Great Meadows Run and Indian Run—meandered through the level bottom to form a natural V-shaped defense position. It was in the fork of these streams that Washington set his men to digging shelter trenches and finishing the rude stockade that had been started, but never completed, after the Jumonville skirmish.

A century of scholarly—and occasionally acrimonious—controversy raged over the exact location and structure of Fort

Necessity. At one time it was declared that the fort was a triangular stockade, with outlying earthworks. Then it was demonstrated that the enclosure was diamond-shaped. Ridicule, in the meantime, was heaped on the head of Col. James Burd, who visited the Great Meadows in 1759, and was naive enough to describe Fort Necessity as he actually saw it—a round stockade with a house in it.

Excavations by the National Park Service in 1952 proved Colonel Burd to have been right. Fort Necessity was indeed a round stockade with a house in it—a poor, ramshackle thing, hardly worthy of even its dubious name.[7]

Archeological evidence has revealed that the stockade was almost perfectly circular, with a diameter of 53 feet. It was made of white oak logs, probably 7 or 8 feet high and about 10 inches thick. Besides its very unusual circular ground plan, Fort Necessity was distinguished by another uncommon feature: it was built of split stockade posts, with the flat sides facing out. This, it has been surmised, was to save the strength of the men: it took less time and muscle to split a log in two than to cut down an oak tree, and half a log was easier to carry than a whole one weighing 300 pounds. Like everything else about Fort Necessity, these split pickets testify to the desperate haste of half-starved men, trying to erect some sort of defense against imminent attack.

Inside the stockade, a crude log house was thrown up, a low structure with a shed roof of bark and skins. Here supplies and ammunition would be stored; and here, when the fighting began, the wounded could be cared for.

Outside the stockade, on the side from which an attack was expected, two shelter trenches were dug. These were no more than ditches behind dirt parapets four or five feet high. In them a man could fire, then stoop and reload without exposing himself.

On the way up from Wills Creek, the Great Meadows had looked very good to Washington; and he was immensely satisfied with the flimsy stockade he had begun to build after the Jumonville incident. "We have just finished a small palisado'd fort," he

[7] Fort Necessity has been restored by the National Park Service, U.S. Department of the Interior, on its original site. Now a national shrine, known as Fort Necessity National Battlefield Site, it is located in Fayette County, Pennsylvania, on U.S. Route 40, 55 miles west of Cumberland, Md. and 11 miles east of Uniontown, Pa.

wrote to Dinwiddie, "in which, with my small numbers, I shall
not fear the attack of 500 men." The Great Meadows, he added,
seemed to him "a charming field for an encounter."

But that was a month ago, and he had grown considerably
older since then. It is probable that, despite his youthful spirit,
he did not find much charm in the situation that faced him now.
Sickness, desertions, and other drains had reduced his fighting
power to only 300 men; he was utterly without Indian support,
Half King and his followers having deserted; he had been able to
mount only two of the nine precious swivels his men had dragged
over the mountains at such cost; there was nothing to eat except
a little flour and cow meat, fast spoiling in the July heat; and his
men were still working frantically on the entrenchments when
Villiers peered at them through the rain.

A stouter heart than Washington's might have quailed at such
an array of embarrassments, but there is no record of the young
Virginian's having taken anything but a practical, if grim, view
of the situation. Methodically, he sent out white scouts in place
of the missing Indians; he posted a great many sentinels, covering
all possible approaches to the fort; and when, on the morning
of July 3, one of these sentries was shot in the heel, he roused his
exhausted men and ordered them to the entrenchments.

There was scarcely room for 200 in Fort Necessity's stockade
and shelter trenches; with 400 jammed into the narrow space,
and many of them too sick to stand, the crowding must have
been intolerable. To add to the discomfort, it was raining now,
a slow, steady rain. The troops in the trenches and at the loopholes huddled over their pieces, trying to keep their powder dry
. . . and waited.

                              • 10 •

Villiers approached Fort Necessity cautiously from the
Northwest, along the Redstone-Wills Creek trail. Finding that
he was marching away from his objective, rather than toward it,
he ordered a turn to the left, in the direction of the woods nearest the fort. This maneuver, exposed his flank to Fort Necessity's
swivel guns, which began to fire. At the same time, the English
were seen coming across the clearing to give battle in the open

field. The French and Indians immediately deployed, "set up the cry," and advanced to meet Washington's men. "But," Villiers reported later, "they gave us no time to make our discharge: they filed off, and withdrew into an entrenchment which lay next to their fort."

Such was the French account of how the Battle of the Great Meadows opened, at about 11 o'clock on the morning of July 4, 1754. Washington's version differs from that of the French only in detail.

The French, according to Washington, fired first, but at an ineffectual range of 600 yards. Washington then arranged his men in front of the entrenchments, apparently hoping for a quick decision in the open. But the French, taking cover behind every bush and rise of ground, advanced very slowly, and did not fire again until they were only 60 yards away.

The English, expecting a rush, grimly withheld their own fire during this interval. When a French attack failed to materialize, Washington ordered his greatly-outnumbered force back to the protection of the rain-filled entrenchments. The French, for their part, retired to the cover of the woods, from which they began methodically to pick off cattle, horses, "even the dogs" of the fort.

After this initial sparring, the Battle of the Great Meadows settled down to a steady exchange of musketry, with perhaps a few rounds from the swivel guns in the fort. Villiers—possibly to make himself and his men look good—may have attributed a little too much importance to Washington's artillery. It now consisted of only two operative swivel guns, very light pieces, one firing a 7-ounce ball, the other a ball weighing only 1¼ ounces. And both, Villiers reported, were soon silenced by his muskets.

This second phase of the battle was described thus by the French commander:

> We then set ourselves about investing the fort: it was advantageously enough situated in a meadow, the wood of which was within musket shot of it. We came as close to them as it was possible, to the end that his Majesty's subjects might not be exposed without necessity: the fire was pretty brisk on both sides, and I repaired to the place which appeared most to favor a sally.

We succeeded in silencing their cannon, I may say, with our
small arms. It is true that the zeal of our Canadians and soldiers
worried me, because I saw that we would in a little while be
without ammunition. M. Le Mercier proposed to me making
arrangements to bolster our positions so as to confine the English
in their fort and entirely prevent them from leaving. I ordered
M. De Bailleul to assemble as many men as possible in order
to help the quarter which would be attacked in case of a general
sortie. At this time we distributed provisions, ammunition, and
goods, which encouraged the Indians and militiamen.

And so, none too sure of themselves and worried about their
ammunition holding out, the French allowed their attack to
slacken off into a desultory sniping action.

On the English side, the situation was complicated by half of
Washington's force having got roaring drunk. Skipping this
detail, Washington's field report describes the second round of
the battle in terms that do not differ much from Villiers':

> Finding that they had no intention of attacking us in the open
> field, we retired to our trenches, and still reserved our fire; as
> we expected from their great superiority of numbers, that they
> would endeavor to force our trenches; but finding they did not
> seem to intend this neither, the Colonel gave orders to fire, which
> was done with great alacrity and undauntedness. We continued
> this unequal fight, with an enemy sheltered behind trees, our-
> selves without shelter, in trenches full of water, in a settled rain.
> . . . and the enemy galling us on all sides incessantly from the
> woods.

The French crossfire was indeed murderous. Before it ceased,
a third of Washington's effectives were killed or wounded. Those
still on their feet, and with weapons in their hands, were fighting
the wettest, dirtiest, most miserable kind of battle imaginable.
The "settled rain" had become a violent downpour—"the most
tremendous rain," Washington wrote, "that could be conceived."
The trenches were knee-deep in a soup of mud. Inside the smoke-
filled stockade, the sick and wounded lay half-submerged in a
bloody pond. Only the dead—of which there were now a score
—could escape the cruel battering from the skies.

Men with powder-blackened faces, in the trenches and at the

loopholes, strained to see what the enemy was up to. Had they crept closer, through the rain-beaten meadow grass and Queen Anne's lace? Were they forming, perhaps, for a final assault? One thing was certain: they were still shooting. It was a marvel how they kept their powder dry. Most of Fort Necessity's defenders had long since found their cartridge boxes soaked, their firearms useless; even the powder under cover in the stockade was wet. Bayonets could still be used, if it came to that; but few out there in the pea-soup mud of the trenches had a bayonet.

As twilight gathered in the woods, and began to settle over the rain-swept fields, the French fire at last slackened. At about 8 o'clock, when it was almost dark, a shout came from the edge of the forest:

"Do you want to talk?"

The amazed young commander of the English troops could hardly believe what Van Braam, his interpreter, told him. When it sank in that the French were, in actual fact, asking for a parley, he took deep thought.

Here he was, his fire-power practically nil, a third of his men out of action, his situation deteriorating every minute. "We could not hope for victory," he himself afterwards admitted; "and from the character of those we had to encounter, we expected no mercy." He had, indeed, good reasons for welcoming a parley.

On the other hand, how could he be sure the French made this offer in good faith? Perhaps they merely wanted to get inside his stockade and look around. It was some sort of ruse, surely; for why should the winning side be first to suggest a truce?

Washington sent back his answer: No, he did not wish to talk. "We determined not to ask for quarter," he later explained, "but with our bayonets screw'd, to sell our lives as dearly as we possibly could."

• 11 •

But Villiers was in dead earnest. He had not suffered many casualties, but he had other worries. His Indians had decided to leave him, and there were rumors of English reinforcements on the way. He set forth his anxieties in his journal:

As we had spent our time all day drying things from the rain, the detachment was very tired. The Indians had announced to me their departure on the next day . . . Rumor said that the beat of drums and the firing of cannon had been heard from a distance. I proposed to M. Le Mercier to offer a parley with the English.

When Washington refused to allow even a single Frenchman inside Fort Necessity's walls, Villiers shouted back a counter proposal: If Washington would send an envoy to the French camp, he, Villiers, would guarantee his safe return. Washington looked around at the fort's drenched, starved, exhausted, drunk, wounded, and dead defenders and decided to take the risk. He agreed to a parley.

There were only two men in the fort who could speak French. One was Captain Van Braam, who had accompanied Washington on his journey to Fort Le Boeuf; the other was a Swiss soldier, Ensign William Peroney. Selected as envoys, they plunged into the rain and blackness, and headed for the French lines.

Captain Villiers shoved a damp, blotted piece of paper at Van Braam—the "articles of capitulation." It would be best if they were signed at once, he suggested; 500 Indian reinforcements were expected in the morning, and he could not, of course, be held responsible for what the savages might do. Van Braam folded the paper and returned with it to Fort Necessity.

Washington must have been surprised at the leniency of Villiers' terms. The English would be allowed to march off with the honors of war, drums beating.[8] They could take with them all their weapons, one swivel gun, and as much property as they could carry. Villiers promised, too, that his Indians would not interfere with the departure; indeed, he would allow a guard to be placed over anything that had to be left behind.

His demands were no less reasonable. All the prisoners taken at the time of the Jumonville skirmish must be returned to Fort Duquesne. The English must promise to keep out of the Ohio country for a year and a day. Finally, two hostages must be

[8] "The honors of war" were not always what they seemed to be. The terms of surrender often stipulated: "The inhabitants shall march out of their garrisons and posts with their arms and colors flying, *upon condition that they afterwards lay them down.*"

surrendered, to guarantee delivery of the Jumonville prisoners.

In view of the circumstances, it was not a bad bargain. The required hostages were selected: Van Braam and Robert Stobo, the latter a dashing young captain whose exploits and adventures were to make him famous—or infamous, depending one's viewpoint—in both America and Europe. After sending Van Braam back to clear up a minor point, the hostages were turned over to Villiers. At midnight, by the light of a candle that could hardly be kept in flame, with the rain spattering the already soggy "articles of capitulation," Col. George Washington and Capt. James Mackay signed.

But now one of those confusions that sometimes besmudge the pages of history arose. In putting his hand to that sodden scrap of paper, Washington did more—and worse—than acknowledge the bitter reality of defeat. He confessed, for all the world to read, that he had murdered the young brother of Coulon de Villiers.

How this came about was long a matter of bitter dispute and conjecture; and, like the death of Jumonville itself, it is something that has never been satisfactorily explained. One thing is certain: in at least two places, the articles of capitulation referred to *the assassination of Jumonville.* If Washington did not realize this when he signed, what led to his misinterpretation of the document?

The answer, perhaps, is found in an eye-witness account of the signing by Capt. Adam Stephen:

> It rained so heavily that he [Van Braam] could not give us a written translation of them; we could scarcely keep the candle light to read them; they were wrote in a bad hand, on wet and blotted paper so that no person could read them but Van Braam who had heard them from the mouth of the French officer. Every officer then present is willing to declare, that there was no such word as assassination mentioned; the terms expressed to us were "the death of Jumonville."

Van Braam, in other words—whether in confusion, or near-ignorance of the French tongue, or perhaps sheer exhaustion—had failed to make the true import of the text clear. He had translated *"l'assassinat du Sieur de Jumonville"* as "the death of

Jumonville." How he translated *"l'assassin,"* also in the articles, nobody knows; but we have Captain Stephen's word that it wasn't as "assassin."

In any case, Washington signed the articles and marched his battered troops away, not just a defeated leader, but—in French eyes, at least—an admitted assassin. And Coulon de Villiers could boast: "We made the English consent to sign that they had assassinated my brother in his camp."

• 12 •

Volleys of musket fire and the boom of cannon welcomed Coulon de Villiers' canoes, as they swept down the Monongahela and up to the water-gate of Fort Duquesne. After a hero's welcome, word of his victory was sped to Quebec and Montreal—and thence to France. "The capitulation . . . will show you the glory our Canadians have acquired on that day," Commissary Varin wrote the Intendant Bigot, "and the humanity with which the English have been treated."

The official French version of what had happened at the Great Meadows did not, of course, coincide exactly with the English account. Washington's field report stated: "Accordingly, the next morning, with our drums beating and our colours flying, we began our march in good order, with our stores etc. in convoy." But Villiers wrote: "The English, struck with a panic, took to flight and left their flag and one of their colors." The French counted 70 or 80 English killed or mortally wounded; while Washington placed his loss at 30 killed and 70 wounded. And so on—as might be expected.[9]

But from any point of view, July 4, 1754, was a black day for the defenders of Fort Necessity; and especially for their young commander, who had met with little but discouragement and disaster since the beginning of his military career. Now he must herd his beaten survivors over the 50 long miles back to Wills Creek, harassed by Indians, carrying the wounded on stretchers,

---

[9] Duquesne, referring to *"la jolie affaire,"* termed the battle of Great Meadows "the most beautiful coup ever brought off in Canada." It was rare, he added, to see open combat, not ambush, in American fighting.

without even a horse to transport the medicine chest—and certain of bitter censure when he reached Virginia.

He could take a little comfort, perhaps, from the kind of fight he and his people had put up. Drunk or sober, sick or well, his officers and men—with the puzzling exception of Major Muse— had acted well under fire. When the chips were down, Captain Mackay and his haughty Independent Company had fought magnificently; their loss, indeed, was even higher than that of the Virginians. And young Colonel Washington had himself demonstrated those qualities of resolution, courage, and leadership that were to carry him through even darker days ahead, to the highest level of greatness. But just now he was going back to Virginia as a beaten and, in the eyes of some, a discredited man. On the way home, Captain Mackay said, he was "not very gay company."

At Fort Duquesne, nothing clouded the perfection of Villiers' victory—except in Indian eyes, perhaps, certain restraints on plundering and scalping. The attack on France's bastion on the Ohio had been repulsed; the first trial of strength against Fort Duquesne had ended in abject failure for the English, triumph for the French. Not only had the enemy been chased ignominiously out of the Ohio country, but they had signed a humiliating stipulation not to set foot west of the mountains for at least a year. What is more, they had confessed to the world their moral culpability in Jumonville's death. And, by the example of their weakness, they had lost whatever Indian support they may have enjoyed.

Such was the tally of gains and losses from the Battle of the Great Meadows. But it is doubtful that either the English in their dejection, or the French in their elation, quite realized what had happened: that here, in a little opening of the great forest that covered America, the first battle of a great World War had been fought.

BOOK FIVE

Round Two: Braddock

Fort Necessity's beaten, frightened survivors had scarcely got back to Virginia before Governor Dinwiddie was calling frantically for 900 men to march back across the mountains at once and clean up the mess that Colonel Washington—as he saw it— had made of things. Fort Duquesne, he insisted, must be taken before the snow flew.

Then the governors of Maryland and North Carolina met with Dinwiddie and concocted a plan to recapture the Forks that same fall with 1000 recruits from all three Colonies. The expedition would be led by Governor Horatio Sharpe of Maryland, an armchair general with a vast inexperience of military affairs.

Fortunately, both these suicidal projects were stymied by the usual complications: feuds between the Colonial authorities, refusal of the Independent Companies to take orders from American officers, mutiny in what was left of the Virginia regiment, desertions, squabbles over rank and pay (with Washington resigning his commission in disgust).

In Paris and London, news of the Great Meadows debacle— or victory, according to the point-of-view—made a profound impression. The French took it with cautious satisfaction. "The movements which took place in the direction of the Beautiful River," Minister Machault wrote Duquesne, "have made considerable noise in Europe, and Sieur de Villiers' expedition has caused a particular ferment in England." Machault surmised correctly that if the English struck again, it would be in the direction of the Ohio, and added, "They will not find our posts defenseless." Le

109

Mercier and Péan, then in France, assured their countrymen that one Frenchman was the equal of six Englishmen, and there was nothing to fear on the Ohio.

But while the French were licking their chops and sitting tight at the Forks, the English were faced with the urgent necessity of doing something constructive. "Military aid" to the Colonies—army supplies, money, professional instruction—was obviously no longer enough. Direct help in the form of regular troops, "hardware," and funds must be supplied, and at once. Prodded by Britain's boy military genius, the Duke of Cumberland, Parliament hastily voted to send two regiments to America and appropriated a war chest of £4,000,000.

A grand strategy for the still-undeclared war in America was carefully worked out in England. First goal would be the capture of Fort Duquesne with a strong force of British regulars and Provincial troops. After Duquesne's fall—no trouble anticipated in that quarter—the army would wheel north to Lake Erie, mopping up Forts Venango, Le Boeuf, and Presqu' Isle on the way. Then it would swing over to Fort Niagara and reduce that stronghold, winding up the campaign with the plucking of Fort St. Frederic at Crown Point.

It was an admirably simple and comprehensive plan, but it had a fatal flaw: the planners had never been in America, were ignorant of its geography, and hence were utterly incapable of visualizing the special problems of wilderness warfare. Advice proffered by the ever-helpful Governor of Virginia only served to mislead the strategists in Whitehall, who persevered in wanting to fight a European war in a country where not even a wagon road existed. Thus were the seeds of disaster sown before the first troopship left England.

Having devised an impossible plan, the Ministry handed it to Maj.-Gen. Sir Edward Braddock, with orders to make it work. "A person worse fitted for the office," Francis Parkman observed, "could scarcely be found." While his courage was ample, Parkman added, he was perverse, profligate, arrogant, and "a bigot to military rules." Nor did Braddock's contemporaries speak much better of him. Horace Walpole went so far as to accuse the General of living on "the infamous wages" of his mistress. Except for the King himself, he seems to have had few admirers, even among his friends.

Yet, it could be said for Braddock that he must have been a superb soldier, as anyone who attained the rank of a general officer in the famous Coldstream Guards had to be. He had seen a lot of hard fighting, was a good organizer, and had a reputation for pounding discipline into refractory troops—such as the Americans reputedly were. Even his best enemy Walpole had to admit that, "desperate in his fortune, brutal in his behaviour, obstinate in his sentiments, he was still intrepid and capable."

Oddly enough, few of the horrid traits charged to Braddock in England came to the surface in America. The worst said of him on this side of the Atlantic was that he was obstinate, stupid, and swore a lot; and history has tended to soften its judgment on at least two of these counts. There probably was some good in Braddock. It is difficult, in any case, wholly to condemn a man who, having had four horses shot from under him, climbed on a fifth to meet his death in battle.

Old and fat, but nevertheless full of energy, Braddock landed at Hampton Roads in February and immediately called the Provincial governors together. It was agreed in council that, instead of knocking off Forts Duquesne, Niagara, and Crown Point, in that order, they should be attacked simultaneously: Fort Duquesne by Braddock, Niagara by Governor Shirley of Massachusetts, and Crown Point by William Johnson's Indians and irregulars. At the same time, New England would send an army to keep the French off balance in Acadia.

In March the British troops assigned to the destruction of Fort Duquesne began arriving from Ireland: the 44th Regiment, commanded by Sir Peter Halkett, and the 48th by Col. Thomas Dunbar. Both had been brought up to strength by drafts on "the outcasts of other regiments" and by much beating up of recruits —many of whom, it was said, would have been in prison if they had not been in the army. Their quality left something to be desired, perhaps; but most of them were trained, seasoned troops, at least, and Braddock was hopeful that some of their discipline would rub off on the unruly Provincials.

In addition to his red-coated Irish regiments—about 1350 effectives—Braddock had some 500 Colonials, consisting of the New York and South Carolina Independent Companies;[1] the Virginia,

---

[1] The Independent Companies were regular troops stationed in the Colonies but maintained out of the royal exchequer.

Maryland, and North Carolina Rangers; and various units of gunners, pioneers, scouts, and other special detachments. Among these were 50 seamen, skilled in the use of ropes and tackle. Their help, Braddock reasoned, might be needed in getting his heavy guns over the mountains, and he couldn't have been more right.

When Braddock's chariot rolled into Wills Creek on May 10, he had in hand a total force of about 2000 men. With their arms, appurtenances, and enough artillery to pulverize the French defenses, they made a brave showing, for a wilderness army. "Fort Duquesne," Braddock assured Benjamin Franklin, "can hardly detain me above three or four days."

The General had some misgivings, to be sure, about the raw colonial troops in their buckskin hunting shirts. As his aide, young Capt. Robert Orme, remarked in his journal:

> The General had now frequent opportunities of seeing and hearing of the appearance and disposition of the Virginia Recruits and companies. Mr. Allen had taken the greatest pains with them, and they performed their evolutions and firings as well as could be expected, but their languid, spiritless, and unsoldierlike appearance considered with the lowness and ignorance of most of their officers, gave little hopes of their future good behaviour.

Well, no matter, his Irish regiments alone would be more than a match for anything the French might bring against him. As for the enemy Indians, he had no worries about them. "Upon the King's regular and disciplined troops," he told a still somewhat skeptical Franklin, "it is impossible they should make any impression." It would be all over by mid-winter, he promised himself, and he would spend a Merry Christmas with his friend Governor Lewis Morris, in Philadelphia.

• 2 •

Thanks to the secret service work of M. Hennessey and other French agents in England and Canada, Paris was probably as familiar with British plans as the British Ministry itself. And it saw these plans as a threat, not just to the Ohio, but to the heart of Canada—to the very existence of New France. In its private instructions to Vaudreuil, April 1, 1755, the Ministry expressed its fears, thus:

> Not content with endeavoring to penetrate in that direction [toward the Ohio] into the interior of the country, and there cut off the communication between Canada and Louisiana, they pretend, further, to have the right to resort to the lakes of Canada, and that the lands which are south of Lake Erie and Lake Ontario belong to them.

In the presence of this massive threat, the French decided, at last, to take all-out measures of defense.

Under an elaborate smoke-screen of rumors designed to convince the English that an invasion of their island was its true objective, a great fleet left Brest for America.[2] Twenty-six ships, armed with 1,612 guns, carried six of France's finest regiments: La Reine, Artois, Burgundy, Guyenne, Languedoc, and Béarn. In command was the celebrated Baron de Dieskau, whose genius was so highly regarded that Louis XV gladly paid him 32,000 livres a year to serve under the fleur-de-lis.

England, of course, did not view the departure of this powerful force for America with equanimity. Both countries were still at peace, both were protesting only the most amicable intentions; but this did not prevent the English from reacting violently and openly to the latest French step toward all-out world war. Seven ships of the line under Vice-Admiral Edward Boscawen were immediately ordered to cruise off Louisbourg, and to fall on any French ship that attempted to land troops.

Storms and fog scattered the French fleet, but at the same time frustrated the British watchdogs. Despite a sudden, savage attack on the French convoy, Boscawen succeeded in capturing only the *Alcide* and the *Lis* with eight companies of troops. All the rest—nearly 3,000 men—were safely landed at Quebec.

For the reception of these reinforcements, Minister Machault instructed Commissary Varin to take the most vigorous measures.

[2] On March 7, 1756, British secret agents in France reported flat-bottomed invasion boats being prepared at Calais and Dunkirk "as a feint to get their own troops to America and prevent the English from sending thither what they might otherwise intend."

No provisions were to leave Canada, not even for use of the returning ships. Wheat and flour were to be seized by force, if
necessary. Salt pork must be had at any cost—even at the exorbitant prices charged by Yankee traders. The chips were down
in Canada, and everything must be sacrificed to the support of
the army and the defense of the Ohio. Everything except, perhaps, the graft to which Canadian officials, civilian and military,
had for so long been accustomed.

With the reinforcements from the mother country, Canada
could now muster 3,800 regular troops, proud regiments, among
the best fighting material in the world. The militia in garrisons
and in the field numbered another 8,000 men, and Duquesne
could write of it: "The militia is in perfect order and submissive.
It is now armed and provided with 20 rounds of powder and ball."

In addition to these 12,000-odd white troops, the French commandants had an immense reserve of Indian power to draw on.
The ignominious defeat of the English at Great Meadows had
caused French prestige to soar in the redman's eyes. Now, besides
the faithful in Canada, the "unmitigated heathen" of the West—
Ojibway and Pottawattamie—were firmly in the French camp;
their leader the same Charles Langlade who had sacked Pickawillany. So were the Shawnee and Delaware from the Ohio; and
the Ottawa from around Detroit, commanded perhaps by Pontiac. Even the hereditary enemies of the French, the tribes of the
Six Nations—had been softened up by Duquesne so that, if not
friendly, they were at least neutral. Nobody could say for sure
what the numerical strength of these Indian allies was. But it
was largely because the French had it, and Braddock lacked it,
that matters turned out as they did.

From a military point of view, indeed, Canada seemed to be
in excellent shape. Duquesne was assuring Machault that there
was little chance of the English crossing the mountains in 1755—
that would require at least a two year campaign. At Fort
Duquesne, Contrecoeur was rather hoping they *would* cross—he
was so well prepared to receive them! And in Paris, Le Mercier
and Péan were still boasting that one Frenchman could lick
six Englishmen any day.

But under this excessive confidence ran a clear undercurrent of
disquiet. Duquesne resigned his post at about this time. He

pleaded ill health and a desire to serve in the navy; but it is possible that he saw how things were really going—that he sensed the coming crash of New France, and had no desire to be buried under the debris. He had done a superb job as Governor General, and under the most trying circumstances. He had worn himself out, in fact, on the service of his King. It was time for someone else to take over now. He demanded his recall, and it was reluctantly granted.

Duquesne's replacement was the Marquis de Vaudreuil, who arrived in Canada with the fleet from Brest. A native son, Montreal-born, he was received with wild cheers by the Canadians; but he was not to be the most illustrious of the Governors General. He would, in fact, turn out to be one of the worst.

Vaudreuil was not favorably impressed with the state of affairs in Canada. He described the situation to Machault in terms that were scarcely complimentary to his great predecessor:

> I find myself much embarrassed, and I think any other person in my place would be equally so. I arrive in a country where I am assured everything is peaceable; I find, in consequence, no stores or provisions laid in, no carriages built, and I must oppose the enemy's attacks on all sides in less than six weeks.

He was especially exercised by the situation at Fort Duquesne, and on July 24, 1755, wrote Machault:

> Fort Duquesne is really threatened. On the 7th of this month the English were within six or eight leagues of it; I am informed by letter that they number 3000, being provided with artillery and other munitions for a siege . . . Unfortunately, no foresight has been employed to supply that fort with provisions and munitions of war, so that the commandant . . . is obliged to employ the major portion of his men in making journeys to and fro for the purpose of transporting these munitions and provisions.

Aside from the ironical circumstance that his pessimistic report was written two weeks *after* the annihilation of the British force before the walls of this very fort, there was a certain amount of truth in what the new Governor General had to say about the way things were going at Fort Duquesne.

• 3 •

During the spring of 1755 the Forks were the scene of feverish preparation for the expected attack. After Great Meadows, Contrecoeur had felt safe in sending most of his force back to Canada, keeping only 250 troops and about 100 Indians to garrison the post over winter. This was in line with the usual procedure for easing the supply problem during the cold months, when military operations were, in any case, suspended by both sides.

But toward the end of May, with Braddock's force mobilizing for its big push, reinforcements began to trickle in from Canada. Duquesne, contrary to what Vaudreuil maintained, did not neglect the defenses of his namesake bastion on the Beautiful River. Despite great difficulties caused by low water in French Creek, reinforcements and supplies were kept coming. In flotillas of from four to sixteen bateaux, detachments left Niagara on one another's heels: May 21, May 24, May 27, June 1, June 11, June 12, June 14 . . . Men and provisions were landed at Fort Presqu' Isle, hurried over the portage to Fort Le Boeuf; then somehow, got through the shallows of French Creek to new Fort Machault at Venango, and on down the Allegheny to Fort Duquesne.

At the same time, Contrecoeur used every man he could spare from the supply service to harden the defenses of his compact little fort. Early spring floods had done extensive damage to the works on the river sides; this must be repaired. A new glacis must be constructed; a powder magazine installed deep under ground, with a four-foot roof of river clay. Quarters must be provided for the new troops.

To make sure that all was done properly, Contrecoeur requested that Lieut. Chassegros de Léry, a military engineer stationed at Detroit, be sent to supervise the work. Contrecoeur's letter to de Léry reflects an atmosphere of urgency, even anxiety:

According to information which reaches us daily by the Indians, the English mean to attack Fort Duquesne this spring. I beg, therefore, that you set out for this place as soon as my letter is received . . . we have the greatest need of an officer capable

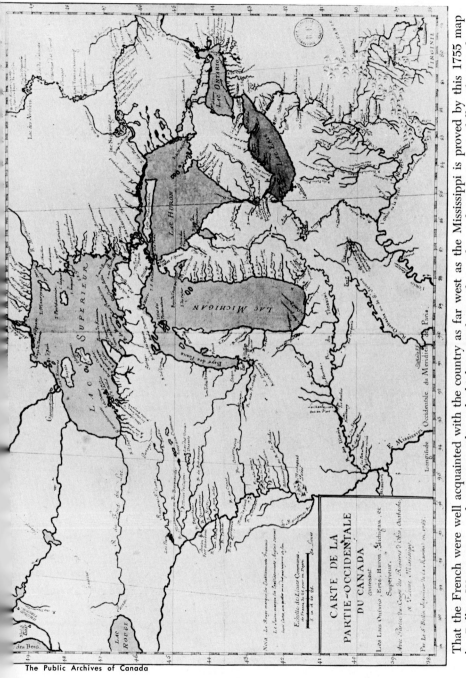

That the French were well acquainted with the country as far west as the Mississippi is proved by this 1755 map by Bellin. Waterways and portages—the only highways of travel in those days—were carefully, if not always accurately, shown.

The Marquis Duquesne, Sieur de Menneville, Governor of Canada, launched the military invasion intended to secure France's lifeline from Quebec to Louisiana.

Robert Dinwiddie, Governor of Virginia, recognized early and resisted vigorously the French incursion into lands claimed by the English on the Ohio.

Charles Wilson Peale's portrait of George Washington in the uniform of a Virginia militia colonel. The large sash, besides being decorative, was intended to serve as a sling in which the wearer could be carried if wounded.

Restoration of Fort Necessity. Right and left, the V-shaped trenches from which Washington's starved, sick and ... "a cruel rain."

Beginning and end of the rain-spattered "articles of capitulation" in which Washington unwittingly admitted his assassination of Jumonville. Capt. James Mackay, outranking Washington as a King's Officer, signed first.

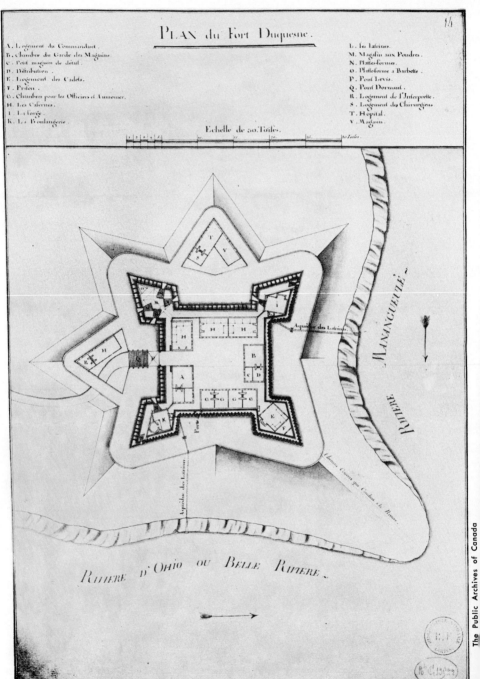

The only known French plan of Fort Duquesne, most of the others having been drawn by English engineers after its destruction. The Allegheny River is designated as the Ohio, in accordance with French usage.

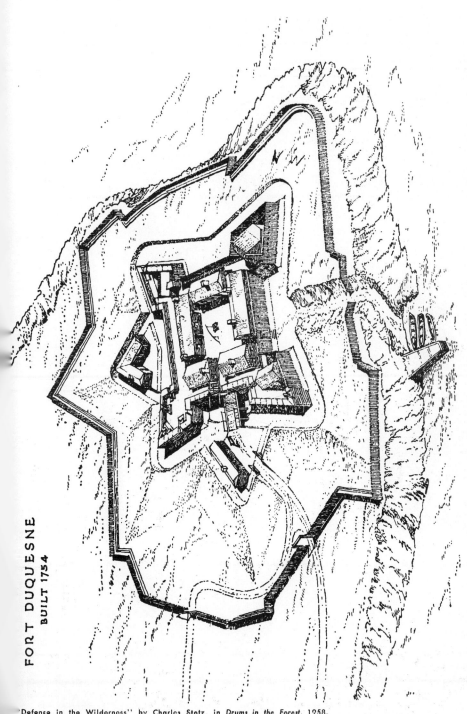

FORT DUQUESNE
BUILT 1754

Conjectural view of Fort Duquesne, drawn by Charles M. Stotz after contemporary plans and descriptions. Note that bastions and walls on river sides are of simple picket construction.

Captain Jean-Daniel Dumas, who took command after Beaujeu's death and inflicted a disastrous defeat on Braddock's overwhelmingly superior force. He afterward became commander of

Captain Daniel-Hyacinthe-Marie Lienard Beaujeu, slated to relieve Contrecoeur of his command at Fort Duquesne, organized and led the French attack on Braddock's force. He was killed

Major General Edward Braddock, supreme commander of the British forces in America, defeated and killed at the Battle of Monongahela.

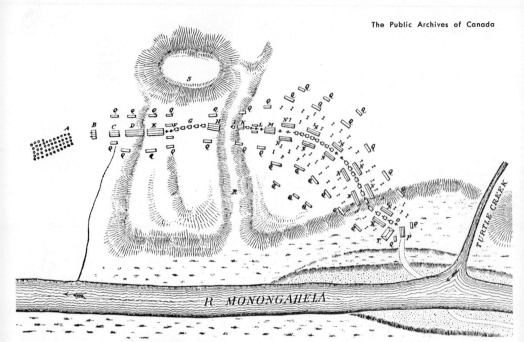

Opening of the Battle of Monongahela, from a sketch by Patrick Mackellar, engineer with Braddock's army. Here the British column unexpectedly encounters the French force (A).

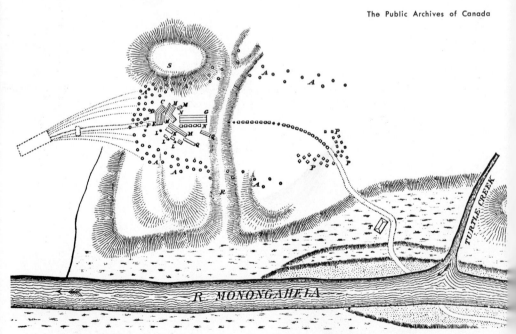

At 2 o'clock Braddock's army has become a panic-stricken mob, desperately fighting to hack its way out of the French-Indian encirclement. Two hours later, it was all over.

Model of Fort Augusta, near Sunbury, Pa. Fort Augusta was one of the more elaborate frontier defenses erected against the French raiders who swarmed south from the Forks after Braddock's defeat.

Zeller's Fort, built with thick stone walls and windows like loopholes, is a good example of the "private forts" designed for protection against French-Indian scalping parties. Perfectly preserved, it is still in the Zeller family, Ches-

Colonel Henry Bouquet, who shared the field command of Forbes' army with Washington. A brilliant European-trained professional soldier, he became one of America's finest wilderness fighters.

General John Forbes, sick and often in great pain, heroically led Britain's third, and this time successful, assault on Fort Duquesne. He died shortly after viewing the ruins of the abandoned French stronghold.

"Defense in the Wilderness" by Charles Stotz, in *Drums in the Forest*, 1958.
The Historical Society of Western Pennsylvania

FORT PITT
BUILT 1759-61

Charles M Stotz 1958

Conjectural drawing of Fort Pitt, by Charles M. Stotz, showing the five massive bastions, thick earthen curtain walls, and elaborate outworks that made this British fort the most powerful stronghold in the West.

All that now remains of Fort Pitt—the so-called blockhouse, an outlying redoubt built by Bouquet in 1763. It is said to be the oldest structure in Western Pennsylvania, and an interesting feature of Point State Park.

Point State Park, Pittsburgh, as it will look when completed. The site of Fort Duquesne is marked on the lawn, just behind the 150-foot fountain. A restored bastion of Fort Pitt can be seen to the right. Beyond the park rises the gleaming office buildings and elegant hotels of Pittsburgh's famous Golden of planning and carrying out works necessary to put this place in a state of defense. Messrs. Dumas and De Ligneris wish you to come as soon as possible.

After a hazardous journey through the woods from Detroit, de Léry spent ten days studying the layout at the Forks, then drew up a discouraging report in which he expressed the dour hope that enough troops would come up from Montreal to beat the English *outside* the walls of the fort.

By May 24, however, he had got the works into fair shape and was supervising the installation of half a dozen new cannon. These guns brought the total armament up to six 6-pounders and nine 3-pound pieces. How good they were is another question: Pouchot claimed that "the refuse arms of all the King's arsenals are sent to this country," and that most of the artillery was rusty.

The post, at any rate, was now as ready as it ever would be to withstand an attack. Governor Duquesne felt justified in writing his successor: "By Sieur de Contrecoeur's letter of 24th of May last, the works of Fort Duquesne are completed . . . it was in want of neither arms nor ammunition." Provisions seem also to have been ample. Despite the difficulties of transportation, "succors of every description" had arrived with the reinforcements—flour, bread, dried peas, salt pork, brandy, and wine. Fort Duquesne, in addition, had already become partly self-supporting. Over 2000 bushels of corn were now being harvested from the fields along the rivers, and the post could boast two cows, a bull, and twenty-three sows with young.

Vaudreuil, however, was still complaining. "I must observe," he wrote Machault in July, "that Fort Duquesne has never been completed; on the contrary, 'tis open to many capital defects . . . I dread with reason, my Lord, the first intelligence from that fort, and shall be agreeably surprised if the English have been forced to abandon their expedition." But at Duquesne, itself, Contrecoeur was now quite satisfied with his situation. Despite the diversion of troops to Niagara, Crown Point and Acadia—troops that could well have been used at the Forks—his post was in a tolerable posture of defense.

A few weeks earlier, the contrary had been true. Had Braddock been able to get his army on the march those few weeks sooner,

Fort Duquesne would have been his for the asking. Now he
would have to fight for it.

• 4 •

In the British camp, an atmosphere of optimism, even exuberance, surrounded the opening of the campaign against Fort
Duquesne. Captain Orme wrote cheerfully:

> Everything seemed to promise so far the greatest success. The
> transports are all arrived safe, and the men in health. Provisions,
> Indians, carriages and horses were already provided; at least
> were esteemed so; considering the authorities on which they
> were promised to the General.

But Orme—like the General himself—was to learn that wars,
alas, cannot be fought with promises. By the time he had reached
his headquarters at Wills Creek, now called Fort Cumberland,
Braddock was beset with vexations.

Most of them stemmed from the continuing reluctance of the
Provinces to do anything about their own defense. Braddock
stormed that in America he had met with "nothing but lies and
villainy." But Braddock was not famous for the sweetness of his
disposition. "To all who know his temper," General Abercromby
remarked, "he seemed more disposed to make war on the people
of Virginia than to defend them."

In the end, Braddock drew on the royal paymaster to finance
his campaign. But he still had with him the problem that had
driven young Colonel Washington to despair—the problem of
wagons. Maryland and Virginia had promised to send 2500
horses and 250 vehicles, but less than a tenth of them had been
delivered. In desperation the General turned to Benjamin
Franklin.

Franklin printed up a handbill that was a masterpiece of
cajolery, appeals to both patriotism and avarice, and a little
judicious arm-twisting. Aware that Braddock's cantankerous
Quartermaster-General, Sir John St. Clair, often wore a Hussar
uniform—symbol of military ruthlessness in Europe—Franklin
capped his appeal with a paragraph aimed straight at the
German-born farmers:

If this method of obtaining the wagons and horses is not like to succeed, I am oblig'd to send word to the General in fourteen days, and I suppose Sir John St. Clair, *the Hussar,* will immediately enter the Province, of which I shall be sorry, because

> I am very sincerely and truly
> Your Friend and Well-wisher,
>
> B. FRANKLIN

Within two weeks, all of the 150 wagons and 600 draft horses that Franklin had requested were on their way to Fort Cumberland, along with 259 pack-animals. Now, at least, the army could move; and General Braddock could turn his attention to other difficulties.

• 5 •

Chief among these was a shocking failure of the food supply. Men campaigning in the wilderness needed food that would stick to their ribs, and plenty of it. The basic ration was salt meat (chunks of whole beef or hog pickled in brine) and biscuit or flour. Seven pounds per man of fresh beef, or four of pork, were issued each week when available. The salt rations were supplemented whenever possible by fresh venison, purchased from the Indians at two pence a pound, sometimes in lots as large as 8600 pounds. And the men often eked out their rations with game on the march. Over and over, the journal of a batman in Braddock's column reads: "We dined this day on dear (*sic*) and bear" . . . "We dined today on bear and rattlesnake."

For the sake of variety, other foods were added when possible; provisions for a winter campaign included:

> flour, rice, corn, salt beef, pork, peas, butter, raisins, turnips, carrots, cabbages, apples dried and green, oats, rum, whisky, wine, salt, barley.

The Colonial troops in particular were heavy eaters at home—plenty of beef, hog-'n'-hominy, game, "risen bread," corn bread and journey cake, salad greens, vegetables, meat pies, fish, bacon

(pork or bear), smoked hams.[3] And they demanded strong food
for the tremendous labor of hacking military roads through the
wilderness and hauling great guns over the mountains.

They also demanded strong drink. On the march, the daily
issue of liquor—rum or whisky—was a gill (half a cup) a day. It
was considered absolutely necessary "to correct the water" and
as a reward after a hard day's marching or road-cutting. Boot-
legged to the troops by sutlers and camp followers, it was also
the source of much drunkenness, to judge from the large number
of whippings administered for that offense.

Colonial commissaries requisitioned huge supplies of hard
liquor—from 10 to 100 hogsheads of whisky at a time. Commanders despaired of getting real work done without the daily
dram; and troops grew mutinous when it was withheld. One
scouting party is on record as having operated for 48 hours on a
biscuit and a gill of rum for each man. Another sent back a
chronologically revealing request for supplies: "Sir, I am reduced
to the necessity of troubling your honor to send me by the bearer
one keg of whisky, 21 lbs. of powder, and 4 lbs. of lead."

As long as the rum held out, troops on the march would put
up with salt horse and biscuit week after week; but in camp they
demanded a more varied diet. Without fresh meat and other fresh
foods, indeed, they were almost certain to fall victim to scurvy
or the dreaded "bloody flux." Braddock's troops had been subsisting on salt meat for two months. At Fort Cumberland, he had
been assured, there would be an abundance of fresh provisions.
He arrived to find an almost complete want of everything.

Worse yet, the salt beef supplied by the backwoods colonel,
Thomas Cresap, arrived spoiled, in casks that had never contained any pickle—or had been drained by the wagoners to
lighten their loads—and had to be buried at once. The Pennsylvania wagons, supposedly laden with flour, arrived empty. The
army was threatened with actual starvation; and dysentery, now
rife in the camp, added to the general misery.

Once again, it was Benjamin Franklin who found ways to
save a desperate situation. He himself wrung funds from the
Pennsylvania Assembly with which to buy food packages. Then

[3] Frontier food was often prepared especially for traveling; for instance,
"journey cake," parched corn, dried and smoked meat. In winter, travelers
sometimes carried condensed and frozen soup; pies were also frozen.

he encouraged the Province's energetic Governor Morris, to round up fifty fat oxen and a hundred sheep from the lower counties. All these arrived at Fort Cumberland, in due time, along with a tempting supply of delicacies for the General's table, including:

> Twelve hams
> Eight cheeses
> Twenty-four flasks of oil
> Ten loaves of sugar
> One cask of raisins
> A box of spices and currants
> A box of pickles and mustard
> Four kegs of sturgeon
> One keg of herrings
> Two chests of lemons
> Two kegs of spirits
> A cask of vinegar
> A barrel of potatoes
> Three tubs of butter
> Eight kegs of biscuit

Finally enough supplies and fodder were accumulated at Fort Cumberland for the army's immediate needs. But meanwhile, a month or six weeks had been lost—during which time Fort Duquesne might easily have been taken and the Colonies spared a long and bloody war.

• 6 •

Along with all these troubles, Braddock had another that led, in the end, to serious consequences: women.

Like every other army of its day, Braddock's was encumbered by large numbers of females who hung around the camps, marched with the troops, and even showed up on the battle-fields. Among the prisoners taken by the French in Braddock's great defeat were eight women, one of whom is rumored to have been the General's mistress. (What they were doing with the advance troops is something that has never been explained.)

Many of these "necessary women," as they are listed on the official rosters, were not camp followers in the usual sense of

the term. They acted—or at least doubled—as washerwomen and
nurses. Thus, in Halkett's orderly book we find this entry:

> Six women of the line to be sent to the hospital immediately
> to attend the sick, to be relieved weekly. They will receive
> provisions and 6 pence sterling per day.

In one case, when the women of Braddock's expedition joined
to demand more than the stipulated six pence and pound, the
General ordered them turned out of camp.

Not a few of the army's womenfolk were married—lawfully
or otherwise—to soldiers; and even the Irish regiments were accompanied by wives, and perhaps children. A heart-rending letter
from one of these army wives has come down to us. It was written by a veteran campaigner named Martha May, from the jail
in Carlisle, Pa., where she had apparently been lodged for speaking her mind too freely about the Colonel. It concludes:

> . . . I have been a wife 22 years and have traveled with my
> husband every place and country the army has marcht too
> and have workt very hard since I was in the army. I hope
> yr Honor will be so good as to pardon me this onct that I
> may go with my poor husband one more time to carry him
> and my good officers water in ye hottest battle as I have done
> before.

The letter bears the straight-faced endorsement of a staff officer: "Petition of Martha May to carry water to soldiers in the
heat of battle."

To judge from the number of women trailing the army on the
march and clustering around its encampments, a tremendous
amount of clothes-washing and nursing was required by the
troops. En route, at least, the situation could be controlled by
refusing rations to all camp followers in excess of a stipulated
quota. At the beginning of Braddock's march, the quota was set
as follows:

> Six women per company are allowed each of the two regts:
> & the Indipendent Companys, 4 women to each company of
> carpenters, Virginian & Maryland Rangers, 5 women to the artil-

lery, 2 women to the detachments of seamen & 2 women to the troop of Light Horse.

This allocation was almost immediately cut to two women to a company; and the new order was enforced with extreme rigor:

> No more than two women per company will be allowed to march from this camp . . . A list of names of them that are allowed to stay with the troops to be given into the Major of Brigade and any woman that is found in camp whose names are not in that list will for the first time be severely punished, and for the second suffer death.

On the march, it was also possible to exercise a certain hygienic control over a problem that has beset all armies from the earliest times. Thus in Halkett's orderly book we find the notation:

> This day all the wimmen that goes up the country was taken to the doctors to see if they was clean and ready to march.

But it was when the army was in camp at Fort Cumberland that Braddock's troubles with women assumed really serious proportions. The sentries were kept so busy flushing soldiers and their girls out of the bushes that a special order had to be issued:

> The provoe is to go his rounds every day through all the roads leading to the camp. Every soldier or woman he shall meet with on the other side of the rivers or beyond the guard of the picquets without a pass from the regt: or the officer commanding the company they belong to, he is to order his executioners immediately to tie them up & give them fifty lashes and to march them prisoners through the camp to expose them.

Most troublesome were the Indian girls who set up for business around the encampment. Led by a chief's daughter who rejoiced in the name of Bright Lightning, they spread havoc among the men, many of whom had been completely out of touch with women since the beginning of their sea voyage four months ago. But even the respectable matrons of the tribes seem to have contributed their share of disturbance with such quaint usages as one described by a bug-eyed sailor in the so-called "Seaman's Journal":

> It is the custom with them, once or twice a year, for the women to dance and all the men sit by . . . Each woman takes out her man that she likes, dances with him, and lies with him for a week, and then return to their former husbands and live as they did before.[4]

Before long, the camp was debauched, the officers and men demoralized; and the Indian warriors not at all amused by the buying of their wives and daughters for gifts and liquor.

Braddock did what he had to do: he ordered the Indian women back to the Susquehanna, whence they had come. This not only aroused the ire of his officers—one of whom later publicly accused him of idling away his time "with his own women and feasting"—but it incensed the Indians, so desperately needed as scouts and guides.

As in almost everything else, Braddock had been let down in the matter of Indian allies. Governor Dinwiddie delivered none of the Cherokee and Catawba he had promised. George Croghan, to be sure, had brought in 50 warriors, but with many women and children; and when Braddock now ordered the women to leave, the men went with them. They promised to return, but only eight kept their word. Those eight were all the Indians that Braddock was ever to have against the French with their hundreds, perhaps thousands.

In these ways, as well as in the shortage of wagons and provisions, preparations for the advance against Fort Duquesne were bogged down. Everything, it seemed, conspired to make one of the most difficult military enterprises in history still more difficult. And it was not until the morning of May 29, 1755, that the army finally began to leave Fort Cumberland on its 110-mile march across the mountains.

[4] David Thompson described a similar ritual practiced by the Mandan Indians on the Missouri: "The women . . . form a line opposite the men; in a few minutes several women advance to the men, each of them takes the man she chooses by the hand, he rises and goes with her to where she pleases, and they lie down together. No woman can choose her own husband; but the women who love their husbands lead away aged men."

• 7 •

Captain Contrecoeur probably did not have to wait long for news that the British were at least on the move. His scouts were keeping a close watch on Braddock's camp; diversionary raids were even being carried out in its vicinity.

Contrecoeur may also have received word that the young Virginia colonel—who had promised on his word of honor at Fort Necessity to keep out of the Ohio country for a year—was again on his way over the mountains. This time it was as a volunteer lieutenant-colonel, serving without pay as an aide to General Braddock. Washington had no command, but as a member of Braddock's official family, his advice was to have an important— perhaps a fateful—bearing on the General's decisions.

Of one thing, however, Contrecoeur could not be sure until Braddock's army was actually on the march: the route it would take to Fort Duquesne. Then, as the long British column began to snake its way northward, it became clear that the road would be the same one that Washington had followed. Whether or not this was the best way to get to Fort Duquesne could be debated. A few years later, General Forbes was to decide that a road directly westward from Philadelphia was more feasible. Indeed, it was argued that a better course was not to march to the Forks at all, but to cut the French lifeline at Niagara—after which Fort Duquesne would have died on the vine. But the matter, in any case, had already been decided by Dinwiddie, Cumberland, et al.—and not without political as well as military considerations. Sir Edward Braddock was merely a soldier carrying out orders. And now, having lost far too much time already, he was in a hurry to get along.

First to take off from Fort Cumberland were 600 pioneers of the 44th. Working parties of 200 axmen, with 100 soldiers covering them, started to widen the road over Wills Mountain. Eight hours of hacking and blasting carried the detachment seven miles. But next day, from four o'clock in the morning until eight at night, it progressed only three miles, and finally came to a standstill.

Clearly, the army would never reach Fort Duquesne at such a

snail's pace. A frantic search was therefore started for an easier way over Wills Mountain. When one was found, it was, oddly enough, not by an Indian scout or frontiersman, but by a young British naval officer, one Ensign Splendelowe, who had never before been in the woods. Once "Splendelowe's Road" was opened—around the mountain, instead of over it—the main body of troops could follow. It marched in three divisions.

On June 7, Sir Peter Halkett's 44th Regiment of British regulars stepped off, resplendent in scarlet coats and pipe-clayed shoulder belts. They were also a little uneasy, perhaps, about the gloomy, Indian-infested forest into which they immediately plunged. It was a state of mind that would not improve as they pushed deeper and deeper into heavily-wooded enemy country.

On the following day, Lieutenant-Colonel Burton marched off the Independent Companies of Virginia and Maryland, and the South Carolina Rangers, escorting the artillery and ammunition wagons. Among the civilian wagoners attached to the buckskin-clad Rangers[5] were two young frontiersmen, Daniel Boone and Daniel Morgan.

Two days later, the last division, the 48th Regiment of regulars, moved off smoothly under command of Colonel Dunbar. With it went the provision wagons, all the pack horses, and a herd of oxen and milk cows. After it trailed the women, and the sutlers with their wares and rum kegs.

The line of march stretched out for three or four miles. Ahead of the column, and on both flanks, a screen of scouts combed the woods. And still farther out, no doubt, still deeper in the forest, skulked Contrecoeur's Indians, watching, waiting, hoping to pick up a few scalps.

When the last man had left Fort Cumberland, Braddock and his staff followed. Among Braddock's papers was a beautifully-detailed plan of Fort Duquesne, made by Maj. Robert Stobo— one of the two hostages Washington had given up to the French

---

[5] Uniforms—if any—varied from Province to Province. Many Colonial troops simply wore their old clothes, perhaps supplemented by a red coat furnished by the Crown. The prevailing uniform color was blue, often faced with buff. Ranger companies wore green (or buckskin) hunting shirts and leggings; or perhaps buckskin breeches and blue coats. Washington was much in favor of "Indian dress" for wilderness warfare—an idea that was enthusiastically accepted by the young frontiersmen.

at Fort Necessity. While at Fort Duquesne, Stobo had drawn the plan and had smuggled it out by a friendly Indian. Whether this made him a patriot and hero, or merely a spy and scoundrel, depended on one's viewpoint. But the plan, at any rate, was of incalculable value to Braddock. He must have studied it often, envisaging the action that would win him the fort. The victory should be an easy one. He had only to get his big siege guns trained on those walls so clearly depicted in Stobo's plan. And now, at last, they were on their way. In three weeks, a month at most, the Cross of St. George would be flying above the Forks.

• 8 •

Braddock's army was burdened, of course, with the incredibly complicated impedimenta of a highly-organized expedition. His Majesty's Office of Ordnance listed no less than 175 separate classes of items, including 140,000 flints for muskets, 10,000 sand bags, 1,000 hand grenades, 54,000 nails, 6200 tacks, 400 spades, 200 shovels, 100 felling axes, 4 scissors, and 2980 swords with brass and iron hilts.

But the greatest trouble was with the big cannon. Washington had been encumbered by only a few swivels, easily carried on pack-horses; but Braddock's artillery train included monstrous 8-inch howitzers and 12-pounders taken from H.M.S. *Norwich.* Even old Admiral Keppel, from whom Braddock had wangled these "Ship Killers" was skeptical about ever getting them over the Alleghenies. "I own I have my own fears," he wrote, "that the heavy guns must be left on this side of the hill." When Braddock persisted, Keppel did the best he could to make the guns portable: he detailed 30 of his seamen to manhandle them "over the hill" with block and tackle.

Braddock was so insistent on having these huge cannon because, once he had got them to the Ohio, the fall of Fort Duquesne would be inevitable. He could then count on the usual siege ritual: a few shattering salvos, followed by surrender of the fort with military honors for its defenders. Or, if resistance were offered, an easy battering down of Duquesne's earth-and-wood walls and massacre of its garrison, according to etiquette.

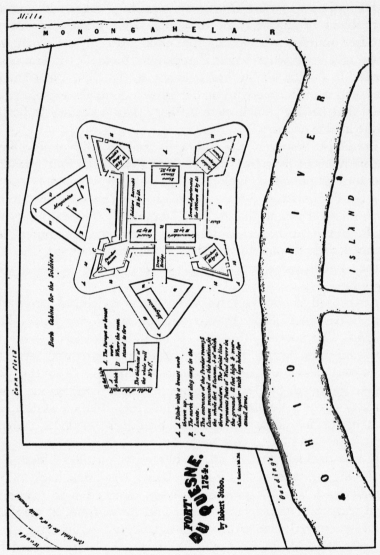

While Major Robert Stobo was being held as a hostage at Fort
Duquesne, he drew up this plan of Fort Duquesne and per-
suaded a friendly Indian to carry it to Braddock. Not far from
the spot marked "Bark cabins for soldiers," visitors to Pittsburgh
now luxuriate in the elegant new Hilton Hotel.

The capture of Fort Duquesne, therefore, narrowed down to a problem of logistics: of dragging eight giant guns over a hundred miles of man-killing mountain roads. The French were quite aware of what would happen to them if Braddock succeeded in getting his big brass cannon to the Ohio. Nevertheless, they had a little quiet fun at the British general's expense; they jibed that he had "much more artillery than necessary to besiege a fort in this country."

Braddock, however, was willing to face the problem of marching with an artillery train that, in addition to the four howitzers and four 12-pounders, included half a dozen 6-pounders and no less than 15 mortars. Seven of the strongest horses were hitched to the howitzers and five to the 12-pounders. The caissons, with loads almost as heavy as the guns themselves, required four strong horses to pull them. The horses were selected, the road cutters put to work, and Burton's artillery began to roll toward the Ohio.

At the end of two days, however, it had rolled only five miles, and Burton sent back frantic appeals for better horse, fitter wagons. The horses—"the offcasts of Indian traders"—were too weak for their work. The King's wagons, moreover, were too large and heavy for these undersized animals. Even the pack horses supplied by the rapacious Virginia contractors, could scarcely carry a hundredweight. Thus the situation at the very start of the march was desperate. Braddock hurriedly called a meeting of his staff to consider what must be done.

It was decided, first of all, to lighten the artillery load. Two of the big 6-pounders and four coehorns[6] were sent back to Fort Cumberland. The King's wagons were replaced with converted farm wagons. The officers—who would never think of marching afoot—sacrificed their extra mounts to carry excess baggage to the rear. And so, after a two-days' delay, the army lurched forward again.

Almost at once, the road pitched upward toward the summit of Savage Mountain, then down the almost precipitous farther side. Wagons shattered on boulders too huge to be blasted away.

---

[6] These deadly little mortars, named after their Dutch inventor Baron Menno Coehorn, were inevitably called "cowhorns" by the Colonial troops. They were often used for throwing grenades.

Horses died on the abrupt grades, and men took their places. Sweating seamen warped guns up and down almost perpendicular slopes. Soldiers, sick and exhausted and driven frantic by swarms of vicious woodticks, keeled over in the unbearable summer heat. And beyond each towering summit stretched other, no less forbidding, ranges of the "endless mountains."

It took Braddock's main force ten days of inching along at the rate of two miles a day to get over these terrible slopes. Then, on June 18, it passed through a cheerless woods known as the Shades of Death, and arrived at a valley called the Little Meadows. Here Sir John St. Clair had thrown together a fortified camp—the only one that Braddock ever bothered to make on this march. And here a council of war was called to decide what to do about an obviously bad situation.

* 9 *

What Braddock was up against, of course, was a kind of war that no self-respecting general would care to be caught dead in.

By all the rules of civilized fighting, it was no war at all. There were not even any roads over which to march your troops to the field of battle. Instead, you must hack your way through a savage, interminable wilderness. You campaigned in country devoid of even a stray shoat to sustain your troops, or a patch of grass on which to graze your horses. You were forced to string your army out for miles in a road scarcely wagon-wide, and nowhere any room in which to deploy and maneuver in case of attack. You knew nothing of what might be lurking in the impenetrable forest surrounding your camps and line of march. Your enemy was invisible.

This was not war, certainly, as Braddock had ever known it. It was a war, nevertheless, that had to be fought; and Braddock waged it the only way he knew how—by the book. With the troops trained to wheel and fire by platoons, instead of taking cover and fighting Indian-fashion. With artillery and baggage far too heavy for his means of transport. And—perhaps worst of all—with almost no Indian auxiliaries to screen and protect his ponderous advance through utterly wild and unknown country.

Yet, it must be said for Braddock that he did the best he could under circumstances largely beyond his control. He was marching to his doom, of course, but he was doing it in proper style. His order of march was correct in every respect, with flankers out, pickets posted, vanguard and rear guard strong, camps carefully patrolled. He was performing something of a military miracle, indeed, in making any progress at all over these first terrible twenty miles. Had it not been for a quirk of fate at the very end of his long drive to the Ohio—and the heroism of a few French youngsters—today's American History students would be reading of Braddock's expedition as a brilliant military exploit.

Braddock himself, nevertheless, was dimly aware that all was not right with his way of doing things; and for that reason he had called the meeting of his officers at Little Meadows. When the meeting was over, he consulted George Washington privately. And it was from the young Virginian that he got what he wanted.

Washington had from the start nursed his own secret idea of how Fort Duquesne could best be approached; but as a mere volunteer aide to the General, it was an idea he must refrain from advancing. Now Braddock had asked for his advice, and he gave it. The important thing, he told the British commander, was to reach the Ohio before reinforcements got through from Canada, while Fort Duquesne was practically defenseless. Corollary to this, Braddock's army must shed some of its burden—the heavily-loaded wagons, sick and disabled men, even some of the precious artillery. Dunbar's supply division must be left behind altogether, and a streamlined striking force must press forward with all possible speed. Washington has given us his plan in his own words:

> I urg'd it in the warmest possible terms I was master off, to push on; if we even did it with a chos'n detach. for that purpose, with the artillery and such things as were absolutely necessary; leav'g the baggage and other convoys with the remainder of the army, to follow by slow and regular marches, which they might do safely, while we advanced in front.

This, of course, was dangerous doctrine. It violated the elementary principle of warfare which forbids division of one's forces in the presence of the enemy. But the enemy had not yet

made his presence known; and nobody, in any case, had come
up with anything better. So Braddock adopted young Washington's plan, and whether this led to his famous defeat or fore-
stalled a still greater disaster is a question that has been often,
and fruitlessly, debated.

On the morning of June 8, accordingly, Lieut.-Col. Thomas
Gage—who would one day win fame as a Revolutionary War
general, on the wrong side—left the Little Meadows with 400
axmen to open the road. He was followed next day by the élite
of the army—800 men of "the old standards," two companies of
Rangers, and special units including a troop of light horse,
pioneers, Indian scouts, and the seamen's detachment. Also an
undetermined number of "necessary women."

Most of the artillery went along with the column, even though
the horses were by this time so weakened that it took nine of
them to pull the howitzers and seven to pull the 12-pounders.
The entire artillery train now comprised four howitzers, four
12-pounders, twelve coehorns, thirteen caissons, twenty gun
carriages, and seventeen ammunition wagons. No other wagons
—except one loaded with Indian presents—accompanied the
troops. All baggage, including provisions for thirty days, was carried on packhorses.

Thus stripped down to bare essentials, the flying column of
picked men plunged once more into the tunnel-like road Gage's
pioneeers were boring through the forest. Dunbar's division, with
all the wagons and most of the supplies, remained in camp, the
men watching the departure of their comrades with gloomy
resentment.

• 10 •

Patrick Mackellar, a British army engineer, has left us an
exact plan of the disposition of Braddock's army on the march.
At the head of the column rode a troop of light horse, followed
by the seamen, then a detachment of 20 grenadiers, some 12-
pounders, more grenadiers, and the vanguard. Almost the same
elements in reverse brought up the rear. In between marched the
main body of troops, with the guns, ammunition wagons, and
packhorses. Far out on each flank, parties of scouts scoured the

woods, with small bodies of light horse thrust out beyond the foot flankers.

It was the classic deployment of troops on the march and, as the army now moved deeper into enemy territory, it seemed to be a wise one. Braddock knew nothing about Indian fighting, but he neglected no security precaution. Whether en route or in camp, he took rigorous measures against surprise attack; and every day, now, the need for the utmost caution became more evident.

Messages were beginning to appear on the trees—grim tallies left by Indians of scalps they had taken, together with obscene jibes and threats calculated to shatter the nerves of the English soldiers. These soldiers, far from home in a savage country, were already in a state of extreme jumpiness. The Americans, who had filled out the Irish regiments, took a sadistic delight in regaling their European comrades with stories of French Indian cruelties —scalpings, tortures, mutilations, indescribable orgies of savagery and cannibalism. And before long, gruesome incidents began to bear out the truth of their tales.

Indian and French raiding parties were soon hanging on the flanks of the column, sometimes causing the whole army to grind to an alarmed halt. Several stragglers were scalped, and a woman "belonging to the General's cows" met the same fate. Finally, Braddock's chief Indian scout Scarroyady was himself bagged by some French and Indians. Scarroyady talked himself out of his predicament—very embarrassing for a scout—and was released. But the harassments continued; and an anonymous British officer's journal reflects the constant sense of peril in which the army moved:

> On our march ye guides imagined they saw some Indians frequently lurking round our line which we had reason afterwards to think true. A wagoner going out next morning to bring back in his horses was surprised by a party of Indians who shot him in 4 places in the belly & his horse in the neck, he made shift to return to camp, but after lingring some days he died; ye same morning 4 people more going out to look after their horses were killed and scalped.

Braddock did his best to counteract the uneasiness that this sort of thing occasioned among his forest-shy troops. He set them

the example of his own contemptuous courage; and he offered
five pounds for each Indian scalp taken by his scouts. But the
danger lurking behind every tree, together with the ever-in-
creasing roughness of the terrain, had now slowed the march
down to a crawl of three or four miles a day.

The army, in fact, was fast approaching a state of something
like demoralization. The men, weakened by a scanty and un-
varied diet of salt horse and biscuit, often fainted at their work.
Many—including Washington himself—were deathly sick; and
some, in fact, died. To make matters worse, the army had run
out of whisky.

Under these conditions, the troops complained bitterly; and
their chronic fear of the forest and what it held grew to panic
proportions. Nor was this deplorable and dangerous state of
nerves confined to the ranks. Among the officers as well, disputes,
intrigues, and jealousies had become rife. It reached a point
where Braddock, for example, was not even on speaking terms
with Halkett and Dunbar.

Thus, beset by every sort of physical and psychological difficulty, the army pursued its slow, painful way toward the Ohio
and Fort Duquesne. It still had almost half its course to go.

• 11 •

On June 28, after having passed the ominous ruins of Washington's Fort Necessity, and having with great trouble got over
the terrible Laurel Range, Braddock reached the Great Crossing
of the Youghiogheny, not far from Gist's settlement.

June 28—this was the date he had set for his appearance before
the walls of Fort Duquesne. He was still 35 ugly, dangerous miles
from his goal; and the chances were every day growing fainter
that he would reach it before Contrecoeur's reinforcements
arrived.

Handicapped by his train of heavy wagons and staggering
horses, Dunbar had in the meantime fallen far behind. On the
30th, a council was called to consider whether a halt should not
be made, to allow Dunbar and his supply division to catch up.[7]

---

[7] Washington was now at the rear with Dunbar, so sick and weak that he
was unable to sit on his horse, but grimly determined to take part in the
battle that was soon to be fought.

The council voted unanimously to push ahead and let him struggle along as best he could. It is probable that this decision was influenced by a fresh intelligence report that 500 French regulars were "in full march to the fort." But the need for speed was, in any case, obvious. Fort Duquesne simply must be reached in the shortest time possible—even if it had to be at the risk of a dangerously divided army. Without further delay, therefore, the march was resumed.

About a week later, on the evening of July 8, Braddock's army camped only two miles from the Monongahela. The troops were, for a change, in high spirits. A herd of a hundred oxen having arrived from Dunbar, every soldier's belly was, for the first time in weeks, full of fresh beef. Their long march was over, the big guns safely across the mountains, the skulking Indians, the wood-ticks, the mired-down caissons, the salt horse and the gut-rotting swamp water all behind them. They could relax now. Tomorrow they would be drinking French wine in the fort down river.

• 12 •

At Fort Duquesne, Captain Contrecoeur was facing a hard personal decision. During the winter of 1754–1755, the torment of his skin affliction had forced him to ask relief from his command. Governor Duquense complied reluctantly with this request of "an intelligent and courageous soldier," and dispatched as his replacement Capt. Daniel-Hyacinthe-Marie Lienard de Beaujeu. Captain Beaujeu arrived at Fort Duquesne in June, accompanied by a detachment of reinforcements.

By this time, however, Contrecoeur's scouts were reporting the British force at the Great Crossing of the Youghiogheny. Unless something happened to slow it up—something beyond Contre-coeur's own power to provide—Braddock would be under Fort Duquesne's walls in two or three weeks. Could he, under these circumstances, relinquish his command? He decided to retain it and await the enemy.

He could have been in worse shape for a defense of his post. When word of Britain's plans for a three-pronged assault on Canada reached Montreal, Governor Duquesne had immediately dispatched some troops over the ice to the Forks. As soon as the water communication was open, he promised, more would follow. Péan, in fact, had rushed a detachment from Chautauqua early in the spring; and after that, small bodies of reinforcements had been arriving every few days since the middle of June.

Then the pressure on other fronts had dried up the trickles of help from Canada. Fort Beausejour, in Nova Scotia, had been taken by Shirley's New Englanders; Fort St. Frederic at Crown Point was threatened; the English had launched two sloops of war on Lake Ontario, and powerful forces menaced Forts Niagara and Frontenac. Fort Duquesne had become—as the English grand strategists had planned it would—merely one piece in a gigantic jigsaw pattern of war. Reinforcements started on their way to Fort Duquesne, indeed, had even been stopped and pulled back for the defense of Fort St. Frederic. It had become quite clear that Contrecoeur would have to make do with whatever men and guns he had at Fort Duquesne.

What he had, now that Braddock was actually at hand with his huge siege guns, suddenly seemed pitifully little.

He had his Indians, to be sure: about 1000 of them against Braddock's eight. All those living in the bark huts around the fort had been loyal from the beginning; and recently they had been reinforced by bands of warriors from the West—hard, tough, heathen fighters from the Ojibway, Ottawa, and Pottawatamie tribes. The Shawnee, too, had at last taken up the hatchet against the English, and were raiding the back settlements. Even the Six Nations, thanks to Duquesne's skillful diplomacy, were remaining scrupulously neutral.

So far, so good. He greatly outweighed Braddock in the enormously important factor of Indian power. In white troops, however, he was far short of the English. His whole command probably numbered no more than 500 officers and men; and many of these were scattered among the upper forts and along the communication. The French soldiers ranked with the finest in the world, and the Canadian militia was a reasonably dependable force. But Braddock also had trained troops—two or three thousand of them!

Contrecoeur's little army was, however, extremely well-officered —a point of vast importance in fighting with Indian allies. Captain Le Mercier had left Fort Duquesne, and Contrecoeur must have missed him; but he had other officers of extraordinary caliber. There was his second in command, Capt. François-Marie, sieur de Ligneris, to be remembered as Fort Duquesne's last commander; and Capt. Jean-Daniel Dumas, who had stood up to Marin at Presqu' Isle, and was destined to be Braddock's nemesis; and Capt. Daniel-Hyacinthe-Marie Lienard Beaujeu, Contrecoeur's assigned successor, talented, courageous, handsome as a Watteau courtier—and with but a few days to live. Fine captains, all of them, and well supported by four lieutenants of the regular army, six ensigns, and twenty young cadets from France.

Additional cannon had arrived, too; the works had been strengthened; and Contrecoeur might have watched Braddock's approach with the grim assurance that if the English wanted Fort Duquesne, they would have to fight for it—if only the weather had played him fair. But the long drought had dried up the rivers again, making it necessary for him to divert many of his men— regulars, militia and Indians—to the work of getting supplies down from Presqu' Isle. As a result, he had too few men at Fort Duquesne even to harass Braddock along his line of march, let alone attack that long, creeping column.

He had not neglected to do what he could, of course. Detachment after detachment had gone off through the woods to hang on the British flanks, shoot a few stragglers, take a few scalps. But so skillfully had Braddock ordered his march, and so carefully had he protected his flanks that not one of those raiding parties had succeeded in turning aside, even for a day, the inexorable approach of the King's guns toward the Forks of the Ohio.

Now those guns had reached the Monongahela and were within two days easy march of Fort Duquesne. Within two days, unless something were done to stop them, they would be lobbing shells and red-hot shot into the fort. All at once, in the virtual presence of those huge howitzers and 12-pounders, the confidence that Contrecoeur had expressed in his letters to Duquesne—and, no doubt, to his officers and men—evaporated. Of what use were his shored-up defenses against the great guns of a British battleship? For how long could his little force stand up against Braddock's huge army?

Contrecoeur could see clearly enough that he was faced with

but two choices. He could surrender Fort Duquesne with the
honors of war: that is, he could march out with drums thundering
and colors flying, leaving behind a single gun mounted on its
carriage with lighted match, according to custom. Or he could
sally out and attack Braddock's column in force, before it reached
the fort. In which case he could expect no quarter.

After consulting with his officers, Contrecoeur elected to make
the second of the two choices. With the help of God and the
element of surprise, he might destroy the English before ever
they glimpsed Fort Duquesne. He decided to ambush Braddock's
army at the ford of the Monongahela.

◆ 13 ◆

The British, who were encamped on the same side of the
Monogahela as Fort Duquesne, now found that a direct route to
the fort led through impossibly rough and dangerous country.
Braddock decided, therefore, to cross the river, march for a few
miles along its west bank, then cross over again. After that, he
would be about eight miles—an easy day's march—from the fort.
Both fords were excellent, and there was still no sign that they
would be disputed.

Braddock was too good a campaigner, however, to let down
his guard at this point. At every halt, his troops now faced outwards with bayonets fixed. With a hundred men, some light
horse, and a few Indian scouts, St. Clair was scouring every foot
of the country ahead of the army. And when St. Clair, finding
everything clear, suggested that a surprise night attack be made
on the fort, Braddock prudently declined to take chances. With
Fort Duquesne practically in the bag, he would play it safe. He
would make absolutely certain that the Monongahela fords were
secure; then he would cross over and attack Fort Duquesne with
every man and every gun at his disposal.

At two o'clock on the morning of June 9, accordingly, Colonel
Gage set off with two companies of Grenadiers, 160 soldiers of
the 44th and 48th, the Independent New York company, and
two 6-pounders, in the direction of the Monongahela. His orders
were to cross over both fords and take his post on the far

side of the second crossing. St. Clair would be close behind
with 250 men to clear the road, for the artillery and main body
of troops.

At daybreak, having drawn their loads, cleaned their pieces,
and reloaded with fresh cartridges, the troops fell in for the last
leg of their march. It had been a long time since they had left
Fort Cumberland, and pretty much a nightmare all the way.
Well, that was over now. By evening they would be at Fort
Duquesne. Tomorrow they would hoist the King's colors over it
—or what was left of it. Then a few days to enjoy the Frenchmen's brandy and the Frenchmen's girls, and home again. Never
had soldiers had so much to feel good about. Never, perhaps, had
troops been more eager to march.

Braddock, it would seem, shared their eagerness. Without
waiting for word from Gage, he started the main army on its way
—about 750 troops with most of the artillery and baggage train.
At the first crossing of the river, the water was so low it scarcely
reached to the soldiers' knees. Braddock, still cautious, posted
400 men on the high ground to secure his crossing.

A mile or so beyond the ford, a messenger from Gage rode
up with the welcome news that the colonel had made the
second crossing without opposition. His guns now commanded
that ford, and St. Clair's men were leveling the banks of the
river so as to assure an easy passage for the rest of the cannon
and wagons.

The far bank at this place was some 12-feet high—a perfect
spot for an ambush. If the enemy were going to attack, this
surely would have been the place. But he had not attacked. Both
advance parties were quickly across the river and safely covered
by Gage's artillery.

St. Clair asked Gage if he wanted the 6-pounders to go along
with the vanguard.

"No, sir," Gage replied. "I don't think we'll have much occasion for them."

Overhearing this breezy exchange, Capt. Robert Cholmley's
batman remembered to note it in his journal, and added:

> So we began our march again, beating the grannadiers march
> all the way, never seasing. There was never an army in the
> world in more spirits.

Captain Cholmley's batman himself was in such high spirits that he decided to celebrate the crossing by milking a cow and making his master a milk punch—the last the young captain was ever to drink.

Indeed, it seemed all over now but the formality of accepting Fort Duquesne's surrender—or battering it down with the great guns. Harry Gordon, the Royal Engineer, noted in his own journal that the men "hugged themselves with joy at our good luck in having surmounted our greatest difficulties."

But it was not until he had posted a strong covering detachment on the slope behind him that Braddock gave the order for the main body to cross over. Then the crossing was made with regimental colors flying and drums beating. By early afternoon the right bank of the Monongahela was brilliant with the gleam of brass cannon and burnished bayonets, the scarlet coats of the King's regulars, and the white tops of the ammunition wagons. It was a brave sight—the most thrilling, George Washington was to recall, of his whole life.

Even the terrain itself now seemed to conform to the smooth completion of the advance. The ground had leveled off and, except for a fringe of underbrush along the river's edge, the forest had become a pleasant grove of large, rather widely-spaced trees through which the officers could ride and the men march with ease. It was necessary, indeed, to cut down no more than an occasional tree in order to open a 12-foot road for the passage of wagons and artillery.

Through this pleasant open woodland the army moved in flawless order. A point of scouts and light horse probed the forest ahead of Gage's advance party. Then came the pioneers, with a strong rear guard and parties of grenadiers well out on the flanks. At proper intervals followed the main army: troops, guns, ammunition wagons, a herd of cattle, even a party of women, all secured and protected in the best style with flankers, vanguard, and rear guard. At three o'clock, Gage, in accordance with orders, called a halt in a fine clearing conveniently provided by the French. When the main force arrived, it would camp here. After the troops had enjoyed a good night's rest, Fort Duquesne would be taken on the following day.

If any fault could be found with this beautifully conceived and faultlessly executed exercise, it could be, perhaps, in the want of a screen of Indians to precede the advance; in Gage's rather cursory examination of the ground ahead of him, and in his almost incredible failure to seize and occupy a certain hill flanking his line of march.

• 14 •

The nearer Braddock and his great guns drew to Fort Duquesne, the clearer it became to Captain Contrecoeur that he must strike the British before those huge siege cannon could be trained against his bastions.

As early as July 6, he began sending out parties under a couple of tough bush-rangers, the Baby brothers,[8] to attack the approaching column; but the Indians, somehow, never got within musket range of Braddock's flankers. Succeeding expeditions brought back plenty of information—all of it alarming. A party of Huron reported Braddock's troops—3,000 of them—within eight leagues of the fort and "marching briskly with their artilery." When another party, under Chevalier de la Parade was sent out to check this report, his Indian guides would not venture more than four or five leagues beyond the fort. Nobody brought back any scalps.

With uncertainty spreading like a ground-fire among his Indian allies, Contrecoeur was faced with the necessity of decisive action. He ordered the muster of a combined force of French and Indians, including every musket that could be spared from the garrison, to make an all-out strike against the enemy on July 8.

To lead this expedition, Contrecoeur chose his successor, Captain Beaujeu. The quality of French leadership was well exemplified in this courtly, experienced, and courageous officer. Beaujeu was descended from a Dauphine family dating back to the eleventh century. He had served brilliantly as commandant at Detroit, and at Niagara, where he had received the Cross of St. Louis. He was greatly respected, even loved, by the Indians, over whom he exercised a kind of influence that almost no English-

[8] Antoine and Jacques Duperont Baby were active in the Great Lakes and Ohio country as traders.

man ever succeeded in commanding. Yet, despite his strong hold
on the redmen, Beaujeu was unable to arouse them to fighting
pitch. Awed by what their scouting parties had observed, the
Indians were reluctant to march.

"No, father," they told him regretfully, "you want to die and
sacrifice yourself; the English are more than four thousand, and
we are only eight hundred, and you want to go and attack them.
We see clearly that you have no sense. Give us until tomorrow to
think it over."

The savage Ottawa and Ojibway from the West were indeed
ready enough to take the war road at once; but they were hardly
enough to attack 1500 well-armed troops. With the precious hours
slipping away, Beaujeu could only put off the attack until, if
possible, he had won the other tribes to his plan.

He could not, however, delay much longer. The last possible
day on which he could hope to take Braddock by surprise was
July 9. He resolved, with whatever followers he could gather, to
ambush the English at the second crossing of the Monongahela
on the morning of that date.

At daybreak, therefore, he stripped to breechclout and leggings
and, with a silver gorget on his breast, prepared to lead his forlorn litle party against the invaders. His handful of regulars and
militia, together with their officers and the cadets, all similarly
dressed for bush fighting, assembled on Fort Duquesne's tiny
parade. They mustered altogether less than 250 men, including
himself and Captain Dumas and de Ligneris, four lieutenants,
six ensigns, and the cadets. There was no music, no drums rolled.
After hearing Mass and receiving communion from Father Denys,
they knelt to accept the chaplain's blessing; then, in the half-light
of the new morning, they fell in and marched to the main gate
of the fort.

Here, as Beaujeu perhaps expected, they found a great crowd
of Indians milling about. Beaujeu halted his men and asked the
chiefs if, by any chance, they had changed their minds.

Their answer, perhaps a little embarrassed, was brief and to the
point: "We cannot march."

"Very well," Beaujeu answered. "I shall attack anyhow. I think
we can beat them." Then, almost as if it were an afterthought,
he added reproachfully: "What! Will you let your father go
alone?"

The question was rather too much for the Indians' pride as fighting men. Suddenly 600 warriors—first the Shawnee and Iroquois—were clamoring for arms and ammunition. Barrels of powder, bullets, and flints—fortuitously at hand—were rolled out and broken open. Each man helped himself. Muskets were issued to those who lacked them. After a short delay for the putting on of war paint and a little dancing, a long column of whites and redmen—all looking exactly like Indians—boiled out of Fort Duquesne.

Almost 900-strong, they swung around the stockade and headed east across the stump-dotted clearing that ringed the fort; through the clutter of cabins, from whose doorways dark-eyed women and children stared in sleepy wonder; past fields of ripening corn along the river, and pastures in which a few cows grazed quietly; then out of the light of the rising sun into the shadowy trail that led, through heavy timber to the Monongahela.

By two o'clock in the afternoon, they were within a mile or so of the river, and Beaujeu exhorted his men to hurry. Everything depended on laying the ambuscade before the English crossed over. The column broke into a run.

Soon afterwards, the scouts relayed back a warning; and a few minutes later Beaujeu glimpsed something through the open forest ahead of him. It was the high pointed hats and scarlet coats of British grenadiers.

• 15 •

On July 25, 1755, Governor Robert Dinwiddie, of Virginia, reported to the Earl of Halifax, President of the Board of Trade:

> I wrote you two days ago the account we had from the Ohio of the defeat of our forces, death of Genl Braddock &c. I then was in hopes these accts were false, but alas! last night I had an express confirming these melancholy news.

It was not easy, indeed, to accept the stunning truth of what had happened on the Monongahela. Even when "these melancholy news" could no longer be doubted, men kept asking one another how it could have happened. This is a question not yet

answered to everybody's satisfaction. But one thing, at least, is
certain: contrary to general belief, *there was no ambush*. Beaujeu
was perhaps as surprised as Harry Gordon—who is reputed to
have first sighted the French and Indians—when he encountered
the grenadiers.

His first thought, perhaps, was that he was too late. His plan
for an ambuscade had failed.

But, having accepted that hard fact, he acted with great cool-
ness and decision. English scouts saw him wave his hat to the
left, then to the right. This was the signal for a tactic the French
commonly used in wilderness warfare: envelopment of the
enemy's flanks by the Indians, while French regulars and militia
held the center.

Beaujeu's Indians responded by deploying among the trees
along both sides of the English column. His regulars then opened
fire on the center of the British advance. The grenadiers responded by forming a line and loosing a volley of musketry. In
one respect the English fire took a devastating toll: at the third
round, Captain Beaujeu fell dead with a bullet through his fore-
head.

Suddenly, it seemed, the battle was over, almost before it had
started. The youthful Canadian militia, unnerved by the death
of their leader, panicked and fled. The Indians began to fade
away. Only the French regulars, true to a proud tradition, stood
firm. At this point, indeed, Gage's grenadiers raised the victory
halloo and pressed forward for the kill.

But they reckoned without the indomitable Captain Dumas,
who now took charge of matters for the French. In the official
French report on the action, it is all made to sound very simple,
almost casual:

> M. Dumas began to encourage his detachment. He ordered
> the officers in command of the Indians to spread themselves
> along the wings, so as to take the enemy in flank, whilst he,
> M. de Lignery, and the other officers who led the French were
> attacking them in front.

But what Dumas actually did, of course, was to turn an imminent rout into an attack—one of the most difficult of all

military achievements. He rallied the militia by a reckless display of personal bravery. The Indians, reassured by his example and thirsting to revenge Beaujeu, returned to the fight. As they slithered through the forest, their deadly crossfire began to converge farther and farther toward the rear of Gage's advance force, their chilling yells came from every quarter. Gage, finding progress against the rocklike French center impossible, and fearing complete encirclement by the Indians, ordered his detachment to fall back on the main body of the British army.

This order was the first, and in some ways the most disastrous, of the many blunders that distinguished British tactics in the Battle of the Monongahela.

It was disastrous because Gage's somewhat shaken troops immediately recoiled into a column of about 800 men (the vanguard of the main force) who were hurrying to their assistance. This column was thrown into confusion, not only by the impact of Gage's troops, but by a murderous enfilading fire that had suddenly begun to rake it from a hill to the right of the road—the hill that Gage, in his exuberant confidence, had failed to seize after crossing the river. To add to the general disorder of the troops, now jammed into a narrow twelve-foot road, Sir Peter Halkett had somehow managed to ram his baggage train against the rear of Burton's column, making maneuver impossible.

About everything bad that could happen had now taken place, and the stage was set for the second, completely disastrous phase of the battle.

• 16 •

General Braddock had scarcely crossed the river with his jubilant rear guard when firing broke out ahead. At first he thought it was his scouts skirmishing with the Indians. But as the rattle of musketry continued, he put spurs to his horse and raced toward the van. Among those who rode with him was his aide, Colonel Washington, still wretchedly weak and scarcely able to keep his saddle.

Braddock galloped wildly through the forest, past Halkett's baggage train, now a heaving mass of frightened horses and

cursing drivers, wedged tightly against Burton's vanguard. The
acrid smoke of black powder was already so dense that the
scarlet coats of the regulars were but a blur of color in the
saffron haze. Spurts of flame—small ones from the musketry,
larger ones from the guns—stabbed the choking gloom as musketeers and gunners fired wildly in every direction. And from
the wooded ravines—ahead and on both flanks, in an ever-tighten-
ing arc—came the morale-shattering yells of a completely invisible foe, quick, shrill shrieks, resembling mad laughter.

Raging into the midst of this confusion, Braddock shouted
orders, commands, imprecations. He beat befuddled men with the
flat of his sword. His horse crumpled under him. He climbed onto
another and raged on. But there was little he could do himself—
or expect from others.

Jammed into a narrow forest road, the disciplined regulars
from Ireland had turned into a frightened, demoralized mob.
They huddled together against the hail of bullets[9] that swept
them from every side. They fired aimlessly into the shadowy
forest—and at one another. Their mounted officers, swearing,
pleading, weeping with frustration, were easy marks for hidden
Indian marksmen. So were the bunched men, now falling by the
score.

From the journal of a nameless British officer we get this eye-
witness account of just what happened on that day of unbelievable disaster:

> The men from what storys they had heard of the Indians in
> regard to their scalping and Mawhawking, were so pannick
> struck that their officers had little or no command over them,
> & if they got a shott at one the fire immediately ran through
> ye whole line though they saw nothing but trees; the whole
> Body was frequently divided into several parties & then they
> were sure to fire on one another. The greatest part of the
> men were behind trees were either killed or wounded by our
> own people, even one or two officers were killed by their own

[9] It was reported afterwards that many of the bullets extracted from
wounded men had been "chewed"—possibly to give them a dumdum
effect, or simply as a result of the Indians' habit of carrying spare bullets
in their mouths.

Platton. Such was ye confusion that ye men were sometimes
20 or 30 deep, & he thought himself securest who was in the
center; during all this time the Enemy kept a continual fire
& every shott took place.

The Americans, for their part, had instinctively broken ranks
and were fighting back from behind rocks and trees. But without
much success. The regulars, mistaking them in the smoke and
confusion for Indians, fired on them repeatedly, on one occasion
wiping out a whole detachment. This, perhaps, was one reason
for the especially high casualty rate suffered by the Provincials.
Washington was rather bitter about this aspect of the battle:

> Our poor Virginians behaved like men, and died like soldiers;
> for I believe that out of three companies that were there that
> day, scarce thirty were left alive . . . It is imagined (I believe
> with great justice, too) that two-thirds of both killed and
> wounded received their shots from our own cowardly dogs of
> soldiers . . .

Back and forth through the melee of terror and slaughter,
Braddock continued to gallop with his flailing sword. He roared
profanity at his terrified troops, striving to drive them back into
some sort of fighting formation. He directed desperate attacks at
the fateful hill from which death spurted without pause. He was
hopeful, perhaps, of pushing through to the open ground beyond
the French center—where he would have room for maneuver. A
stubborn old man, he seems never to have thought of retreat.

Braddock had four horses shot from under him in this night-
marish fight against a phantom enemy. All the mounted officers,
indeed, were prime targets for the Indian snipers: of 86 who went
into the battle, only 23 were neither killed nor wounded. Of
Braddock's staff, Washington alone escaped without hurt, although he lost two mounts and had his hat and clothes riddled
by bullets. Whatever had to be said about the behavior of the
bewildered rank and file, all of Braddock's field officers seem to
have fought bravely. And in vain.

For there was nothing they could do to save this battle. The
troops had not yet broken in uncontrollable panic, but they were

on the verge of it. Isolated groups, to be sure, were putting up a stubborn, if hopeless, fight against unimaginable odds. But the battle, plainly, was ready to fall apart.

And now Braddock was down for the fifth time, mortally wounded but still trying to rally his battered troops. The wagoners—including Boone and Morgan—had long since cut their horses free and scuttled. All of the artillery was out of action. Most of the officers and almost two thirds of the men were either dead or wounded. And the fire from the ravines was creeping farther and farther toward the rear—closer and closer to complete encirclement.

When the break came, it took the form, not of a retreat, but of a complete rout. The gay army that had so blithely crossed the Monongahela with banners flying and drums beating, only a few hours before, now clawed its way toward the narrow strip of ground that still lay open between it and the river. There was no rear guard action. The great guns, so prized by Braddock and brought hence with such infinite toil, were abandoned. The badly wounded were left to be scalped. The women cried in vain for help. It was each man for himself. "They behaved," Washington recalled, "with more cowardice than it is possible to conceive . . . they broke and ran as sheep pursued by dogs."

A stark picture of the battlefield, after the last of Braddock's beaten troops had got clear of it and regained the far side of the Monongahela, has been left us by a young French militiaman:

> The bodies of a great number of men killed, and those of eight women or girls, entirely stripped, lie promiscuously with the dead horses for more than half a league.

Statistically, the English loss was staggering. Out of a total force of 1460 men, 456 were killed and 421 wounded. Among the severely hurt were such important officers as Sir John St. Clair, Lieut.-Col. Ralph Burton, Lieut.-Col. Thomas Gage, and Capt. Horatio Gates. The killed included Sir Peter Halkett, his son Lieut. James Halkett and, of course, Gen. Edward Braddock, himself.

Whether the fault lay in the quality of leadership or in the men, the Battle of Monongahela added nothing to the luster of

British arms. "Our disgrace," an English major commented laconically, "thereby added to the glory of the French and to the fury of the Indians; and so ended the Virginia campaign of 1755."[10]

• 17 •

As the sun sank toward the Ohio on the afternoon of July 9, anxious watchers peered eastward from the ramparts of Fort Duquesne. Nobody knew for certain what had happened on the Monongahela.

At four o'clock, a terrified Indian had brought dismaying news: a battle had been fought, Captain Beaujeu had been killed, the Indians had fled, and the British would be along at any moment. After that, two long hours of ominous silence.

But now, at six o'clock, a party of French soldiers emerged from the dusk of the woods beyond the clearing. Carrying their wounded, they limped heavily toward the fort; and the watchers on the walls observed apprehensively the smallness of their number, the weariness of their progress . . . By nightfall, however, all the regulars and militia—all but Captain Beaujeu and a few others—were back inside the walls, recounting the story of incredible victory.

Besides a thousand dead, they said, the British had left all their artillery on the field of battle, all their provisions, supplies, and stores, besides 100 oxen and some 500 horses. Even the British general's military chest, containing £25,000 in gold, and all of his official papers, had been left behind. Never had a victory been more complete! Never the spoils of battle richer!

And all this the French had purchased at the trivial price of only sixteen casualties. Three officers had been killed—two of whom, Lieutenant Carqueville and Ensign La Parade, had died after returning to Fort Duquesne; two officers and two cadets had

---

[10] Who was responsible for Braddock's defeat was a topic of bitter argument immediately after the battle, and has been a subject of debate ever since. Of eight known eyewitness accounts of the battle, four blamed the men; four blamed the officers, directly or indirectly. Stanley M. Pargellis, in "Braddock's Defeat," *American Historical Review*, Vol. XLI, No. 2, Jan., 1936, concludes that tactical mismanagement was a major cause of the defeat, and that the fault lay in quality of leadership, not in the men.

been wounded; five soldiers had been killed and four wounded. And besides the French losses, 27 Indians were reported killed or wounded.

It was not until the next day that the Indians began to arrive. As their ponies, loaded with dripping scalps and booty, plodded toward the fort, red-coated savages waved swords, shot off muskets, and raised the scalp halloo; while cheers and answering musket fire welcomed them from the walls of Fort Duquesne. Ahead of the Indians stumbled a dozen British regulars and seven white women.[11] The soldiers' faces had been painted black—a sign that they were reserved for torture.

Captain Dumas had not pursued his fleeing enemy. Even if he had wished to, it is doubtful that he could have restrained his blood-maddened Indians from indulging in the greatest orgy of scalping and plundering that the frontier had ever offered. Besides, he could not be sure that the British reserve, under Dunbar, might not cross the Monongahela and fall on his disorganized force. Most of all, he was concerned about the artillery being retaken and—who could tell?—being used against Fort Duquesne after all.

Contrecoeur shared this anxiety. "If the English had returned," he wrote afterwards, "with the 1000 fresh troops they had in reserve at some distance from them, how far we did not know, we might perhaps have found ourselves distressed." He accordingly sent Dumas, de Léry, and 100 men to guard the guns until they could be brought in. Next day, the big brass cannon—which would one day be used by Montcalm to batter down Oswego—arrived at the fort they had been intended to destroy.

On the 12th, the battlefield was again visited to kill horses, destroy wagons, and scatter gunpowder and flour over the corpse-littered ground.[12] The Indians, having scalped and looted beyond their savage dreams, left for home. And so peace, and the silence of the wilderness, settled down once more on the Beautiful River.

The official French account of so momentous an engagement was remarkably restrained—almost as if the defenders of the

[11] One of the women is said to have been kept at Fort Le Boeuf, the others sent to Montreal.
[12] Beaujeu's body, oddly enough, was searched for in vain on the day of the battle, and was not found until the day following, when it was brought back to Fort Duquesne and buried in the post's cemetery.

Forks were aware that, although they had won a battle, they were still to lose the war:

> The rout was complete. We remained in possession of the field with six brass twelves and sixes, four howitzer carriages of 50, eleven small royal grenade mortars, all their ammunition, and generally their entire baggage . . . The enemy have left more than 1000 men on the field of battle. They have lost a great portion of their artillery and ammunitions, provisions, as also their general whose name was Mr. Braddock, and almost all their officers . . . Such a victory, so entirely unexpected, seeing the inequality of the forces, is the fruit of M. Dumas' experience, and of the activity and valor of the officers under his command.[13]

But it was a spectacular victory, in any case, and one that spread consternation from Williamsburg to London, and sowed panic along the whole frontier. For the time being, at least, the white banner of the Bourbons was the only flag flying west of the mountains; the Ohio was still securely in French hands.

---

[13] About the kindest word spoken by anyone for Braddock's poor, bewildered troops were those of Contrecoeur in a letter to Vaudreuil: "The English fought in order of battle and with brave countenance."

BOOK SIX

Blood on the Moon

After what the British Ministry described as "the unfortunate miscarriage of His Majesty's forces in the designed attack on Fort Duquesne," the frontiers of the Middle Provinces found themselves naked against a torrent of death and destruction pouring down from the North.

It need not have been so. If a more determined officer than Colonel Dunbar had succeeded to command of the British troops, a defense of the frontier could have been organized—even a new offensive against Fort Duquesne mounted. But when Braddock's terrified survivors reached his camp, Dunbar himself seems to have panicked. He promptly burned, destroyed, or buried everything in sight—wagons, supplies, ammunition, even the great guns that were to have shattered the French stronghold. Then he back tracked as fast as he could to Fort Cumberland.

Governor Dinwiddie reminded the colonel that he must still have some 1600 effectives, and urged an immediate return to Fort Duquesne. But Dunbar had other ideas. Although it was only the middle of summer, he decided to go into winter quarters! On August 2 he abandoned Fort Cumberland, taking with him about 1500 men, including not only the uninjured survivors of the Irish regiments, but the Independent American companies as well, and marched off to Philadelphia.

"He appears," Dinwiddie fumed, "to have determined to leave our frontiers as defenseless as possible."

At Fort Duquesne, the French command had come to the same conclusion. Swarms of raiders were loosed against the back settlements, left unprotected by Dunbar's ignominious departure for "winter quarters." Yet, it was not until they had sweated out a period of anxious uncertainty that the French launched their "hairdressers" southward with tomahawk and torch.

After the incredible victory on the Monongahela, nobody at Fort Duquesne quite knew what to expect. Would Dunbar, with his reserve of trained troops, come and take revenge for Braddock's destruction? Now that the way was open, the roads cut, what was to prevent the English, with their enormous resources, from mounting another swift offensive from Fort Cumberland?

The state of affairs at Fort Duquesne was not, indeed, reassuring. Immediately after Braddock's defeat, many of the regulars and militia were pulled out of that fort and hurried to other danger points—Fort Frontenac, Fort Niagara, Fort St. Frederic. France was fighting her North American war on many fronts now; and victory on the Monongahela had not eased the threat to her other St. Lawrence-Mississippi defenses. For the moment, Fort Duquesne would have to make do with a garrison of only 250 men, including 10 officers and 15 cadets.

As was their custom after a big victory, the Indians had returned to their villages; and not all of them in an amiable mood. Inevitably, quarrels flared up over the division of plunder. The Ottawa—whom even the Ohio Indians feared—turned especially ugly. Throwing the symbolic hatchet of alliance at Contrecoeur's feet, they threatened to join the English. Before taking off for their distant lodges, they killed and scalped two Frenchmen within sight of the garrison.

Montreal, meanwhile, was taking a somewhat jaundiced view of the situation on the Ohio. Vaudreuil was sure the English would attack again, and that Fort Duquesne would this time be a push-over. He wrote Moras:

> Fort Duquesne, in its present condition, could not offer any resistance to the enemy; 'tis too small to lodge the garrison necessary on such an occasion. A single shell would be sufficient to get it so on fire that 'twould be impossible to extinguish it, because the houses are too close. The garrison would then find itself under the painful necessity of abandoning that fort.

The engineer Le Mercier was in agreement. "That post," he admitted, "is too small to be able to sustain a siege."

General Montcalm put it even more emphatically: "Fort Duquesne is not worth a straw."

All this, however, was really nothing new. Fort Duquesne had always been a small, undermanned fort; but twice she had confounded her enemies—not by withstanding a prolonged siege, but by going out and destroying her attackers. The High Command decided that this would have to be the strategy now. New orders were therefore dispatched to Captain Dumas who, in September, had succeeded Contrecoeur as Commander of the Ohio forces.

"Whenever advised of their marching against him," Captain Dumas's orders read, "he is to call his forces together again, in order to proceed to meet them, as in the present state of the fort, it would be impossible to make resistance for any length of time."

And Dumas's own on-the-spot decision was: "To go out and meet the enemy and give him battle appears inevitable."

As soon as fear of imminent attack had passed, accordingly, long-range operations against the English settlements began. The technique—originated by Frontenac in the preceding century—consisted of sending a strong force of Indians and French soldiers, commanded by a regular officer, deep into enemy territory. The approach was usually made along a large river. When the settlements were reached, the main force split up into several small parties. Then, to make mutual defense more difficult, a number of houses or forts were attacked simultaneously. The attack, always made at dawn, was sudden, short, and hideous. After it was over, the striking parties rendezvoused to count scalps and plan another raid.

So long as the English were kept busy rushing from one place to another in defense of their 300-mile frontier, it was reasoned, they would have litttle time, energy, or money left for another advance against Fort Duquesne. And so Captain Dumas assured Vaudreuil, "I will offer them everywhere the most active resistance." Which was another way of saying, "I will kill, burn, scalp, destroy, and spread terror in every direction."

It would be a war of attrition, of course, and could lead to nothing decisive. But Vaudreuil hoped "it would disgust the colonists and make them yearn for peace." It would keep the Indians happy, at least—and the English away from Fort Duquesne.

• 2 •

"Dunbar's decision to march to Philadelphia," Governor Sharpe wrote Dinwiddie, "has alarmed the frontier more than Braddock's defeat."

At Fort Cumberland, Col. James Innes saw himself making a last stand, if need be, against hordes of French and Indians descending from the Forks of the Ohio:

> I have at this moment received that melancholy account of the defeat of our troops, the general killed and numbers of our officers, our whole army taken. In short the account I have received is so very bad that, as please God, I intend to make a stand here, it's highly necessary to raise the militia everywhere to defend the frontiers.

Nor was the general alarm unfounded. For the next two years there was hardly, in the grim parlance of the frontier, "a dry settlement" along the western border, hardly a night but what there was "blood on the moon."

In Pennsylvania the storm broke at the little settlement of Penn's Creek, on the Susquehanna. Here, on October 16, the Delaware suddenly swooped down and killed or carried off 25 people. Soon afterwards, the same Indians wiped out 47 families along the Maryland border, and razed 27 plantations.

These two raids were enough to throw the Pennsylvanians—hitherto concerned chiefly with how to profit most from army contracts—into wild dismay. The rumor spread that 1500 French and Indians were killing and burning their way down the Juniata and the western branches of the Susquehanna. Hollow-eyed fugitives swarmed into Carlisle, York, and Lancaster. "This town is full of people," Col. James Burd wrote from Shippensburg, "they being all moving in with their families." And Franklin sent a graphic picture of how things were in Bethlehem:

As we drew near this place, we met a number of waggons, and many people moving off with their effects and families from the Irish settlements and Lehi Township, being terrified by . . . the burnings and murders committed in the Township on New Year's Day. We found this place fill'd with refugees, the workmen's shops and even cellars being crowded with women and children; and we learned that Lehi Township is almost entirely abandoned by the inhabitants.

In a short time, indeed, the whole Juniata Valley was empty of everything but the smoking ruins of cabins; and the line of settlements had been pushed back a hundred and fifty miles. But still the attacks continued, and not only against defenseless families. Armed patrols were engaged; at Dietrich Six's, half a dozen men were killed and the surrounding country then ravaged. Soon a belt from 20 to 40 miles wide along the Pennsylvania border had been laid waste.

South of the Potomac things were no better. Almost immediately after the departure of Dunbar's regiments, French and Indian raiders began to murder isolated settlers on the Maryland border. Soon the bloody tide had swept toward the Blue Ridge, and the mountain passes were clogged with people "flying as if every minute was death." Washington arrived in Winchester to find that town jammed with refugees from the West, while the residents themselves were fleeing still farther eastward. Almost a year after Monongahela, he wrote to Dinwiddie: "Desolation and murder still increase, and no prospects of relief. The Blue Ridge is now our frontier, no man being left in this Country except a few that keep close with a number of women and children in the forts, which they have erected for the purpose."

In one of these "forts" on the Greenbrier River, 60 settlers and their children sought safety from an approaching band of raiders. They stood off the Indians for four days, at a cost of some 13 lives. Then the savages murdered a dozen other settlers who had not made it to the fort, carried off two girls and, after burning every house and barn, departed with all the settlement's horses and cattle.

This sort of thing happened week after week. The story repeated itself so often that one report was often confused with another—so that all the massacres seemed more or less alike. Which, in fact, they were.

Before the end of the summer, the French were striking as far south as the Carolinas. Captain Dumas, reporting a raid by Capt. Marie-François Picote, Sieur de Bellestre, gives us an idea of the scale of some of these "visits." Bellestre, with 300 marines, Canadians, and Indians, surrounded a Palatine settlement protected by five forts, took the strongest blockhouse by assault and, after putting the garrison to the sword, accepted the surrender of the others. In this raid alone, 40 English were killed and 150 taken prisoner; 60 houses burned, and all outbuildings, barns, and a mill destroyed. The total damage was reported as: more grain than the Isle of Montreal produced in a year of abundance, and the same quantity of hogs; 3000 cattle, 3000 sheep, 1500 horses; property, including liquor, to the value of 1,500,000 livres; also a great amount of wampum, silver bracelets, scarlet cloth, and other Indian trade goods. Quebec suspected this report was much exaggerated, and could probably be cut in half; but even at that, such a blow—dealt in only 48 hours—was a staggering one.

The French, of course, were well pleased with these bloody doings. Marquis Montcalm could truthfully write to Vaudreuil in June, 1756:

> Pennsylvania and Virginia are really desolated. Letters found on officers who have been killed admit not a doubt of the alarm prevailing in that quarter.

And a French "Abstract of Dispatches from Canada" comfortably reported:

> Letters of the 23rd March assure us that the French and Indians have, since Admiral Braddock's defeat, disposed of more than 700 people in the provinces of Pennsylvania, Virginia, and Carolina, including those killed and taken prisoners.

Captain Dumas wrote from Fort Duquesne, indeed, that for eight days he had been so busy taking in scalps that he had found litttle time for anything else. And Vaudreuil—never one to play down good news—reported enthusiastically:

> On the 8th of June the grass was growing in the roads communicating with Cumberland. Expresses no longer came any farther than Winchester, on account of our Indians, who are always

in the field. The entire frontier of the three provinces is in
the like condition. It was thought that Fort Cumberland would
soon be abandoned; more than three months have elapsed since
a wagon or bateau came there. The English are in daily dread
of being attacked . . . they propose blowing up Fort Cumberland and retiring.

So well was the strategy of terror succeeding, in fact, that
Paris thought it proper to caution Vaudreuil against carrying
things too far; French troops, as well as Canadians, must be
spared for more decisive actions.

• 3 •

It is a cliché of American history that all the atrocities in
this cruel wilderness war were on the side of the French; and
it is true, of course, that the French-Indian sweep of the frontier was a fiendish business. Behind each official report of a
successful foray there was a nightmare of sudden, horrible death;
or, even worse, of a prolonged one under torture.

The Indian allies of the French were not only consummate
raiders; they were also sadistic killers.[1] Even French officers were
sickened, sometimes frightened, at their ferocity. "Humanity
groans at being forced to use such monsters," a Colonel Bougain-
ville confessed. And a Quebec priest, Father Claude Godfroy,
was expressing a feeling of guilt, as well as of horror, for most of
his countrymen when he wrote sorrowfully to his brother:

> The Indians do not make any prisoners; they kill all they meet,
> men, women, and children. Every day they have some for their
> kettles, and after having abused the women and maidens, they
> slaughter or burn them.

If the French officers often gloated, it can also be said that
sometimes they had no choice but to stand by with averted
eyes when the fires of torment were lighted. There is nothing to

---

[1] It is sometimes rationalized that Indian cruelty was, in fact, a compliment
to a brave enemy—a chance for him to display his fortitude. A viewpoint
shared by few frontiersmen!

show that, as a matter of policy, they approved the refined cruelties so dear to the Indian heart. On the contrary, there is evidence that they took specific measures to prevent them. Thus Captain Dumas' instructions to a leader of his raiding parties:

> The Sieur Douville will employ all his talents and all his credit to prevent the savages from committing any cruelties upon those who may fall into his hands.

French commanders were not always successful, of course, in restraining the Indians' blood lust; but not even the savages were invariably murderous, and alongside the tales of horror can be placed the story of a young French militiaman named Michael La Chauvigniere.

With a scalping party from Fort Duquesne, Chauvigniere had penetrated far into the settlements. He told of passing ruined houses, "some with peach trees." The first unharmed cabin the raiders came to was inhabited by Germans. Only five children, four girls and a boy, were at home, the parents having gone to visit a neighboring fort. "We took some clothes for the children," Chauvigniere related, "and some provisions. We took some horses at another place, about three leagues away, and put the children on them." After passing many deserted houses, with chickens running through them, Chauvigniere dropped a piece of bread on the trail, and stopped to look for it. The rest of the party left him behind, and he lost himself in the woods. After wandering for seven days, he came on Fort Henry and, rather than starve, gave himself up.

It was not the most exciting of frontier stories. But against a background of flaming settlements and shrieking victims, one remembers: "We took some clothes for the children . . . We took some horses and put the children on them." It was so seldom, alas, that even such a fitful little light of human compassion gleamed in the smoky blackness of America's cruelest war.[2]

---

[2] The ferocity with which it was waged is reflected in a letter from young Beaujeu de Vilmonde to his father, March 27, 1747: "I attacked a house where there were twenty five English, all armed to the teeth. Rushing to the door, I came suddenly upon a sentry and I killed him. I entered the house and they fired three or four shots at me, which only passed through my greatcoat. I fired my pistols at the captain, whom I killed, then I gave

When the English, at last, succeeded in gathering their own force of Indians, the necessities of survival forced them into a course of conduct no different from that of the French. Savage allies must be kept happy; and it is not difficult to detect the ominous undertones in one of William Johnson's victory dispatches:

> I divided among the several nations the prisoners and scalps amounting to two hundred and forty-six, of which ninety-six were prisoners. The officers I with difficulty released from them by ranson, good words, etc.

The Indians, for their part, killed white men on either side with about equal pleasure.

• 4 •

For a while, the English colonies fully expected a full-scale French invasion, probably by a force from the Illinois and Mississippi; and at one point troops were rushed to Fort Cumberland to repel such a thrust. But as this threat faded, England decided to let the frontier shift for itself, and to concentrate on the campaign in the North. Fort Duquesne could be disregarded for the moment; in any case, it could not long outlive the fall of Niagara.

But in the North, too, things had gone badly. Under Governor Shirley of Massachusetts, who had now been named supreme commander of the British forces in America, an attempt to carry out the original plan of attacks on Niagara, Crown Point, and Acadia got nowhere.

Col. Robert Monckton, to be sure, easily took Fort Beausejour, in Acadia, after which some 7,000 Acadians were packed into transports and sent off to various British provinces. But the

---

the sergeant a bayonet thrust in the stomach and ran my gun through his body. He fell, his intestines protruding from his stomach, and I withdrew my gun, which was all broken. I snatched the gun from another Englishman who had caught me by the neck; happily, I was the stronger, and I killed him. I clubbed another one to death, and outside I fired on a fleeing Englishman and broke his arm."

Crown Point expedition ran head-on into disaster at Lake George,
where a detachment of frontiersmen was ambushed and routed
by Dieskau's French regulars. Although the French were then
repulsed, and the brilliant and expensive Dieskau himself captured, Colonel Johnson thought it best to abandon the Crown
Point campaign and pull back to Albany. As for Niagara, Shirley
got no closer to that vital French stronghold than Oswego. After
dallying there through the summer, he too went into winter
quarters at Albany.

All in all, the year 1755 was not a very successful one for the
English. Nothing that happened between July and November,
indeed, did much to wipe out the disgrace of Braddock's debacle
—and the even greater ignominy of Dunbar's retreat to Philadelphia. Except in Acadia, the French were everywhere still in
command.

And on the western frontier, forgotten in the drama of larger
events, hundreds of defenseless settlers were dying horribly on
lonely backwoods farms.

◆ 5 ◆

Feeling themselves abandoned by their governments, the
frontier people made shift, at last, to organize their own defense.
They armed themselves and tightened up their cabins. They built
small "private forts," places to which neighbors could flee in times
of alarm; and they raised bands of rangers, professional Indian
fighters, to protect the setttlements and pursue the Indians after
a raid.

The fort soon became the most important feature of frontier
life, and the word "fort" one of the most common and versatile
words in the border vocabulary. It had many meanings—all of
them heavy with the sense of danger and death. "Fort" was a
noun, signifying anything from a stronghold with cannon to a
miserable old cabin with loopholes. It was an adjective; people
spoke of a "forted settlement" or even a "forted house." And it
was a verb; in time of trouble, a settler and his family "forted"
to the nearest blockhouse.

Typical of the "private fort"[3] was one erected by John Harris

[3] Montcalm contemptuously called them "pretend forts."

on the site of present Harrisburg, Pa. In the fall of 1755, after the massacre at Penn's Creek, Harris wrote:

> I have this day cut holes in my house, and am determined to hold out to the last extremity if I can get some men to stand by me.

The house, at that time already an old one, was solidly built of notched logs, with huge fireplaces and a spacious cellar—room enough to shelter families from twenty miles around when the Indians came. As a further defense, Harris enclosed it with a strong stockade. In such a "fort" a dozen resolute men could stand off a lot of Indians.

Pennsylvania soon had some fifty private forts scattered along her border. They included ordinary settlers' cabins, mills, meeting houses, taverns, even a large stone boarding school for girls at Nazareth, Pa. Almost any building, favorably located, could be turned into a fort, just as any backwoods farmer could become an Indian fighter.

As the flood of destruction from Fort Duquesne rose higher, however, the need for specially-built blockhouses, capable of protecting a large number of families, became pressing. And here again, in the absence of help from provincial governments busy elsewhere, the frontier looked to its own defense.

A good contemporary description of the kind of fort that was built, often in frantic haste, has been provided by the frontier clergyman, Joseph Doddridge:

> The fort consisted of cabins, block houses, and stockades. A range of cabins usually formed one side at least of the fort . . . The walls on the outside were ten or twelve feet high, the slopes of the roofs being turned wholly inward . . . The block houses were built at the angles of the forts. They projected about two feet beyond the outer walls of the cabins and stockades. Their upper stories were about eighteen inches every way larger in dimensions than the under one, leaving an opening at the commencement of the second story to prevent the enemy from making lodgement under their walls.
>
> In some forts, instead of block houses, the angles of the fort were furnished with bastions. A large folding gate made of

thick slabs, nearest the spring, closed the fort. The stockades, bastions, cabins, and block houses were furnished with port holes of proper height and distances. The whole of the outside was made completely bullet proof. It may be truly said that necessity is the mother of invention; for the whole of this work was made without the aid of a single nail or spike of iron.

Benjamin Franklin describes the erection of a frontier fort— a rather second-rate one—at Gnadenhut, Pa.:

Our first work was to bury more effectually the dead we found there, who had been half interr'd by the country people . . . The next morning our fort was planned and marked out, the circumference measuring four hundred and fifty-five feet, which would require as many palisades to be made of trees, one with another, of a foot diameter each. Our axes, of which we had seventy, were immediately set to work to cut down trees, and, our men being dexterous in the use of them, great despatch was made. Seeing the trees fall so fast, I had the curiosity to look at my watch when two men began to cut at a pine; in six minutes they had it upon the ground, and I found it of fourteen inches diameter. Each pine made three palisades of eighteen feet long, pointed at one end. While these were preparing, our other men dug a trench all round of three feet deep . . . When they were set up, our carpenters built a stage of board all round within, about six feet high, for the men to stand on when to fire thro' the loopholes. We had one swivel gun, which we mounted at one of the angles, and fir'd it as soon as fix'd, to let the Indians know that we had such pieces; and thus our fort, if such a magnificent name may be given to so miserable a stockade, was finished in a week . . .

Such forts were placed wherever the danger seemed greatest, without any general plan of frontier defense. They served not only as places of refuge, but as stores where supplies, ammunition, and food could be held in reserve. And they were often designated as distribution centers for that all-important frontier commodity, salt.[4]

[4] As a preservative of meat, salt was so vital to Colonial economy that the discovery of new salt licks or wells was an important factor in the westward advance of the frontier.

In time of danger, families from the surrounding country crowded into them, while the men gathered crops, scouted, or fought. Usually, one fully-armed party worked in the fields, while another covered it from behind trees, or scoured the neighboring woods for Indian sign. A lookout on the roof kept a watch for scalping parties, and often enough saw his own house go up in flames while the Indians cavorted and filled the air with feathers from his beds.

When an actual attack on a fort came—usually just before dawn—every person rushed to his assigned station and task. If the main building were two-storied—as many were—the women and children crowded into the windowless room on the first floor, while the men fired through the portholes in the upper story. But when the fighting grew hot, wives and daughters took their places beside the men, reloading and priming their rifles, tending the wounded, melting down pewter plates and running bullets, if need be.

Each man knew which was his own loophole, and fired through it with his own rifle and whatever ammunition he was spared from the common supply. Axes and mattocks were distributed for use in case of hand-to-hand fighting. Nothing—including kettles of water at strategic points to put out fires—was overlooked. The Indians did not relish attacking a fort thus prepared to receive them; and they seldom tackled one without the help of white men.

But such "forthouses" were too few along the extended frontier, too far apart, too thinly manned; and the long stretches of wilderness between them were almost completely unpatrolled. Supplied and equipped at Fort Duquesne, the Indians were making inroads even in the winter now; and by the end of 1755 it had become apparent to the governments of Pennsylvania and Virginia, preoccupied though they were with adversities in the North, that something would have to be done about the almost-forgotten frontiers.

• 6 •

With his strong sense of public duty and unlimited capacity for punishment, George Washington undertook the thankless job of organizing the frontier defenses of Virginia. Governor Dinwiddie appointed him commander-in-chief of the Province's military forces and instructed the 23-year-old colonel to run a line of forts along the east slope of the Alleghenies. These forts, covering the principal passes, were to be spaced from 20 to 30 miles apart, with patrols operating between them.

Washington himself was by no means convinced of the usefulness of such a defense system. It was necessary, he believed, to take the offensive and strike at the source of the frontier's woes —namely, Fort Duquesne. But he had his orders, and he carried them out with his usual dogged dedication to duty, making long and dangerous rides across the mountains, doing all he could to rally the frontier and bolster its haphazard defenses. By mid-1756, the Province was sketchily protected by about 25 Provincial forts, reaching from Fort Cumberland to the Carolina border, and connected by roads cut through the wilderness. Many of them were nothing more, however, than "private forts" now garrisoned by Provincial troops; none was strong enough to withstand artillery.

Pennsylvania took similar measures under the capable direction of Benjamin Franklin and George Croghan. The Pennsylvania plan also called for an unbroken chain of forts, rather than a few large ones, garrisoned by paid troops, and with intervening patrols. By 1756, such a chain, supplemented by local blockhouses, extended along the Blue Ridge Mountains from the Susquehanna to the Delaware and west of the Susquehanna, more thinly, to the Maryland border.

Some of these frontier forts were very small, very badly run, and very dirty—damp, vermin-ridden holes in which women and children crowded miserably while their menfolk scoured the woods for Indians. No compliment, for example, was paid Benjamin Franklin in naming the fort at Allemengle, Pa., for him. On this particular bastion an inspector reported:

> The Lieut assured me that he has been obliged to carry several cart loads of horse dung & litter out of the fort before he could get it tolerably clean, that he found most of the men full of vermin and was obliged to discharge two of the nastiest of them to get all the blankets wash'd and scoured upon that acco't.

Of Fort Henry, on the other hand, the same inspector could write:

> This fort is very well built, the palisades are spiked together at the top, the houses within are all covered with tyle, and the whole is kept clean and in very good order. There is a convenient room within the Fort to parade and exercise all the men.

A few forts were impressive. Fort Augusta, at the forks of the Susquehanna, was even larger than Fort Duquesne—to which it bore a striking resemblance. Fort Frederick in Maryland was a substantial work of masonry, designed to thwart the Indians' talent for setting fire to wooden stockades. And Fort Cumberland, although poorly-built and poorly-located, was a "King's fort" and the north bastion of the whole Virginia system.

Few major offensives were ever launched, however, from even these large establishments. The role of the Provincial forts, large and small, was chiefly to harbor refugees and accommodate the "ranging companies" that operated between them. It was the border patrol that was the mainstay of the frontier defense.

* 7 *

Every morning, "as soon as it was light enough to see an Indian," a party of rangers set out from its fort and made a thorough search of the surrounding woods. At some points on the frontier, where the forts were only 10 to 15 miles apart, the "scout" covered the entire space between posts. The objective of the scouting activity was twofold: to rout out any Indians that might be lurking in the vicinity, and to "accustom the men to the woods."

In the smaller forts, scouting was conducted on a regular but rather informal basis, and the journal of the commanding officer was likely to be a repetition of such entries as:

> I went to scout with six men, and went about six miles from the fort and found the snow in many places half a leg deep; we discovering no enemy, all returned safe to the fort.

At the larger posts, however, the technique was sometimes an elaborate one. The patrol plan at Fort Augusta, for example, required a line of five parties abreast, each under an officer or non-com which swept a wide semicircle of ground in front of the fort. Capt. Joseph Shippen, in a letter from Fort Augusta, tells how it was done:

> Every morning before sun-rise a party of 50 men goes out to reconnoitre the ground for a mile & a half around the fort they take different routs every time & march at the distance of 6 or seven yards apart & all a breast in one rank entire, so as to sweep a large space of ground.

In addition to these routine "scouts," the garrisons of the forts were expected to protect reapers during the harvest, pursue raiding parties after a strike, and take the field against reported marauders. Not infrequently, of course, they ran into trouble.

In the spring of 1756, Capt. John Mercer, with 40 or 50 men, was unfortunate enough to be ambushed by a party of Indians he had gone out to scout. Mercer, a subaltern, and 15 men were killed and scalped in the ensuing skirmish. On the French side, one Indian was unaccounted for. Not an encouraging score.

The life of a ranging company was, indeed, hard, dangerous— and often short; and it is not to be wondered, perhaps, that few aspired to it. Washington was immediately up against the old problem: frontiersmen who did not want to be in the army; and if they were in it, wanted out. In Pennsylvania, Franklin was confronted by other problems, peculiar to that Province—including a deep-seated tradition of pacificism.

But somehow, by some means, a defense of the miserable back country people had to be contrived; and, fortunately, both Provinces found leaders equal to the challenge.

• 8 •

In Virginia, Dunbar's withdrawal had stripped the Province of both men and arms. It would be necessary, Governor Dinwiddie decided, to organize five companies of rangers at once, and

call out the militia. Then he ordered Washington to work out
the details.

Washington promptly encountered mutiny, rioting, wholesale
desertion, and an almost complete lack of volunteers. There was
also a lack of food, clothing, arms, money, almost everything
needed for even a makeshift defense of the blazing frontier. In
the meantime, settlers were being murdered daily from Fort
Cumberland to the Carolinas: at Greenbrier, 25; near Cumberland, 6; at Patterson Creek, 3 whole families . . . Washington
wrote Dinwiddie:

> I am too little acquainted, Sir, with pathetic language, to at-
> tempt a description of the people's distresses . . . But what can
> I do? . . . I see their situation, know their danger, and partici-
> pate their sufferings, without having it in my power to give
> them further relief than uncertain promises.

But the young colonel finally got himself an army. He had to
hang deserters and send whole companies of worthless militia
home; but, with Dinwiddie's backing, he gradually acquired a
fighting force of sorts, and a string of forts to cover their ranging
operations.

In Pennsylvania, Franklin had equally rough going. Aside from
an extralegal force of volunteer militia, the Province had no
troops whatever. Since the days of William Penn, the Quakers
had depended on a policy of friendship with the Indians to keep
the peace. Up to 1755 it had worked. Presents and good will had
taken the place of troops and forts. And now, even with the backwoods reeling under the tomahawk and torch, the Quakers found
it hard to believe that the Indians were really their enemy.

It was not until mid-winter of 1755–1756, that the Assembly
appropriated funds with which Franklin could pay a militia. By
the spring of 1756, however, the Province had cast loose from its
long tradition of pacifism. Soon she was to have a striking force
on the frontier of some 1400 troops—more than all the French
forces on the Ohio.

With Pennsylvania's militia, Washington's Virginia Regiment,
and a battalion of regulars in the field, the situation along the
frontier began to assume more the character of a two-sided war.
The Provincial troops could not prevent sporadic raids between

forts, but they were increasingly successful in blocking deep penetration of the settlements. Where marauders from Fort Duquesne had once found only defenseless farms, they now encountered well-built forts, garrisoned by government troops. Where they had roamed the woods at will, they now had to be on the alert against ranging parties out for their own scalps. Raiding was not quite the fun it once had been.

• 9 •

At Fort Duquesne the French believed, indeed, that the English were actually planning another expedition to the Ohio. They were not wholly mistaken. Governor Shirley was certainly toying with the idea of an attack on Fort Duquesne. Four thousand men and 1000 Cherokee, he figured, could turn the trick. The time: summer of 1756.

At this moment, Captain Dumas had at most 800 men—hardly enough for even a token defense against such a force. He had been harassed by smallpox. And he was worried about feeding such troops and Indians as remained at the fort. Canada was starving again, and had little to send to the Ohio. Dumas made shift to bring provisions up the Ohio from New Orleans and the Illinois country, but it was a long, back-breaking pull; and how could he be sure the English would not attack his bateaux at the Rapids?

With little but moral support coming from Canada, Dumas was left to work out his own plan of defense against the expected blow. It would come, he reasoned, from the direction of Fort Cumberland. Therefore, he would continue his policy of harassment. If he could not defend Fort Duquesne, at least he could make it difficult for the English to get set for an attack on it.

His patrols were soon probing the wilderness to within musket range of Fort Cumberland. The first party sent out, in October, 1755, consisted of 250 Indians and some French officers. It had orders to attack Fort Cumberland itself, if possible; but after lying in ambush for some time, it returned to Fort Duquesne "with sixty prisoners and a great number of scalps."

In April, 1756, the first French officer was killed. The officer,

Ensign Dagneau Douville, was on scout beyond Fort Cumberland, with instructions to raid English ammunition dumps. While attacking a small fort on the Cacapon River, Douville was jumped by a detachment of Virginians led by a backwoodsman named Pearis. One of Pearis' men was killed, and two wounded; but several of the French Indians were hit and their leader slain. Washington gleefully sent Douville's scalp to Governor Dinwiddie.

In July, 1756, the second French officer was killed—Ensign Louis-Jean-Baptiste Céloron de Blainville, a younger brother of the Céloron who had buried the King's lead plates along the Ohio. Ensign Céloron's raiders had previously accounted for eight Englishmen in a small fort near Cumberland. The fight, in which Céloron lost his life, was described in Vaudreuil's report of the action to Paris:

> A party commanded by Sieur Céloron de Blainville attacked enemy scouts six leagues beyond Fort Cumberland. These two parties met unexpectedly. They fired point-blank; the enemy yielded at once. We killed 3 of them and the savages brought back the scalps, but we lost Sieur de Blainville, a Huron, a Loup, and a Montague.

The winter of 1755–1756 was a severe one, and Dumas's Indians, wary of being tracked in the deep snow, were reluctant to leave Fort Duquesne. Nevertheless, scalping parties were continuously in the field, with officers and cadets at their head. A raid led by Sieur de Rocheblave was typical of many:

> Sieur de Rocheblave, with another Cadet, a corporal, a militiaman, and twenty Chauoanons [Shawnee], knocked at the gate of a small fort three leagues from Fort Cumberland, where there remained some families and thirty militiamen. He killed four Englishmen, whom the Indians scalped, wounded three, who dragged themselves into the fort, and took three prisoners.

With monotonous regularity, dispatches of this nature flowed back to Paris—not always accurate, but fairly illustrative, perhaps, of what was going on along the desolated frontier during the hard winter of 1755–1756. In December, Dumas reported the

Indians at Fort Duquesne had turned in 500 English scalps, and had taken 200 prisoners. Vaudreuil wrote smugly to Paris:

> The news from Fort Duquesne and Beautiful River are very favorable. M. Dumas has laid waste with his Indians a good part of Pennsylvania, Virginia, and Maryland . . . We learn that the sufferings throughout the English colonies could not be greater.

Particularly favorable was the news of the burning of Fort Granville. This fort was an important link in the chain of strongpoints on the west side of the Susquehanna, commanding the pass where the Juniata falls through the mountains. On July 22, Dumas sent Capt. Coulon de Villiers—the same Villiers who had defeated Washington at Fort Necessity—to attack it. With 23 Frenchmen and 32 Indians, de Villiers began his assault on the morning of August 2. Most of the garrison was away, protecting harvesters in the vicinity; but a Lieutenant Armstrong and 24 men held off the attackers until the next morning. Then, with the fort afire and Armstrong killed, a sergeant named John Turner opened the gates and surrendered the garrison, three women, and a number of children.[5]

But, depressing as such disasters were, the frontier was not entirely supine. The ruins of Fort Granville had scarcely stopped smoking before the brother of the post's slain defender, Lieut.-Col. John Armstrong, was gathering a force of aroused frontiersmen for a retaliatory attack on Kittanning. This Delaware Indian town was the base from which, under the leadership of Captain Jacobs and Shingas, many of the bloodiest raids on the settlements were launched. Colonel Armstrong surprised Kittanning with 300 Pennsylvanians, killed Captain Jacobs, and scattered the Delaware. It was a blow that did nothing for French prestige along the Ohio.

By the spring of 1757, the Virginians had recovered the initiative to the extent of making raids of their own. Defensive measures, it was finally admitted, were not enough. The Indians' villages must be attacked, and the Indians cut off from their hunt-

[5] Early chroniclers (English) of this event note with some satisfaction that Villiers' savages tortured Turner by thrusting red-hot gun barrels through his body.

ing grounds. The Cherokee were, at last, willing to go along on raids against their northern brothers; and for the first time the Provincials were now striking back with Indian aid.

Maj. Andrew Lewis led a band of Cherokee against the Shawnee villages on the Ohio—250 miles beyond the Virginia border, and returned with a few prisoners but no scalps. Another expedition under Lieut. James Baker had better luck. When Baker, with a party of five soldiers and fifteen Indians, reached Turtle Creek, only twelve miles from Fort Duquesne, they came on the tracks of a party of French raiders. Baker prepared an ambush in which three French soldiers were killed and two ensigns captured. The ensigns, Douville de la Saussaye and de Saint Ours, were murdered and scalped by the Cherokee after they had surrendered.

Another expedition toward Fort Duquesne, led by Capt. Robert Spotswood, came to grief. Spotswood and a number of his men never returned from it.

One could hardly conclude from these sporadic forays that Pennsylvania and Virginia had really taken the offensive. The raw, undisciplined, underfed, and poorly-armed provincial troops were still deserting in droves, fleeing at the first sight of an Indian, and giving up forts without a fight. But the commandant at Fort Duquesne could no longer send his raiders south to burn, kill, scalp, and rape without meeting some show of resistance. The frontier, if only feebly, was beginning to strike back.

• 10 •

As Washington, Franklin, and other leaders had discovered, it was no easy thing to make soldiers out of American colonists. They did not like to fight. They did not know how to fight. And, once in the army, they wanted nothing so much as to get out.

Recruiting in Pennsylvania was hampered, of course, by Quaker and German pacificism. But what totally defeated professional soldiers like Col. Henry Bouquet was the reluctance of frontiersmen to defend their own homes. "For my own part," Bouquet wailed, "I am so much disgusted at the backwardness of the frontier people in assisting us in taking revenge of the savages who murder them daily with impunity, that I hope this will be the last time I shall venture my reputation and life for their sake!"

Washington, as we have seen, was dogged from the beginning of his career by recruiting troubles. But even more exasperating, perhaps, was the difficulty of keeping a backwoodsman in the army, once he had been enrolled. Desertions often outran daily enlistments. The Virginians went over the hill 20 or 30 at a time; and on occasion the troops took mass leave—as at Winchester, when rumors of approaching Indians threw the militia into such a panic that Washington's entire "fighting force" disintegrated.

The penalty for desertion was severe—1000 lashes, sometimes hanging. "Any soldier who shall desert, though he return again," reads a paragraph in Halkett's Orderly Book, "shall be hanged without mercy." At one time, Governor Duquesne and Governor Peregrine Thomas Hopson, of Nova Scotia, agreed to return each other's deserters, "and deserters so returned shall on either side be punished with death."

But the enforcement of rigorous punishment for so common an offense—and with public sympathy generally on the deserter's side—was not easy. Once, when 114 of his 400 drafted men took French leave, Washington was driven to desperate measures. He wrote to Col. John Stanwix:

> I have a gallows near 40 feet high erected (which has terrified the rest exceedingly) and I am determined if it can be justified in the proceedings, to hang two or three on it, as an example to the others.

A couple of weeks later he did hang two of the most notorious of the deserters. The immediate effect was salutary; but soon his ranks were again thinning so fast that he found it difficult to garrison all the frontier posts. Many were left with a force barely sufficient to protect the fort "and to keep the women in heart."

Nor was the quality of the troops finally enlisted and kept in the army all that might have been desired. Drunkenness was a problem second only to desertion, often immobilizing whole companies. Fighting, unruliness, malingering, brought officers to the brink of despair. "I have served over 22 years," Capt. Simeon Ecuyer wailed, "but I have never seen such a tribe of rebels, bandits, and hamstringers . . . In the name of God let me retire to private life!"

Contrary to tradition, the frontier troops were not always good marksmen. Some there undoubtedly were who could cut the head off a running turkey; but a better idea of frontier shooting can be obtained, perhaps, from a report by James Young, who made an inspection tour of the frontier forts in 1756. At Fort Lebanon he found that only half the soldiers could come within two feet of a bull's-eye at 80 yards; not over four in twenty-five could hit a tree at the same distance. Two years later, Col. James Burd reported no improvement.

As for their Indian-fighting competency, perhaps Washington himself said what had to be said when he wrote Dinwiddie: "The timidity of the inhabitants of this County is equalled by nothing but their perverseness." His dim view of the Virginia militia was amply supported a couple of months later, when a detachment was attacked by Indians while escorting an express from Winchester to Fort Cumberland. The detachment proceeded in an exemplary manner until word was passed back that Indians had been sighted. Capt. John Rutherford shouted orders to deploy; but at the first fire from the savages, half his force did not even pull a trigger—they ran, without stopping, all the way back to Winchester!

The garrisons at the frontier forts also came in for their share of contemporary criticism. They were accused of holing up safely inside their stockades and shirking dangerous patrol work. When Indians attacked settlers in the neighborhood, it was charged, they refused to send out rescue parties. Deaths of settlers, it was pointed out, far outnumbered those of soldiers—an obviously unfair comparison.

The frontier farmer had not yet developed the woodsman's skill, the rawhide toughness, and the cold hatred of Indians, that would one day make him a bush-fighter as cunning and ruthless as the red man himself. That would come in another generation—after the Big Leap over the mountains that would separate the men from the boys, and turn quiet settlers into hard-eyed Indian killers. It would not be until the Men of the Western Waters took up the long rifle and tomahawk in defense of their lonely clearings that America would have her "fighting frontier."

Yet, it would be grossly unfair to suppose that all Provincials, even at this early time, were poor soldiers. British officers recognized the native skill of many of them in bush-fighting. One of the war's most brilliant tacticians, Lieut.-Col. John Bradstreet, had so much confidence in the backwoodsmen that he proposed a special regiment of 800 rangers, to be led by himself. And even Colonel Bouquet, in one of his calmer moments, wrote:

> I can truly assure you that you will find no other fault than ignorance and inexperience, which I cannot remedy—but they are loyal and will not abandon you.

Maj. Andrew Lewis, the magnificent but almost unsung leader of innumerable hard, dangerous expeditions, was not the only hero on the frontier. In spite of desertions, drunkenness, and general orneriness, the backwoods soldier put up with an incredible amount of cold, hunger, and misery for his six dollars a month—often paid, if at all, in rum, tobacco, or even wampum. And if he sometimes showed his heels to danger, it was probably more a lack of discipline and leadership than a want of courage that impelled him to "git." It is worth noting that one body of Pennsylvania volunteers insisted on a promise of dangerous patrol detail rather than soft, safe garrison duty as a condition of enlistment.

There is, after all, a ring of truth in the simple tribute that a Captain Walker paid his troops:

> One third of our men ware constantly imployed as guards to the inhabitants, and I may aferm in harvest the one half ware imployed the same way, nor can any man in the county say he ever asked a guard (when he had a just occasion) and was denied. Dureing this time the troops ware not supplied even with ration whiskey, allmoste neaked, for want of blankets and cloathes, and yet I have the satisfaction to inform you they done their duty Cheerfully.

The men who manned the blockhouses and patrolled the bush did, on the whole, "do their duty Cheerfully." They did provide places of safe refuge for harassed settlers, and protected them in the harvest fields. They combed the woods between forts, at-

tacked marauding bands, and definitely discouraged the French
and Indians from raiding very deeply into the settlements. And,
as the first terrible months of terror passed, they did their job
better and better.

Toward the close of the year 1756 the commandant at Fort
Duquesne was receiving fewer scalps from the Blue Ridge,
sending fewer glowing reports to Paris. On the frontier, at least,
the English had begun to hold their own. The same could
hardly be said of other quarters.

◆ 11 ◆

In July, 1756, a British general in New England wrote with
true English reserve to a friend at home: "This part of the world
does not abound in good news."

The war we call the French and Indian War had finally been
made official by formal declaration; and for the English, indeed,
it could hardly have gone worse. Grandiose plans for an expedition against Louisbourg, led by the new Commander-in-Chief,
Lord Loudoun, came to nothing. Fort William Henry was destroyed by Montcalm and many of its garrison massacred. Most
shattering blow of all, perhaps, Oswego crumpled under Montcalm's artillery—some of it left-overs from Braddock's debacle.

Without doubt, 1756 and 1757 were catastrophic years for
the English; and, on the surface, highly satisfactory ones for
the French. At Fort Duquesne, despite a falling off in scalps,
the little garrison shared the general elation over unbroken
victory. On June 2, 1758, M. de Hugues wrote to Maréchal Belle-
Isle:

> Intelligence has been received that everything is going well
> around the Beautiful River. That post has abundance of pro-
> visions from Illinois; our Canadians and Indians are doing
> wonders there.

The official view was that a serious attack on Fort Duquesne
was highly unlikely; and dispatches to Paris made much of the
supplies of flour and meat reaching that fort from the Illinois.

A new commander, Capt. François Marie de Marchand, Sieur

de Ligneris, veteran of the Battle of Monongahela, had replaced Captain Dumas at Fort Duquesne. He was very busy with the pressing business of his remote post. Too busy, and too lulled by official reports of spectacular victories in the East, perhaps, to sense impending disaster.

As spring came to the Ohio, and his Indians made moccasins for their summer journeys to the English settlements, it is doubtful that de Ligneris even knew that a powerful force was gathering in Philadelphia for a third attack on Fort Duquesne. A far greater army than Braddock's, this time, under the leadership of a truly brilliant general.

BOOK SEVEN

Round Three: Forbes and Bouquet

• 1 •

The winter of 1757–1758 was a gay one in Montreal, now the virtual seat of the government and Canada's social center—"a sparkling fragment of the reign of Louis XV, dropped into the American wilderness." Grand balls, dinner parties, assemblies, "great suppers with ladies," dancing until seven o'clock in the morning. So many victories to celebrate! Such good news from every quarter! And so many rich plums for the commissariat to pluck from the pie of a hugely successful war!

For more than two years, now, those stuffy British generals in their red coats and laced hats—Braddock, Shirley, Webb, Loudoun—had stumbled from one disaster into another. In the West, too, the whole English frontier was prostrate with terror. And, what with the disgraceful loss of Minorca and the Duke of Cumberland's defeats, things were not much better across the sea.

At Quebec, the lilies were flying high, indeed, over the citadel atop the Rock. Only in the town below—and all over the wintry reaches of Canada—was there any lack of cause for rejoicing. And there, as usual, the people were starving.

By spring, the situation had become so alarming, indeed, that dispatches to Paris reported:

> After having passed a part of last autumn and winter on a quarter of a pound of bread per person per day, we are reduced these six weeks past to two ounces . . . The supply of animals is beginning to fail; the butchers cannot supply a quarter of

183

the beef necessary for the subsistence of the inhabitants of this
town, though they pay an exorbitant price for it . . . We are
on the eve of dying of hunger.

And General Montcalm, for all the brilliance of his victories—
Oswego, Fort William Henry, Ticonderoga—saw their hollow-
ness. By the middle of summer, matters had reached such a
low ebb that he wrote, in cypher, to Massiac:

> The situation of the colony is most critical, should peace not
> intervene . . . With so small a force, how preserve, without a
> miracle, from the Beautiful River to Saint Sacrament [Lake
> Champlain], and attend to the descent on Quebec; 'tis an im-
> possibility. Whoever will write to the contrary of what I ad-
> vance, will deceive the King.

He cited the overwhelming superiority of English numbers—
50,000 men in the field against his own 15,000; the uselessness of
the Canadian militia; the fickleness of the Indians. "We are resolved," he wrote, "to bury ourselves under the ruins of the
Colony." And in his mind there could have been only the question: *"How long before that time comes?"*

In England, a man named William Pitt was preparing his
answer.

Pitt—a singularly unattractive and widely popular genius—
became Prime Minister in the summer of 1757. He immediately
set in motion the astonishing land and sea operations that were
to raise Britain from the depths of defeat to the peak of victory
and power. Soon his fleets and armies were striking everywhere
—in Europe, in India, in Africa, wherever the fleur-de-lis flew.
And the hardest blow of all was being readied against the
French in America.

It was in America, Pitt was convinced, that his World War
would be won, and he shaped his global strategy accordingly.
When he came to power, however, it was too late in the summer
to launch a new offensive there; for the rest of the year, General
Loudoun would have to bumble along his unhappy way. But in
the meantime, during the winter, Pitt pushed his preparations
for the final defeat of the French in the New World.

His strategy followed the general lines of previous North American campaigns. It again called for an attack on Louisbourg, the great sea bastion of Quebec and Montreal; an expedition against the Hudson River-Lake Champlain forts; and a march— this time in overwhelming force—against Fort Duquesne. It was the same old plan: the difference was that this time a man of flashing intellect, explosive energy, and spectacular oratorical powers was in charge.

For his leaders Pitt chose young and, with one exception, able men. Against Louisbourg he sent Gen. Jeffery Amherst and Gen. James Wolfe. To Gen. James Abercromby—unfortunately— he assigned the job of taking Ticonderoga and Crown Point. And for a third try at Fort Duquesne, he selected Brig. Gen. John Forbes.

Forbes—whom the Indians, for some unexplained reason, called "Ironhead"—had studied medicine before entering the army. He arrived at Halifax as a colonel of the 17th Regiment, with a good deal of European soldiering under his belt. Now, as adjutant and advisor to hard-pressed General Loudoun, he began to pile up valuable administrative experience. When Pitt looked around for a man to lead the most important, perhaps, of his three American campaigns, he settled on Forbes and made him a brigadier. He could hardly, as it turned out, have made a better choice.

Forbes received his appointment at New York in March, and began immediately to shape up an army and work out his plans. He was overwhelmed at once with the usual difficulties and frustrations; but by the first of May he had obtained promises of at least 3,000 Provincial troops from Pennsylvania, Maryland, Virginia, and North Carolina. In addition to these, he could count on some 1600 regular troops—13 companies of Highlanders and several of the newly-formed Royal Americans. He had hopes, too, of enlisting some 600 Cherokee and Catawba. His total force, if all went well, would add up to some 6,000 troops.

Before the end of May, Forbes had begun to send companies of regulars to the frontier. By the middle of June, 1758, his drive against the small wooden fort at the Forks of the Ohio—a massive offensive dwarfing even Braddock's—was well under way.

• 2 •

While the Royal Americans were mustering at Philadelphia, and Col. Archibald Montgomery's Highlanders were beginning to arrive from England, the Virginians were gathering at Winchester. The problem facing General Forbes was: how to get them all together and march them, as a combined force, to the Ohio? And this, in turn, boiled down to a question of what route the advance against Fort Duquesne should take. It was a question that split Pennsylvania and Virginia into bitterly-opposed factions. It even threatened to wreck the campaign before it was fairly started.

Two routes were possible. One was over Braddock's old road from Fort Cumberland. This, of course, was the one favored by the Virginians. Why clear a new road over the mountains, they asked, when a good one already existed? Why waste precious time? To Washington, commander of the First Virginia Regiment, the idea seemed little short of insane.

But the Pennsylvanians were equally sure that the shortest and best route was one directly west, through their Province. Why take a round-about road that was never much good, anyhow? Why not drive straight over the mountains?[1]

General Forbes was inclined to agree with the Pennsylvania viewpoint; and Col. Henry Bouquet, his second-in-command, urged him strongly to adopt it. This roused Washington to a high pitch of indignation. He wrote to his friend, Maj. Francis Halkett:

> If Colonel Bouquet succeeds in this point with the General all is lost! All is lost by Heavens! Our enterprise ruined; and we stopped at the Laurel Hill this winter . . .

But when Forbes made his decision—one that Washington continued to oppose to the end—it was for the direct route through the Pennsylvania passes.

[1] Since future trade would undoubtedly follow the military road, Virginia and Pennsylvania accused each other—and perhaps not without some justification—of a commercial interest in its choice.

That having been settled, he began at once to cut his new road to the Ohio. He not only rejected Braddock's old route, but completely reversed that unfortunate general's strategy. Braddock had gambled on a swift thrust from Fort Cumberland, without a single supply base on his 110-mile line of communications, and without a fortified post on which he might fall back in case of a reverse. Had it succeeded, his headlong plunge through the wilderness would undoubtedly have gone into the history books as a brilliant military coup. But it had not succeeded —and the lesson was not lost on General Forbes.

This time, Forbes decided, the army would march swiftly, if possible, but in any case safely. He would go only as fast as he could set up supply depots. As he neared Fort Duquesne, he would establish a strong fortified base from which to launch the attack—one that he could retreat to, in case of defeat. Everything would be methodical, systematic, secure.

Carlisle, Pa., long the gateway to the West, was the natural staging area for the Pennsylvania troops. From here, the route— worn deep by the iron-shod hooves of traders' packhorses— trended through Shippensburg, Loudon, and Lyttleton to Bedford, then called Raystown. At Raystown, Forbes decided he would build his rear base—a fort, storehouses, and a hospital. And at Raystown, only 30 miles north of Fort Cumberland, the troops from Virginia, Maryland and Carolina would join the Pennsylvanians. Then all would march together, over the new road, to the Ohio.[2]

This was Forbes' plan. But, like all campaign plans, it was immediately complicated by the old problems of unruly troops, politics, money, supplies, the weather, and wagons—always wagons! "The farther I go away from the settlements," Forbes cried, "the more I see that the expedition, which I believed so easy, is full of almost insurmountable obstacles."

Besides, General Forbes was a sick man, often in pain, a victim of that scourge of armies, the bloody flux. On some days he was better, on others so weak that he could not leave his bed. Before long, he would have to be carried wherever he went in a

[2] On a modern road map, the route is approximately: the Pennsylvania Turnpike from Carlisle to Bedford, thence Route 30 (the Lincoln Highway) to Pittsburgh.

litter. He bore his suffering with iron courage and saintly patience; but often with little strength for the gruelling problems of wilderness war.

He was fortunate to have, as his chief lieutenant and field officer, Col. Henry Bouquet.

• 3 •

Bouquet was a Swiss soldier of fortune who wrote his letters either in beautiful English or French, sometimes in both. At the time he became Forbes' chief executive officer, he was 39 years old, and already a seasoned veteran of many European wars. Besides having served as a lieutenant in the famous Swiss Guards, he had studied military tactics and strategy at the University of Leyden. He not only knew the theory of war, but quickly adapted it to bush fighting and became, in the end, a wilderness campaigner without peer. Characteristically, it was from the Romans that he learned how to fight Indians.[3]

When Colonel Bouquet arrived at New York in June, he was given the job of forming a new force of regulars, "The Royal American Regiment."[4] On this assignment he proved his ability as a military organizer—and a talent for making himself popular with everyone, including the troops, Philadelphia society, and even the close-fisted Pennsylvania Assembly. It was inevitable that Forbes, already gravely ill, should choose him to carry on as the actual field commander of the expedition against Fort Duquesne.

Arriving at Carlisle, Bouquet found the initial stages of the campaign already in an unbelieveable snarl of red tape and petty detail. One may glean from his dispatches the state of affairs as that suddenly teeming base:

[3] The ambush and destruction of three Roman legions by Arminius had its obvious parallel in Braddock's disaster on the Monongahela. The English, fighting Indians in the forests of America, faced problems not unlike those confronted by the Roman leader in the Teutoburger Wald.
[4] The Royal Americans, or 60th Regiment of regulars, was recruited chiefly from recent German immigrants to America. Henry Bouquet was commissioned lieutenant-colonel in the new regiment, becoming its senior officer in America and commander of the first battalion.

The troops from Virginia have no canteens nor tomahawks.

We are waiting for saddles and pistols, but they say there are neither brushes nor curry combs.

I have collected a dozen poor horses which belonged to General Braddock's expedition.

We have only about 40,000 cartridges which for 2000 men is only 20 shots each . . .

About 140 barrels of pork was opened, of which we found 60 fit for use.

I have ordered only 10 hogsheads of whisky. About 50 will be needed for the expedition, and as much rum.

The advance got under way in June, a month of vile weather, and reached Raystown on the 24th. Raystown, on the Juniata River, was the logical place of rendezvous for General Forbes' two armies. One of these armies consisted of the First and Second Virginia Regiments, under Colonels Washington and Byrd, together with a few Carolina and Maryland troops. The other comprised the Pennsylvania Colonials, the Royal Americans, and Montgomery's Highlanders. The first was gathering at Fort Cumberland, the second at Raystown. A north-south road between the two points was started immediately, with axmen working from both ends, to facilitate the juncture of the two forces at Raystown.

At the same time, the little settlement on the Juniata was being rapidly turned into a strong rear base for the British advance. By July 11, construction of the fort was well along, with a third of the stockades in place and storehouses ready to receive more than three months' provisions for 5000 men. Fort Bedford, as it was called, was a regulation frontier fort, with five bastions and a couple of redoubts. Maj. Joseph Shippen wrote of it:

We have a good stockade fort here, with several convenient and large storehouses. Our camps are all secured with good breastworks and a small ditch on the outside, and everything goes well.

As well as could be expected, that is. Bouquet was having the usual headaches with raw troops and shortages of almost everything. "One is not through with one difficulty," he exclaimed, "before falling into another." His letters to General Forbes reflect his troubles:

> Our men are very weary, and I hope we may soon receive some new recruits.
>
> We are very shamefully supplied with wagons. Some who had good horses when they were appraised, kept them and sent nags who were unable to drag themselves along.
>
> You will not find things as far along as I should have wished; but I hope that, with a little indulgence for the provincial troops, you will not be dissatisfied with us.
>
> I beg you to send me a warrant for general courts martial. An example must be made to stop desertion. We have a man here who has offered his services to do the hanging.

But Col. Henry Bouquet was a philosopher as well as a brilliant captain. "As the wine is drawn," he observed, "so it must be drunk." And at Raystown, despite a thousand harassments and annoyances—ranging from the violent road dispute to a plague of rats—preparations for the destruction of Fort Duquesne went forward methodically.

There were even a few bright spots. The provincial troops, Bouquet was discovering, were not half so bad as he had feared. Both the Pennsylvanians and Virginians, he assured Forbes, were on the way to becoming real soldiers—if they could only be spared "the overbearing spirit of the others, chiefly your countrymen."[5]

• 4 •

At the Forks of the Ohio, Marchand de Ligneris, Fort Duquesne's new commandant, was having some difficulties of his own. He was finding it very hard to figure out British intentions. There was no longer any doubt that a huge force—estimated in Quebec at 12,000 men—was on its way to the Ohio. But by what route? Scouts reported great concentrations of troops at both Raystown and Fort Cumberland. Axmen, they revealed,

[5] Antagonism, often bitter between the officers of the British regular and Provincial militia regiments, extended to the rank and file; and it was one of Bouquet's signal achievements that he succeeded in smoothing out the long-standing differences between the English and American troops.

were brushing out Braddock's old road from Wills Creek. Would
the attack come from that direction? Or would it come from
Raystown, through the Pennsylvania passes? Or from both directions at once? Until he knew, there was little he could do to
block the British advance.

In fact, there was little he could do in any case. Marchand de
Ligneris, Captain of the Marine Troops, had learned his trade
of soldiering in the hard school of the Western Posts. Twenty
years of campaigning against the Kickapoo, the Mascouten, and
the Fox had taught him about all there was to know about bush
fighting—as the survivors of Braddock's disaster could well
remember. He brought to the command of the Fort Duquesne
garrison experience, energy, steadfastness, and courage; but not
even all these fine qualities were enough to offset the lack of
practically everything necessary to hold the post.

"On the Ohio," it was being said in Quebec, "everything is
to be apprehended and little to be hoped." The brilliant Dumas,
indeed, observed glumly that Fort Duquesne was "fit only to dis-
honor the officer who would be entrusted with its defense."

At the moment, this officer happened to be Capt. Marchand de
Ligneris; and, though he may have secretly agreed with Dumas,
it could not be said that he gave way to despair. On the contrary, he turned all his energies to putting his despised post in a
posture of defense. During the summer, a flood had nearly carried Fort Duquesne off the Point; canoes, in fact, had been
paddled about inside the walls, removing men and supplies!
De Ligneris not only repaired the damage as best he could, but
constructed a "second fort" in which to store supplies and lodge
most of the garrison. By every means at his disposal, he patched
together, shored up, and overhauled the forlorn little fort in
which he must make shift to defend his country's claim to half a
continent.

He was not, at least, embarrassed by want of room in which
to garrison his troops. He had so few!

For a time, Fort Duquesne had been well-manned. As soon
as it became certain that the English were mounting a major
offensive, Vaudreuil and Montcalm had done what they could to
reinforce de Ligneris' command. About 350 Canadian militia
were rushed to the Forks; and the other Ohio posts were ordered

to rotate their forces, so as to be always ready to send aid in case of attack. An appeal for help was sent to Detroit and Michilimackinac; and Capt. Charles Aubry had actually arrived from the Illinois with 600 men.

It is unlikely that de Ligneris himself knew exactly how large a force he had at Fort Duquesne. Many of his men were scattered along the communications, and stationed at Fort Machault (Venango), Fort Le Boeuf, and Fort Presqu' Isle. The number of Indians fluctuated from day to day. The Canadian militia, and even the French regulars, were constantly on the move with the supply bateaux and canoes. The only way the total force, white and Indian, could be estimated, indeed, was in terms of the daily rations issued; these averaged 3500 during the summer of 1757.

Things were happening fast, however, to reduce the force at de Ligneris' disposal. After Kittanning, the French Indians were showing less enthusiasm for raiding the frontier—especially since the flow of merchandise, liquor, and even their customary rations, had dried up. Practically nothing was getting through from Canada now, and de Ligneris found himself hard-put to feed his troops, let alone a horde of voracious Indians and their families. Most of his food supply was coming from the Illinois, where the government had contracted with one Sieur Gradin to provide 150,000 livres worth of flour. And it was far from enough.

But de Ligneris, watching his Indians fade away, and calculating the number of days before he would have to send his regulars and militia back to Canada for want of food, tried to put the best possible face on a grim situation. He reported cheerfully to Quebec that he would be able to resist an attack, although "he had learned from deserters that the English were encamped at Fort Cumberland in pretty considerable numbers." He was short of provisions, he said, but added hopefully that "the Intendant had promised him some."

In Quebec itself, the *Journal of Occurrences in Canada,* reporting the enemy's moves against Fort Duquesne, commented rather forlornly, " 'Tis hoped he will meet a warm reception, as there are a number of Indians there."

But nobody was being fooled. Montcalm wrote to the Chevalier de Lévis, "If you had interrogated Babaty about the actual state of Fort Duquesne, you would have said: Poor King!"

During the summer, indeed, Captain de Ligneris received orders to burn Fort Duquesne and remove the artillery, stores, and provisions on the approach of the English force.

· 5 ·

The month of July witnessed the cumulation of great projects on other fronts: disaster for the English at Ticonderoga, where General Abercromby took a terrible beating at the hands of General Montcalm; and victory at Louisbourg, where Amherst evened the score by taking the great sea gate to New France. Meanwhile, little mindful of great events otherwise, Bouquet's sweating, fly-bitten troops continued to drive the road westward.

Forbes was still at Carlisle, fighting the bloody flux and wrestling with the perennial problems of supply, logistics, and Indian relations. Impatient to be with the advanced forces, he planned repeatedly to leave for Raystown. "Make the best Hutt you can for me," he wrote Bouquet, "if it is not too much trouble." But always he found himself too weak to travel.

The dispute over the route was at its height, with Washington raging honestly against the insanity of hacking a new road over Laurel Hill, and close to the point of insubordination. Forbes settled that argument, at last; but Bouquet continued to have his hands full with other distractions. So many of his troops were sick that only 800 were fit for duty. The Virginians refused to work without pay; so Bouquet gave them guard duty while the Pennsylvanians labored with pick and shovel—an arrangement that did nothing to promote good feeling between the Provincials. The storehouses were completed, but where were the stores? Horses provided by the Pennsylvania farmers were too weak to pull the supply wagons. "The roads are strewn with broken wagons," Bouquet lamented. "The wagon masters for the most part are good for nothing." So the storehouses remained empty.

Sir John St. Clair, "the Hussar," was in favor of employing "violent measures," lest the expedition break down completely for lack of transport; and Forbes actually threatened to turn his ferocious Quartermaster-General loose on the Province unless sound vehicles and horses were forthcoming.

Forbes was beginning to despair, indeed, of getting his army to the Ohio before snow flew—let alone by the original target date of September 1. The task ahead of him was staggering. After detaching fifteen per cent of the Pennsylvanians for defense of the frontier, he must assemble at Raystown about 5,000 troops, plus 1000 wagoners, sutlers, and camp followers. The total number of men—and women—of all descriptions would be close to 6,000. All these people—with artillery, baggage, food, ammunition, and equipment of all kinds—would have to be moved in four months over more than a hundred roadless miles of the roughest country in Eastern North America. Without—it was hoped—any rude interference on the part of the enemy.

West of Raystown towered the Allegheny Mountain, then the even more formidable heights of Laurel Ridge, and beyond that the great barrier of Chestnut Ridge. Every mile was heavily timbered and tangled with laurel thickets; and, as Forbes himself wrote to Pitt, "impenetrable almost to any human thing save the Indians."

Bouquet's immediate problem, as field commander, was to discover the best—or, at least, the likeliest—approach to Fort Duquesne over this fearsome terrain. With the Virginians still crying lustily for Braddock's road, he secretly dispatched a hundred men to find, if possible, a direct route from Raystown to the Ohio. The party returned on July 20 to report that such a road could be opened. It would not be easy; merely possible.

This was enough for Bouquet. Two days later he dispatched a detachment of Pennsylvanians to blaze the route and select a site for a forward base on the far side of Laurel Hill. Maj. George Armstrong, commanding the detachment, reported that Loyalhanna would be an excellent spot for such a base.[6] He was, in fact, quite exuberant about it:

> The situation is undoubtedly good for nature has supplied it with all the conveniences, and what makes it more desirable is the western breezes carrying with them the smell of French brandy.

[6] Loyalhanna (or Loyal Hannon) was the name of a small Indian village on Loyalhanna Creek, between Laurel Hill and Chestnut Ridge. Its site is on the Lincoln Highway, U.S. Route 30, about 40 miles from Pittsburgh.

On the same day—July 31—Bouquet received the final go-ahead from Forbes to begin cutting the new road. He was now free to prepare a base for the climactic assault on Fort Duquesne; and he lost no time. By August 11, some 600 men were hacking, grubbing, and blasting their way westward, while another 600 covered them with guns. In a somewhat sarcastic mood, Bouquet wrote Washington:

> Sir John went forward this morning, and sent me back word . . . that as far as he had gone he found the road good, and every other thing answering our expectations. I cannot therefore entertain the least doubt that we shall now all go on hand in hand and that the same zeal for the service that has hitherto been so distinguishing a part of your character will carry you by Reas Town over the Allegheny Mountains and to Fort Duquesne.

But Washington, if he were not to have the last laugh, was at least to have the next one.

• 6 •

As soon as the road crews hit the slopes of the Alleghenies, cries of distress could be heard all the way back to Raystown. Frantic appeals for men, tools, and liquor poured in from Sir John St. Clair: "The work to be done on this road is immence . . . pick axes crows and shovels is what is most wanted. Likewise more whiskey . . . Send me as many men as you can with digging tools, this is a most diabolical work, and whiskey must be had." Col. Adam Stephen pleaded, "Please send us three or four cross cut saws to seperate the numberless, damned, petryfyd old logs hard as iron, & breaks our axes to pieces." As for Bouquet, he at last admitted, "It is a difficult and long task to build the road."

But it is a soldier's privilege to grouse; and despite everything, the road did go forward, foot by foot, mile by mile, through Edwards Swamp, the Shades of Death, the endless laurel "slick." It reached the crest of the mountains. Each day it pushed a little closer to Fort Duquesne.

From Fort Cumberland, in the meantime, Washington was sending his axmen and covering parties to brush out Braddock's old road. But the work was mainly an elaborate feint; the idea was to keep de Ligneris guessing, to divert his attention from the route the English were actually following to the Ohio.[7]

As his army pushed ahead, General Forbes was still compelled by his malady to remain at Carlisle. On August 9 he wrote Bouquet:

> I am now able to write, after 3 weeks of the most violent and tormenting distemper, which thank God seems now much abated as to pain, but has left me weak as a new born infant.

He attempted to join Bouquet a few days later, but got no farther than Shippensburg, where the intolerable torment of his flux forced him to remain for several weeks. It was not until the middle of September that he finally reached Raystown, in a sling between two horses.

Meanwhile, however, the build-up at Raystown had gone ahead almost on schedule. By the middle of August, 4000 troops were encamped there, with another 1000 or so at Fort Cumberland, waiting to join them. Others—notably Montgomery's Highlanders and Pennsylvania contingents—were stationed at various posts all the way back to the Susquehanna.

But all was not well by any means. The shortage of supplies was still critical. The road went forward more and more slowly. By September 1, it was still far from finished; what Bouquet called "the break neck passage of Laurel Hill" had wrecked his time-table.

The troops, moreover, were growing restless. Bouquet, in some disquietude, wrote Forbes:

> The army is beginning to become visibly bored and impatient. Their ardor is cooling, and I am afraid that the discontent may very soon be followed by murmurs and other annoying consequences.

[7] At one point Washington's crew was only 16 miles from those working on Forbes' new road, and he received orders to "reconnoitre where the junction of the two roads could be made."

Bouquet even took the unheard of liberty of reminding his superior officer that "both America and England have eyes on you." Plainly chafing, he asked permission to abandon the cautious, step-by-step plan of advance and send a strong striking force over the mountains immediately. Forbes, with complete confidence in Bouquet's judgment, gave his consent. Without waiting for the road over Laurel Hill to be finished, Bouquet then ordered Col. James Burd to march 1000 men to Loyalhanna and establish a base only 40 miles from Fort Duquesne.

• 7 •

Captain de Ligneris had his scouts out along Forbes' road, of course, and now and then a small party returned to Fort Duquesne with a few scalps. But de Ligneris was hardly prepared for what his "ears" now reported to him from Loyalhanna.

The French had been quite confident that the assault on Fort Duquesne—if it came at all during the summer of 1758—would be from the direction of Fort Cumberland, over Braddock's old road. The English would hardly be fools enough to build a new road over the worst part of the mountains when a good one already existed. In this the French and Virginians saw eye to eye.

De Ligneris was well aware that a strong column of English and Provincials was advancing from Eastern Pennsylvania; but he also knew that a large concentration of troops was gathering at Winchester and Fort Cumberland—and that Washington's soldiers were busy with ax and shovel on Braddock's road. What more natural than to expect these two forces to join, not at Raystown but at Fort Cumberland, and then march as a single army by the old route?

De Ligneris accordingly kept a close watch on everything in that direction. He sent out as many parties as he could spare, to harass Washington's road crews and keep the settlements in terror. When he learned that the Cherokee had gone over to the English, he raided their towns in an effort to divert them from helping their new allies. He had even begun to fortify the fords and passes along the expected route. Forbes was not far wrong, in fact, when he wrote General Abercromby as late as August 11:

> The Enemy has as yet given us no disturbance, nor do I believe
> that they suspect my coming this way whereas along Mr.
> Braddock's route from the Great Meadows [Fort Necessity] to
> the Great Crossing of the Yoghegenny, they have reconnoitered
> every pass and defile, and have proceeded so far as already
> to have a *Batis de bois* where of necessity we must have passed
> had we been confined to that road entirely.

But with the sudden appearance of Colonel Burd and 1500 men
at Loyalhanna—deep in his own end zone—de Ligneris could no
longer doubt what the English were up to. The establishment of
a strong base only a few days march from the Forks could mean
but one thing—a strike at his fort directly over the one remaining
mountain range, Chestnut Ridge.

From Fort Duquesne, therefore, scalping parties immediately
began to cross this ridge and swoop down on work crews and
outposts in the vicinity of Loyalhanna. It was the only riposte
possible. Unable to withstand a siege, de Ligneris had to fall
back on the offensive-defensive strategy so successfully employed
by Contrecoeur and Dumas against Washington and Braddock.

He could hardly hope for another Great Meadows or Monongahela—although he was to come closer to it than ever he dreamed
possible—but he could stab at Forbes' flanks, slow up his methodical advance, and sow confusion in his ranks. He could never,
with his limited resources, win more than limited victories, of
course. But he could quite possibly delay the English advance
until snow blocked the passes, and thus force Forbes into winter
quarters. He could delay a decision, at least, until spring.[8]

So he hurled his raiders at Loyalhanna, and the results must
have startled even himself. Within a few days the whole British
camp was in what Bouquet himself described as a state of abject
terror. On September 11, the colonel—who had reached Loyalhanna on the 7th—wrote Forbes:

> Scarcely had I arrived in this camp when a soldier of the
> Pennsylvania troops with fear marked on his face came up

[8] In Canada, General Montcalm was taking a cynical view of the situation
on the Beautiful River: "The abandonment of Fort Duquesne would, in my
opinion, in the present circumstances, be more advantageous than not to the
Colony. It is a branch that exhausts the tree. But has consent ever been
given for the abandonment of a source of such riches to the Grand
Societe?"

to tell me that, having gone out to hunt (without orders) with one of his comrades and a soldier from the Highlanders, they were attacked by four Indians. The Highlander stood his ground and fired three shots, but was killed and scalped. The two others fled like cowards, throwing away their weapons. He had scarcely finished his story when a Virginia soldier arrived and said that, having gone to hunt (with permission) with another soldier, they had been attacked by nine Indians, who had taken his comrade prisoner; and he had escaped also by throwing away his weapons. I had them both arrested in order to put an end to such cowardly conduct at once.

How to check the raiders and calm his frightened men thus suddenly became Bouquet's most pressing problem. One of his officers, Maj. James Grant, of the 77th Regiment of Highlanders, came forward with a solution. Grant was the perfect pattern of an officer—courageous, energetic, gentlemanly, a thoroughly professional soldier whose counsel was valued by everyone from General Forbes down. What Grant proposed was "to go straight to the source," that is, to Fort Duquesne itself. He asked permission to raid the French stronghold.

The scope of his plan rather surprised Bouquet, who had in mind nothing more ambitious than the dispatch of a couple of small parties "to hold the paths" and maybe take a few prisoners. But this, Grant maintained, would only serve to lose men and discourage the troops. What was needed was a night attack on Fort Duquesne with at least 500 men.

Grant must have been a very persuasive salesman. Before he was through, Bouquet had agreed to give him 800 men. And what had started out as a simple raid became a fearfully complicated operation—completely at variance with Forbes' careful, methodical approach to his goal.

What, one must wonder, would the General have thought of it all? What, for that matter, had come over the incomparable Bouquet?

• 8 •

Early on the morning of September 14, de Ligneris was aroused from sleep and, hastening to the rampart, was astonished to see one of his storehouses in flames.

Grant had arrived about midnight, and after a brief reconnaissance, had ordered Maj. Andrew Lewis to proceed with 400 men and "attack everything that was found about the fort." Lewis, an expert woods fighter, must have questioned the feasibility of such an action in pitch darkness, but he was too good a soldier to protest an order, even an impossible one. With his men wearing white shirts over their uniforms—to distinguish them from the Indians—he marched his frontiersmen off through the woods.

Grant waited uneasily until close to daybreak for the noise of an attack. Then, to his astonishment, he saw Lewis' men returning through the woods, in what he called "complete disorder." They had not been repulsed by the fort garrison; they had simply lost contact with one another in the darkness and, like honest woodsmen, had decided to get back to familiar ground. Grant ordered them to the rear to guard the baggage and form a reserve.

Then, incomprehensively,[9] he sent fifty of his Highlanders to attack an Indian camp near the fort. Finding no Indians, the Highlanders set fire to a storehouse and withdrew.

At this point—according to Bouquet's own wry version of the affair—Grant got the idea that the French were too weak to attempt a sally. Stationing himself on a rise of ground with 200 Highlanders, 100 Marylanders, and 100 Pennsylvanians, he sent 100 of the Highlanders, with drums beating and pipes skirling, across the open ground—possibly to cut off a sortie from the garrison.

It was seven o'clock now, and de Ligneris, listening to Grant's drummers lustily beating out the reveille, and watching his kilted Highlanders marching straight at his fort, came to terms with his unbelieving senses. He opened the gates of Fort Duquesne and turned his Indians, and a few troops—possibly 800 in all—loose on them.

Yelling and firing as they came on, the savages and French

[9] Grant himself could offer only this explanation: ". . . tho' I was reduced after all my hopes of success, to this melancholy situation, that something at least might be attempted, I sent Lieuts. Robinson and McDonald with 50 men to make an attack at a place where two or three fires had been seen the night before. I desired them to kill a dozen Indians if possible, & I would be satisfied."

overwhelmed the little company of Highlanders, killing Captain McDonald and throwing his men into disarray. The Pennsylvanians turned and made off without firing a shot. The rest of Grant's force soon found themselves surrounded and milling about in complete confusion. "Fear had got the better of every other passion," Grant afterwards wrote, "and I hope I shall never again see such a pannick among troops."

To complete the confusion, Major Lewis, in attempting to come to Grant's aid, arrived just in time to become inextricably entangled with the fleeing Provincials. All of Grant's desperate efforts to rally his troops were futile. It was the Virginians, under Capt. Thomas Bullit, who saved the rout from becoming a massacre. Bouquet, in his report of the action to Forbes, described the heroic stand of the Americans as the one bright spot in a day of otherwise unbelievable disaster:

> They would probably have been cut to pieces but for Captain Bullet of the Virginians who with 100 men sustained the battle with all their forces until, having lost two-thirds of his men, he was pushed in the direction of the river . . . They were soon surrounded, and the Frenchmen, calling him Major Grant by name, offered him quarter. He did not wish it. They did not want to fire on him, wishing to take him prisoner. Captain Bullet still fired, and in the end they fired, too, and routed his party into the Ohio, where a large number were drowned.

So, with a loss of almost 300 killed or captured out of 800 engaged, ended Major Grant's strange attack on Fort Duquesne. It was an action that Forbes could never understand, and Bouquet never tried to explain.[10]

De Ligneris, whose loss amounted to only eight killed and another eight wounded, did not pursue the enemy. After his Indians had finished with the scalping, and looting, he bolted the gates of Fort Duquesne, raised the drawbridge, and awaited developments. In about a week, a small party with a drummer and flag of truce appeared, halted under the walls of the fort, and beat for a parley. Ensign Blane delivered to de Ligneris a

[10] The Indian chief Tecaughretango simplified everything with the surmise that Grant had been drunk.

letter from Colonel Bouquet. It asked for information about the
English prisoners, Major Grant and Major Lewis, and added:

> I am fully persuaded that the wounded will receive the same
> assistance from you that the Troops of His Most Christian
> Majesty have in like circumstances always met with from the
> British officers, who without any distinction, have treated them
> as their own . . .

To this de Ligneris sent back a somewhat indignant reply,
which began:

> Sir:
> A recommendation from you was unnecessary to induce me
> to give civil and humane treatment to the English officers whom
> we captured in the action of the fourteenth of this month.
> The French nation has never followed any other course in deal-
> ing with prisoners, and I am very certain, Sir, that if you had
> some of ours, you would do as much as I have done for
> yours . . .

Bouquet then wrote de Ligneris a gracious note of thanks, and
another to Lieutenant de Rocheblave, who had escorted Lieutenant Blane and his party back to the English lines. It was a
very polite war, and only one incident marred the amenities:
during the parley at Fort Duquesne, Private Cloine had his rifle
stolen by the Indians.

· 9 ·

The aftermath of Grant's disaster was not what might have
been expected. Forbes, of course, was at first unbelieving, then
disgusted; but he was not discouraged. Even a defeat could have
its bright side. This one had proved his system of strong forward bases a sound one: Grant—unlike Braddock—had something, at least, to fall back on. The behavior of the Virginians had
been excellent. Bouquet went so far as to write: "The Provincials
seem to have done very well, and their good men are more
suitable for this warfare than the regular troops." Finally, the
army was not at all disheartened. "The Troops now breathe

nothing but revenge," Major Shippen wrote home, "and are in high spirits."

Otherwise, the month had been marked by developments favorable to the English cause, and in one case disastrous to French hopes.

At Loyalhanna, work on the fort was progressing apace under direction of Engineer Harry Gordon. In Forbes' estimation, it was progressing too well. "You know we want nothing but a strong post," he reminded Bouquet, "So for God's sake think of both time money and labor and put a stop to all superfluitys." The road was improving every day, the supply wagons rolling on schedule. Washington and his Virginia Regiment had arrived from Fort Cumberland. The expedition was back on the track.

Meanwhile, far to the rear, a staggering blow had been struck at Fort Duquesne.

At the eastern end of Lake Ontario, the French had built Fort Frontenac to guard the St. Lawrence River route to the Interior. Over this route passed all troops and supplies destined for the Ohio River and Great Lakes posts. Whoever controlled it, controlled the West; and Fort Frontenac was the key to its mastery.[11]

Late in August, Lieut.-Col. John Bradstreet, of the Royal Americans, made a surprise attack on Fort Frontenac and destroyed it.

Worse news could hardly have been received at the Forks. With Fort Frontenac in British hands, every French post in the West was now cut off from Canada—including, of course, Fort Duquesne. Captain de Ligneris might have reflected wryly that this really meant little to him. Canada, in any case, did not have much to send him now. They were eating horses in Quebec, and even the French troops were on flour and salt rations.

For some time, indeed, de Ligneris had been wholly dependant on Louisiana for provisions. But even that trickle had dried up. The flour-laden bateaux no longer labored up the Ohio to his hungry fort. Soon he would be under the dire necessity of sending away the Illinois and Detroit militia. With a force of

---

[11] For all its importance, Fort Frontenac was, in Captain Le Mercier's words, "one of the worst posts that one could see." A major of the Bearn battalion stationed there reported, "When one of the guns is discharged, the whole fort shakes."

6,000 English closing in on him, hunger would force him to reduce his own garrison.

To make matters worse, many of his Indians had deserted him after Grant's defeat. It was not what one might have expected, but you could never tell what Indians would do—especially the wild ones from the West.

And now Fort Frontenac had fallen, and no prospect for food or help from that quarter, not this fall, nor perhaps ever. In Montreal, de Ligneris knew, they had already given up his post as lost. "The English are perhaps at this very moment," Doriel, the War Commissioner in Canada, was writing to Belle Isle, "masters of Fort Duquesne and the whole of the Beautiful River. At least they will be in a short time." Nor did de Ligneris doubt that, in case of an attack on Quebec, Montcalm would pull every available man back to the defense of the Capital. Montcalm would willingly sacrifice everything—Fort Duquesne, the whole Ohio country, and all the Great Lakes posts—to save Canada.

Pondering these grim facts, and reviewing the odds against him—he had no more than 500 troops now, and a very uncertain number of Indians against an army of at least 6,000 with siege weapons—de Ligneris considered what course he should take. Except for a faint hope that he might force Forbes into winter quarters, there was not much logic in what he decided to do. He decided to attack.

◆ 10 ◆

Besides killing a lot of English, de Ligneris had made a definite strategic gain in defeating Grant. He now knew fairly well the strength of the enemy, and where he could be hit.

He knew, for example, that Forbes had set up an advanced base about nine miles west of Loyalhanna—as a jump-off point for the final assault. At Loyalhanna itself, a fort of considerable strength was building. It was the familiar square fort, with bastions at each corner, not unlike Fort Duquesne in design. The exposed faces were built of horizontal log ramparts, the others of strong stockades, and the whole surrounded by fraised entrenchments. Further protected by redoubts and outer batteries,

Fort Ligonier—as it was later called—lacked nothing to make it a strong defense against a French counter attack. Still quite ignorant of the true strength of the enemy, Forbes was taking no chances. The Loyalhanna works must be capable not only of repelling an assault with musketry, but artillery-proof and "fitt to stand a siege."

Against this formidable stronghold de Ligneris sent 500 Canadians and about a hundred Indians.

Under command of Capt. Charles Aubry, of the Louisiana troops, this force spent almost three weeks in marching from Fort Duquesne and reconnoitering the English camp. Then, at eleven o'clock in the morning of October 12, it opened hostilities with an attack on an English grass guard a short distance from the fort. Colonel Burd, commanding in Bouquet's absence, sent out a couple of parties to surround what he supposed to be a few marauders. These soon came scurrying back, and the woods began to rattle on all sides with musket fire.

Burd then hastily mustered 500 Highlanders and Provincials, and launched them against the attackers, only to see them hurled back into the retrenchments. A battle in the open now developed, with English cannon and coehorns playing on the French troops. Aubry's men, armed with nothing but muskets and bayonets, were finally forced to retire; but Colonel Burd's own description of the fight reflects little glory on the fort's defenders:

> This day at 11 A:M the enemy fired 12 guns to the South west of us upon which I sent out two partys to surround them but instantly the firing increased, upon which I sent out a large party of 500 men they were forced into camp Immediately a regular attack insued which lasted a long time I think above two hours, but we had the pleasure to do that Honr. to His Majesties Arms to keep the camp at Loyal Hannon . . . I have drove them from the field, but I don't doubt of a second attack, if they do I am ready . . . Excuse this scrall being in a little hurry at present—since writing we have been fired upon.

Captain Aubrys troops kept up a derisive fire during the night, then made off next morning with practically all the horses belonging to the Loyalhanna post. They had lost, by their own

account, 2 killed and 7 wounded. The English casualties were
12 killed, 18 wounded, 31 missing.

The troops at Loyalhanna fired a general *feu-de-joie* to celebrate what they considered a victory. But Bouquet's secret
thoughts were far from jubilant when he wrote Forbes:

> A thousand men [actually about 500] keep more than 1500
> blockaded, carry off their horses, and retire undisturbed with
> all their wounded and perhaps ours, after burying their dead.
> This enterprise, which should have cost the enemy dearly, shows
> a great deal of contempt for us, and the behavior of our troops
> in the woods justifies their idea only too well.

Whatever the feelings of the French may have been, they
must have known in their hearts that the success at Loyalhanna was an empty one. The dice of war were loaded against
them; their time was running out.

• 11 •

It was running out for General Forbes as well. The cold
was setting in, snow covered the tops of the mountains, and the
campaigning season was hurrying to a close. Moreover, there was
a good chance that most of his troops would leave him on
December 1, when their terms of enlistment would expire. Too
weak to sit a horse, he had himself carried to Loyalhanna in a
litter, and from there began to direct the final stage of his campaign. He poured out the last remnant of his strength in a
desperate effort to get within striking distance of Fort Duquesne
before the end of November. It was a discouraging business. The
weather was abominable, the Indians disheartened, the troops
ready to go home, and a prisoner reported 1000 French and
Canadian troops waiting to receive him at Fort Duquesne.

On November 11 he called a meeting of his officers to review
the situation. A careful balance sheet of advantages and disad-
vantages was drawn up. The council decided that, "the risks
being so obviously greater than the advantages," an attack on
Fort Duquesne should be put off until spring.

The events of the very next day did nothing to relieve the
gloom that now enveloped Loyalhanna. The French struck

again, this time with only a small force but with dismaying
results. When the approach of the enemy was reported, Forbes
sent 1000 men to oppose them—500 Virginians under Washington and another 500 under Mercer. Meeting unexpectedly in the
gathering darkness, the two parties mistook each other for the
enemy and opened fire. Fourteen men were killed, 26 wounded;
and Washington himself had another of those razor-edge escapes
from death that were already part of his growing legend. For
the English, the episode was another humiliating and dishearten-
ing demonstration of their ineptness in woods fighting. "Why
waste powder?" the French might well ask. "The English will
shoot each other!"

But November was not altogether a black month. On the 17th
a remarkable man, a Moravian missionary named Christian Frederick Post, arrived at the Forks of the Ohio as an emissary to the
Indians from General Forbes. At the imminent risk of his life,
Post actually confronted the French on their own grounds and
made his bid for Indian support in their presence. At Easton,
he told the redmen, a great conference had just been held with
the Six Nations and nine other tribes. By solemn treaty, the
English had promised not to settle, or even hunt, beyond the
mountains.

The Indians at the Forks no doubt surmised—and correctly—
that this was a hollow promise. But they were weary of involve-
ment in the white men's wars; and they respected, even loved
Post, and wanted to believe what he told them. Many of them
now broke openly with the French and began to drift back to
their hunting grounds. To Forbes, indeed, the mild-mannered
Moravian missionary was worth at least a regiment.[12]

Another stroke of good luck resulted, oddly enough, from the
tragic clash of Washington's men with Mercer's. During this
ill-fated operation, a prisoner was taken, a renegade Englishman
named Johnson. As a member of the Fort Duquesne garrison,
Johnson was well-informed on the situation at the fort. He was
given an interesting choice: rum and riches if he told all he knew
about the French strength; death "in an extraordinary manner"
if he refused or falsified.

[12] Bouquet remarked that Post's success with the Indians on behalf of the
English was "a blow which knocked the French in the head."

Johnson readily told the truth. Instead of the supposed 1,000 men and innumerable Indians at Fort Duquesne, the garrison had been reduced to a handful of French and Canadian troops—not more than 500—and almost no Indians.

Upon receiving this welcome intelligence, Forbes wasted none of his precious time. The decision of the War Council was reversed. Forbes ordered a special force of 2500 picked men to start immediately for the Forks. It would march in three divisions: Montgomery, with a brigade of axmen, would clear the road; Washington, with his Virginians, would cover him; Bouquet and the Royal Americans would bring up the artillery.

The advance would be made with all possible speed. Nothing but weapons, ammunition, and provisions would be taken—on the men's backs; no tents, wagons, or other unnecessary gear. The men would sleep on their arms. All women would be sent back to Loyalhanna. No fires at night; 100 lashes on the spot for any soldier who fired off a gun; all dogs to be hanged. Nothing must be allowed to impede the final thrust, or to betray it to the enemy.

The three brigades took off from Chestnut Ridge on November 15. By the 22nd, they had lunged to within 12 miles of Fort Duquesne. It had been a lightning advance—which meant simply that the men had chopped faster, shoveled harder, sweat more; it was the same old business of felling trees, clearing brush, letting daylight into the swamp—only at an accelerated pace.

At the end of it, the troops were wet, cold, and exhausted; and they welcomed a halt at Turtle Creek to make a fortified base and wait for the rear division of the army. Fort Duquesne was now so near—only a day's march away—that scouts were sent out to scour every foot of intervening ground. As they prepared for the final assault, officers—and doubtless men—were not unmindful of what had happened to Braddock.

• 12 •

In Montreal it was thought that the Battle of Loyalhanna had effectively checked Forbes' advance. As late as November, indeed, Montcalm was writing to Paris that, although the Detroit and Louisiana troops had gone home, Fort Duquesne could be considered safe for the winter. On the 19th of the same month, a scout named de Linctot reported to Captain de Ligneris that Forbes' advance column was encamped only 12 miles away.

With what could only have been stoical calm, the French commander called a council of war. It was no more than a matter of form, this meeting of the French officers. Everyone at Fort Duquesne, if not at Quebec, knew well enough what had to be done.

De Ligneris, nevertheless, carefully reviewed the situation with his staff. Only four months ago, he had commanded 1,000 troops; now, having been forced to send the Illinois and Detroit troops home, he had a bare 300—two thirds of them sick and hardly fit for duty. Most of his Indians had left after Grant's defeat; the rest were at that very moment meeting with the missionary Post at Kuskuskas—they could be written off. No more supplies could be expected from Canada, what with Fort Frontenac in English hands; and probably none from Louisiana. Unless someone—Montcalm, perhaps—performed a miracle, Fort Duquesne was lost.

The officers of the garrison reviewed these painful facts and came to the obvious conclusion. "All these gentlemen were of the opinion that they should prepare to evacuate the place." Accordingly, the work of dismantling the fort was begun. Roofs were removed from the buildings, stockades were cut down, and everything that would burn was piled against the walls of the fort.

In the midst of this activity, de Linctot returned from a second reconnaissance and reported the English army only half a day's march away.

De Ligneris reacted to this news automatically. He had his orders from Quebec. They were "to use all means in his power to annoy the enemy, embarrass their communications, and intercept their convoys"; but also, "to burn and remove the artillery, warlike stores, and provisions" on the approach of the English. Well, he had never failed to carry out the first half of the order; now he would have to obey the second.

The small store of trade goods still remaining in the King's warehouse he packed up and sent off to the Indians at Con-

chake, "to induce them always to take our side and attack the
English." The artillery he loaded into bateaux and sent down the
Ohio to Fort Massac and Fort Chartres. To the best of his fighting
men he gave eight days' rations and ordered them to prepare for
a retreat to Fort Machault. All this was accomplished in less than
three hours.

To blow up the fort, 50 or 60 barrels of spoiled powder were
left in the magazine. When all was ready, the fleur-de-lis was
hauled down, and de Ligneris sent away his men. The time had
come for him to order the destruction of the fort he had defended
so valiantly against insuperable odds.

It had never been a very strong fort, but at least it had been
a brave one. It had never waited for its enemy to come to it,
but had always gone out to meet him. Twice it had destroyed
its attackers, and only a little while ago had dealt them another
grievous blow. It had never stood siege, and it would not stand
siege now . . .

> When everyone had embarked [Vaudreuil wrote to the Minister
> of Marine] when the scouts had returned, and when all the
> bateaux had left, except the one which he had kept, he had
> the fort set on fire. After this, he embarked to join his force
> of 192 men who had orders to wait for him a league above
> the fort.

Thus, in a roar of flame, died Fort Duquesne of the Blessed
Virgin at the Beautiful River. When Forbes' scouts reported great
columns of black smoke rising from the vicinity of the Forks, he
sent a detachment of light horse to discover their cause. The
English troops arrived to find thirty gaunt chimneys standing
amid a smoking ruin.

BOOK EIGHT

Fort Pitt

• 1 •

General Forbes did not remain long at the dismal scene of his triumph. After providing shelter and defense of a sort for his troops, he gave the name of Pittsburgh to the desolation at the Point, and began his slow, painful journey home. At Fort Ligonier his strength gave out and he had to pause for a while; but, carried all the way in a litter, he reached Philadelphia at last. And there, in March, 1759, he died.

"After God," Bouquet wrote to Chief Justice Allen, of Pennsylvania, "the success of this expedition is entirely due to the General."

But the great prize that a sick and harassed man had gained, largely by sheer patience and dogged courage, was not yet secure. The Ohio was not yet firmly in British hands, the frontier not yet freed from the ghastly spectre of Indian terror.

It was possible—indeed probable—that the French would return.

To oppose them, Forbes left only 200 Virginians under Colonel Mercer. With winter at their heels, the rest of the army retraced its march with all possible haste. It was that or starve. For on the blackened Point, amid the ashes that de Ligneris had left behind him, there was nothing that could sustain even a squad of soldiers until spring.

Neither was there anything left of Fort Duquesne that could serve as a defense for Mercer and his men. De Ligneris had done a thorough job of demolition. He had promised the Indians he would leave nothing but "bare ground" at the Point; that the

213

English would find it impossible to build a fort there over winter.

"We will be back early enough in the spring to destroy them," Post had heard his officers assure the Indians at Logstown. "We will come with seventeen nations of Indians and a great many French, and we will build a stone fort."

Nobody at the Point doubted that de Ligneris would try to make good his boast. Even William Pitt in England looked for a counter attack. "Lose no time," the Premier wrote urgently, "in concerting the properest and speediest means for completely restoring, if possible, the ruined Fort Duquesne to a defensible and respectable state, or for erecting another in room of it . . ."

To Mercer, on the ground, there was no question of which course to take. After attending to a few gruesome chores—such as burying the bones of Braddock's dead, still strewn about the battlefield—he set to work on the construction of a new fort. Activity continued on it during the winter at a feverish pace. Despite the frozen ground, which had to be broken with old axes, pickets were set, barracks raised, bastions enclosed, and finally the gates hung on December 19. Mercer wrote to Bouquet:

> I expect in four days to have the place made capable of a tolerable defense, and I am fully determined to maintain the post, or at least, make it as dear a purchase by the enemy as possible.

The new fort, which was never to be accorded the dignity of a name, was of the simplest design and construction. It consisted essentially of four log buildings arranged in the form of a square, with palisaded bastions at each corner. Perhaps its most significant feature was its location—as close as possible to the banks of the Monongahela, with special works to defend the river landing. Despite Mercer's resolute words, the main idea was to get out of the fort and across the river as quickly as possible, in case of a strong attack.

Mercer's instructions were, in fact, to burn the fort, cross over, sink his boats, and march to Fort Ligonier or Fort Cumberland. In preparation for such an evacuation, he was to conceal a cache of coehorns, arms, and stores on the opposite bank of the Monongahela. So large and so dark loomed the threat of a French attack on the northern horizon!

With the coming of spring, anxiety at the Forks mounted. Mercer's force had now been increased to 400 men, and innumerable Indians were once again flocking to the Point. But 400 men were not nearly enough to meet the expected assault from Venango—no less than 1,000 to 1,500 would be needed, Bouquet maintained; and the Indians, while eating Mercer bare, were far from dependable allies.

The new commander of the Ohio forces, Brig.-Gen. John Stanwix, was taking vigorous measures, to be sure, for the consolidation of the English position. He was raising—or hoped to raise—a force of 7,200 men, with 1,000 pack horses to carry supplies to the Forks from Fort Bedford, plus a shuttle service of 100 wagons between the Forks and Fort Ligonier. With all these men and resources he planned to replace Mercer's feeble little post with a fort, the like of which had never been dreamed of in the West: a mighty bastion of English power on the Ohio, to be called Fort Pitt.

But both men and supplies were slow in coming; and Mercer's spies were bringing in more and more alarming reports of French troops and vast numbers of Indians massing at Venango. Early in July, the imminence of attack seemed so clear that the English at the Point panicked and burned all houses outside the walls of the fort. It was not an irrational fright: the peril to the little garrison—"300 miles from any aid," as one of its members wrote, "and surrounded by merciless savages"—was real enough, and near at hand.

• 2 •

At Venango, Captain de Ligneris was putting together a formidable force for the retaking of the Forks. White troops and Indian warriors were pouring in from all quarters. Pouchot sent reinforcements from Niagara. Aubry arrived from the Illinois with no less than 600 militia. A hundred French and 150 Indian fighting men reported from Detroit. Indians from twelve tribes, including the fierce Chippewa, Sioux, and Fox from the Great Lakes region, were being fitted out, and bateaux built to carry them down the Allegheny to the Forks.

While all these preparations were going forward, softening-up attacks were launched against the 300-mile lifeline between Pittsburgh and the East. As early as May, raids were begun on the convoys moving between Fort Bedford and Fort Ligonier. In that month, Ensign Duverger St. Blin attacked a wagon train, killed 40 out of 100 guards, and forced the rest to flee. On July 6, an attempt was made to storm undermanned Fort Ligonier itself, but was beaten off by Colonel Stephen's artillery.

A week after this, de Ligneris called together his entire striking force—about 700 French and Canadians, with perhaps 2,000 Indians—in a great council at Venango. He threw down the war belts and told everybody to be ready to start the march on Pittsburgh in the morning.

At this precise moment, however, fate chose to play one of her wayward tricks. Two Indians suddenly broke into the meeting with letters from Niagara. Capt. François Pouchot, commanding there, had unexpectedly found himself threatened by a great force of 2,000 English and 1,000 Iroquois.[1] With a garrison of less than 500 men, he needed all the help he could get—at once. The attack on Pittsburgh must be abandoned.

"My children," de Ligneris sorrowfully told his astonished Indians, "I have bad news for you . . . I have received orders to go directly to Niagara and take you with me."

De Ligneris was nothing if not thorough in carrying out his new orders. The water in French Creek was too low to transport the heavy stores; so—after the Indians had helped themselves to what they wanted—everything was piled up in the fort and set afire. The bateaux, lined up at the river bank for the trip to the Forks, were destroyed. The swivel guns were buried. At Fort Le Boeuf a similar demolition was carried out. At Presqu' Isle, de Ligneris' force, consisting now of about 700 troops and 1,000 Indians, embarked on Lake Erie and headed eastward to the relief of Pouchot's desperate garrison.

As they approached the fort on the Upper Niagara River, they appeared as "a floating island, so black was the river with bateaux

[1] Pouchot had only 150 French regulars, 180 colonial marines, 133 Canadian militia, a few artillerymen and a handful of faithful Indians with which to oppose 2,000 soldiers and 1,000 Indians under Brig.-Gen. John Prideau and Sir William Johnson.

and canoes." De Ligneris and Aubry were supremely confident, indeed, of their ability to scatter the English besiegers; and their Indians, after destroying a British patrol and sticking their heads on poles to terrify their comrades, seemed equally eager to join with the enemy.

At this point, however, the French Indians learned that Sir William Johnson had succeeded in drawing a large force of Iroquois to the English side. Not even the Fox or Sioux had any desire to tangle with the ferocious warriors of the Six Nations. After a little parleying, they decided to declare themselves neutral. They deserted de Ligneris, almost to a man.

In spite of this demoralizing set-back, de Ligneris and Aubry, with their 700 French regulars and Canadian militia, moved forward along a road leading to Fort Niagara.[2] About a mile from the fort, they were faced by 600 English regulars and Provincial troops, backed up by 600 of Johnson's Iroquois.

While Pouchot and his pitiful garrison watched from the battered ramparts of Fort Niagara, the French advanced against a British barricade of fallen trees. Waiting with fixed bayonets, the British troops fired several volleys, then leaped the barricade and charged. The attack quickly developed into a rout, the rout into a slaughter. Johnson's Indians—no less frightful than the French savages—fell on the fleeing relief force "like so many butchers." When it was all over, fewer than 100 prisoners were left alive—17 of them officers, including de Ligneris and Aubry.[3]

After this destruction of the western relief, there was but one course open to Pouchot. For days, his garrison had been without sleep; he was wadding his cannon with blankets and shirts; bales of precious furs were being used to plug the great holes torn in the parapets by the English howitzers; and now the Canadian militia were refusing to expose themselves on the ramparts. There was only one thing to do: surrender himself and his completely exhausted garrison.

With the fall of Niagara, not only was the French lifeline to Louisiana and the West severed, but the whole Army of the Ohio

[2] This place was called La Belle-Famille, and from it the ensuing battle took its name.
[3] Johnson claimed credit for saving the officers from the Indians; he was discreetly silent about what happened to the rest of the prisoners.

was destroyed beyond hope of replacement. And so, too, ended French hopes of ever again raising the white banner of St. Louis above the tiny triangle of land on which had once stood Fort Duquesne.

• 3 •

Elimination of the French forces on the Ohio did not, however, lessen British determination to dominate the vast, fertile valley of that river with the most powerful fortress ever to have been built in the West.

William Pitt, in his wisdom, had demanded a stronghold that would "maintain His Majesty's subjects in undisputed possession of the Ohio"; and, with the French still in control of the Lakes, and the Indians' intentions by no means a sure thing, no time was to be lost in building it. Almost before the pitiful remnant of de Ligneris' army had dragged itself back to the safety of Detroit, the walls of Fort Pitt began to rise.

Around the first of August, Capt. Harry Gordon—General Stanwix's Chief Engineer, who probably drew the plans for the fort—arrived on the ground with a small crew of artisans. The experts wrangled for a while over selection of a site, but actual pick-and-shovel work got under way on September 3. Within a few weeks, the Point swarmed with an antlike activity that soon overflowed into the surrounding country. On what is now Mount Washington miners were digging for coal and limestone. Far up the river, trees were being felled and the logs turned into boards and timbers, first in two-man sawpits, then in a sawmill. Along the Monongahela, bateaux—hundreds of them—were being built and caulked to carry supplies from Virginia. The smoke from lime and brick kilns drifted across the Point and mingled with the smells of bake ovens, blacksmiths' forges, tar kettles, and Indian camp fires. From daylight to dusk, seven days a week, Gordon drove his army of artificers and laborers; and gradually, as the tremendous job of dirt-removal progressed, the huge outlines of Fort Pitt began to take shape.

An idea of the magnitude of the new works may be got from the fact that the whole of Fort Duquesne, bastions and all, could have been dropped onto the parade of Fort Pitt—with room to spare!

On paper, the new fort was of conventional design—a series of bastions connected by curtain walls. But instead of four bastions, Fort Pitt had five; and its shape, therefore, was pentagonal rather than square. The bastions were not of precisely uniform size, and the curtain walls were of unequal length; but the overall appearance of the trace was that of a surprisingly regular pentagon.

That it would be, on the ground, a pentagon of immense size is shown by the scale of the plan. The length of the curtains, we find, varied from 188 to 272 feet; the distance between bastions, from tip to tip, 416 to 476 feet. Two acres of ground were enclosed by the ramparts, and sentries walking their posts would pace off almost a mile along the perimeter of the main works.

No other fort on the British frontier, indeed, was quite as impressive as Fort Pitt, although Crown Point was as large, and Oswego only slightly smaller.

For Fort Pitt was protected by an astonishing system of outworks: a complex of ditches, walls, ramparts, ravelins, and redoubts that expanded the total area of the fort to almost eighteen acres. These outworks, with their nuclear citadel, fitted snugly into the triangular pattern of the Point. On the landward side, a deep ditch, known as the "Isthmus," extended from the Allegheny almost to the Monongahela. This ditch, with a fortified embankment called the "Epaulement," provided a strong advance line of defense from river to river. Three ravelins—the largest guarding the entrance roads across the Isthmus—provided extra protection on the landward and Monongahela sides of the fort.

Fort Pitt itself lay close to the shore of the Monongahela, leaving about five acres free for buildings on the Allegheny side, within the protection of the Epaulement and a stockade extending around the Point. This area was known as the Lower Town—a term that acquired a somewhat unsavory connotation in later times.

More than a dozen contemporary plans of Fort Pitt are extant. The earliest—a sort of archetype of the final plan—was found by the French among Braddock's papers. This plan, although

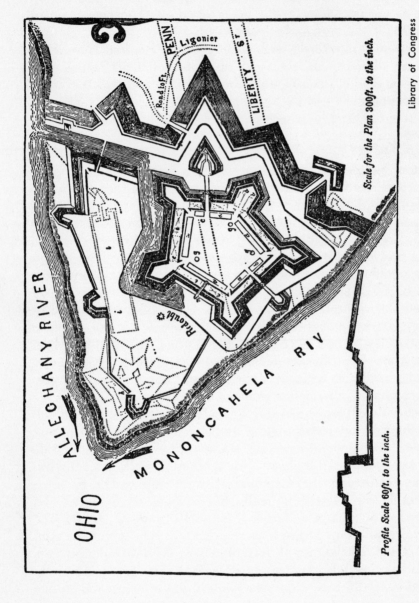

In this plan of Fort Pitt, adapted from Lieut. Bernard Ratzer's drawing, the relative positions and sizes of Fort Pitt and Fort Duquesne are indicated. Mercer's fort is also outlined near the shore of Monongahela; it is partly obscured by Fort Pitt's walls.

220

labeled "Fort Duquesne," has been identified by Charles M. Stotz as a rough sketch of the great fort the British had intended to build at the Forks—had not Contrecoeur, Beaujeu, Dumas, et al. rudely interfered with their program.[4] These beautifully rendered "blueprints," the work of professional draftsmen, give us a great deal of precise detail about Fort Pitt; but none of them can remotely suggest the enormous amount of labor that went into the building of this great work 300 miles deep in the wilderness.

Probably because the supply of near-by timber had been exhausted, General Stanwix directed that Fort Pitt should be a "dirt fort." Its walls and bastions were built neither of pickets nor horizontal logs, but of earth. It was constructed almost precisely as the Romans built their legionary fortresses and walls (including the great Antonine Wall), right down to sodded slopes and brick or masonry revetments.

Fort Pitt was, in effect, a great five-sided ditch, with the earth of the ditch thrown up to form a rampart over 20 feet high and 60 feet wide. It has been estimated that the total amount of dirt moved in its construction was 66,000 cubic yards. Even in our own day of bulldozers and earth-movers, the work involved in such an operation would not be inconsiderable. With picks, shovels, handbarrows, and wheelbarrows, nothing made it possible, perhaps, but regular issues of rum.

Because weather, burrowing animals, grazing cows, and small boys digging for worms quickly erode an earthen rampart, those of Fort Pitt were protected in two ways. On the landward side they were supported by heavy brick retaining walls, with the tips of the bastions further reinforced by cut stone. On the less-vulnerable river sides, the walls and bastions were sodded, i.e. covered with squares of turf laid perpendicularly to the slope of the wall and secured with long wooden pins. On top of the ramparts, a sodded parapet 18 feet thick was erected for protection of artillery and soldiers firing small arms. Behind this parapet ran a level space 20 feet wide, providing a platform for cannon and the necessary room for recoil after firing.

[4] For a detailed discussion by an architect and engineer, see Charles M. Stotz's magnificent study of Fort Pitt in *Drums in the Forest*, Historical Society of Western Pennsylvania.

A sentry walking his post on the high, windy ramparts of Fort Pitt looked down on a kind of walled city inside the great pentagon of earth and masonry. Around the central parade, indeed, could be housed from 700 to 1,000 men. Two-storied barracks—one of brick 190 feet long, and two others of frame construction—provided lodgment for the men; another quartered the officers. The commandant's house was the show-place of the establishment—a fine brick building with cut-stone steps. All these long, narrow buildings could be seen grouped symmetrically around the parade, parallel to the curtain walls. But hidden away in the immensely thick ramparts were even more spacious storehouses, magazines, and casemates. Excepting some flour, most of the provisions and, of course, all of the ammunition, were stored underground. The capacity of the subterranean facilities may be judged from the fact that each of two magazines provided room for the storage of 2,000 barrels of powder.

Underground, also, was the guardhouse, and the dungeons in which prisoners awaiting trial for their lives "mouldered away" in utter darkness.

Such was the fort that Harry Gordon was building at the Forks. He was building it, as usual, under the most frustrating of conditions: without proper tools and supplies; bedeviled by hordes of idle, always-hungry and often-drunken Indians; plagued by reprobate soldiers and a riff-raff white population that cluttered up the Point and demoralized the workers. But he drove everyone—including himself—unmercifully; and by March, 1760, supplies and men were all under cover, and the defensive works well-advanced, with 18 guns mounted in the bastions.

The garrison celebrated Christmas in a practically completed fort. The brick revetments around the so-called Music, Grenadier, and Flag bastions were finished, the intervening curtains in place, and the drawbridge giving entrance through the Gate Curtain operative. Most of the other walls and bastions had been sodded, parapets set up, and firing platforms installed. Only the bastions and curtains on the Point side of the fort were still in a somewhat indefensible condition.

By this time, too, the troops at Pittsburgh—as the new fort, as well as the village around it, was commonly called—were sheltered in a comfort, even luxury, that soldiers on the Point had never before known. The long brick barracks, and the wooden ones of weatherboard and shingles, were provided with chimneys that served four rooms and furnished cooking facilities. In the brick barracks there was "a closet in each room, and other accommodations for the officers." And, at last, there was plenty to eat.[5]

In mid-summer, 1761, however, Captain Gordon was still driving his work crews. A glimpse of the intense activity on the Point is afforded by the journal of the Quaker storekeeper at Fort Pitt:

> I think they are very diligent ye drum beats as its light in ye morning to set all to work and holds it until ye gun fires late after sun down. Mostly ye works going on are ye fort banks raising higher, a fine stone house, a building in ye S.E. corner for a governor's house, stone quarrying for lime and burning ye same, making & burning brick, & farming & gardening, having a fine incloasure under Indian corn and divers things, mowing and haymaking abroad up both rivers.

Before it was completely finished, Fort Pitt was to suffer a series of batterings from flood waters of the Ohio, and much of what was so laboriously wrought by Harry Gordon and his sweating builders was undone. Still later, the great fortress would sink into a desuetude of disrepair and uselessness. But now it stood as William Pitt had intended it should stand—a bastion of British power on the French flank, and a symbol of British dominance on the Ohio.

Before long its trial of strength would come. But it would not be the French, marching down from Canada to regain lost possessions, who would put it to the test. It would be an Indian who, some said, had helped to destroy Braddock. A war chief of the Ottawa, from around Detroit. A man named Pontiac.

• 4 •

On September 8, 1760, the Chevalier de Lévis burned his battle flags to save his troops from the humiliation of surrender-

---

[5] The December, 1759, return of provisions included 146,740 pounds of flour, 212 beef cattle, 66,415 pounds of salt beef, 5,800 pounds of butter, and 3,285 pounds of cheese.

ing them, and Vaudreuil yielded New France to the British
Crown. So the war was over.

But it took the commandants of the western posts a while to
grasp the staggering fact that Canada was no longer French. The
fleur-de-lis continued to flutter over such wilderness posts as
Detroit, Michilimackinac, Green Bay, and St. Joseph. And it was
not until Maj. Robert Rogers appeared with his Rangers, followed
by a detachment of the Royal Americans, that the unbelieving
garrisons of those remote posts laid down their arms.

But the Conquest was neatly consummated, at last, and there
was only one slightly sour note in the smooth take-over of half a
continent by a few British foot soldiers: a low rumble of unrest—
unnoticed or, if noticed, ignored—among the aboriginal inhabitants of the subjugated lands.

The British, in truth, did little to make the transition easy
for the Indians. Now that red allies were no longer needed, the
old arrogance surged to the surface. British traders resumed
cheating Indian hunters of their eye-teeth. They refused them
guns, ammunition, and blankets on which life itself depended.
British officers kicked Indian visitors out of their posts, dis-
honored their wives and daughters, heaped insult and indignity
of every kind on the heads of their old men and sachems. Worst
of all, the English quickly forgot the promises they had solemnly
made in dangerous times to allow no settlements beyond the
mountains.

What the Indians now faced was loss of their hunting lands—
that is to say, their total extinction as a people.

They saw this clearly, just as clearly as a white man would
have recognized a similar threat to his own existence. It was
written everywhere: in the sudden abrogation of long-honored
treaties; in the rising tide of settlements up the eastern slopes of
the Appalachians; in the planting of arrogant British garrisons
across the ancient routes of Indian travel; in the implacable advance of hard-eyed long hunters into the Indian's best game
preserves.

What could be done about it? Nothing, of course; but there
were some who were willing to try. A messiah, the Delaware
Prophet, arose and preached destruction of the whites—before it
was too late. Alarmed Seneca chiefs tried abortively to organize a

general blood-letting. In the West, war councils met and debated fruitlessly the desperate measures of survival.

But it was not until the gigantic figure of Pontiac emerged from the western forests that the tribes united to strike their blow.

Pontiac was a war chief of the Ottawa, a nation closely related to the fierce Chippewa. He had learned to fight white men with the French—at Monongahela, it was said, and later with Montcalm. He was a man of awesome dignity, apparently, a powerful orator, as well as a great warrior; and when he sent out the belts of black wampum and the tomahawks stained red, tribes a thousand miles away responded to his call for action.

In the spring of 1763, Pontiac summoned the chiefs of practically every warlike tribe east of the Mississippi to a great council near Detroit. He gave them his plan for a concerted blow at every British fort in the West; and simultaneously, a devastation of the border that would forever roll the white man's frontier back to the mountains. Then he sent the excited chiefs home to organize their parts in the uprising.

In May, like a drum-roll of horror, blows began to fall on the whole line of British forts. Pontiac himself, with about 800 Ottawa, Chippewa, Pottawattamie, and Wyandot, led the assault on Fort Detroit. After some preliminary reconnaissance and an attempt at stratagem—foiled, it is said, by the British commander's Indian mistress—an all-out attack was made on May 10. Six hours later, the Indians, beaten off by musket fire and cannon loaded with red-hot spikes, settled down to a grim investment of the fort.

Lesser outposts in the Great Lakes country suffered swift destruction. Fort Sandusky was taken by treachery on the 16th and its troops slaughtered by the Wyandot. The weak, undermanned forts at St. Joseph, Miami, and Ouiatanon were captured by surprise or stratagem and their garrisons tomahawked. The little force at Green Bay was saved only by the miraculous intervention of the Sioux, who hated Pontiac and his Chippewa even more than they hated the white men.

But it was at the great British fortress and trading post of Michilimackinac that Pontiac's savages made their most devastating strike. Capt. George Etherington, commander of that fort, seems to have possessed rather more than his share of military

stupidity. Disregarding all warnings, he allowed large numbers
of Chippewa and Sac to concentrate around his post, and even
to wander in and out at will. On June 4, the savages, stripped to
their breech-clouts, gathered on the plain before the fort to play
a game of la crosse. Suddenly, while the amused garrison watched
in the shade of the ramparts, the ball soared toward the open
gate, and all the players swarmed after it. An idea of what
happened next may be had from the journal of Alexander Henry
the Elder, a New Jersey fur trader who had hidden himself in an
attic inside the fort:

> Through an aperture, which afforded me a view of the area
> of the fort, I beheld, in shapes the foulest and most terrible,
> the ferocious triumphs of barbarian conquerors. The dead were
> scalped and mangled; the dying were writhing and shrieking
> under the unsatiated knife and tomahawk; and from the bodies
> of some, ripped open, their butchers were drinking the blood,
> scooped up in the hollow of joined hands, and quaffed amid
> shouts of rage and victory. I was shaken not only with horror,
> but with fear.

So, indeed, were a great many other soldiers in lonely little
forts still to be visited by Pontiac's demons, and hundreds of
settlers who, after the fall of Fort Duquesne, had felt it safe
to return to their abandoned farms. For even before the sack of
Michilimackinac, havoc was spreading down the Allegheny and
eastward to the old border settlements. On June 22, Fort Pitt
itself was under hot attack.

• 5 •

The assault on the main British stronghold in the West was
preceded by a series of lightning thrusts at the auxiliary forts upriver. After capturing Fort Duquesne, the British had rebuilt
the French posts at Venango, Le Boeuf, and Presqu' Isle. These
were now feeble, weakly-garrisoned places, and Bouquet urged
that they be abandoned. He was overruled by General Amherst,
with the consequent destruction of the posts and massacre of
their defenders.

First to fall was Presqu' Isle. It consisted of little more than a stockade and a log blockhouse in which Ensign Christie and his garrison of twenty-seven men holed up when the attack came. With their little citadel on fire, their water gone, and the men deathly sick from smoke poisoning, Christie's command held off 200 Indians for two days. When he surrendered the fort (much to Bouquet's disgust), the haggard survivors were sent off to Detroit, and Presqu' Isle was razed.[6]

Venango was next to go, although not a man of Lieutenant Gordon's command lived to tell the story of its destruction. Long afterwards, an Indian related how a large band of Seneca gained entrance to the fort by a ruse and butchered all the garrison except Gordon, whom they roasted to death for several nights over a slow fire.

At Fort Le Boeuf—which, like Presqu' Isle, consisted of little more than a wooden blockhouse—Ensign Price, 2 corporals, and 11 privates found themselves with only 20 rounds of ammunition and their shelter aflame from fire arrows. When Price proposed fighting to the end, his men sensibly overruled him. They broke for Venango, got lost in the woods, but finally made it to Venango, where they found nothing but smouldering ruins. Three days later, they staggered up to the gates of Fort Pitt with the harrowing news of what was happening up river.

Less successfully, the Indians also attacked Fort Ligonier, made a pass at Fort Augusta, and even threw a fright into stockaded settlements as far east as Carlisle. Scores of backwoods families and isolated traders, needless to say, perished under the unprecedented storm of desolation that now swept over the mountains.

With these preliminaries out of the way, the savages turned their attention to their main objective, Fort Pitt.

Since its completion in 1761, Fort Pitt had been regularly garrisoned by 300 to 400 troops, but they had rested idly on their arms. The French had been disposed of. The Indians were happy—or thought to be. Councils were held with the Delaware, Shawnee, and Miami; treaties signed with much smoking, drinking, speech-making, and giving of gifts. And around the fort mushroomed a thriving center of trade and commerce.

Pittsburgh was the natural reshipment point for furs from the

[6] A notable example of the Indians' keeping their word after promising quarter on condition of surrender.

Illinois and Great Lakes posts. It swarmed with Indians eager to trade pelts for goods and liquor.[7] Wagoners rolled in every day from Philadelphia with merchandise and provisions, and left with bales of valuable furs. The great trading house of Boynton & Wharton stood ready to supply every need of white man or savage, from beaver hats to ear bobs.[8]

It is significant too, perhaps, that B & W's account books record the sale to one William Guthrie of "4 yards of linen for a winding sheet for his wife, 24 boards for a coffin, and a quart of rum." For Pittsburgh had become, not just a fort and trading post, but a town in which people were born and died, and carried on the ordinary business of living in between. It was a town inhabited largely by reprobate traders and other doubtful characters— among them the infamous Girty brothers—with their Indian wives and half-breed children. But there is a wistful note of hope in Storekeeper Kenny's journal when he writes: "I think drunkenness and fighting is much abated in this end of ye town to what it was, and some of ye ordinary houses is moved from here." It was a poor sort of town, no doubt; but it was a start, at any rate—a start toward what has turned out to be one of the western hemisphere's most magnificent cities.

It was also a problem to Capt. Simeon Ecuyer, the new commander at Fort Pitt. There were at this time well over 200 houses and huts clustered around the walls—every one of them possible cover for an Indian with a gun. In them lived not only a horde of traders and other non-army males, but about a hundred women and an even greater number of children—all of whom would be ready victims of the tomahawk when the fighting began.

When it became clear that Pontiac's uprising was general, and Fort Pitt in imminent danger of attack, Ecuyer acted decisively. He burned everything outside the walls and bundled the whole population, men, women, and children, into the fort. Although a

[7] To feed the 400 to 500 Indians at Pittsburgh, George Croghan, the Indian agent at the fort, drew 17,000 pounds of beef and flour in one month.
[8] Among the items listed in B & W's books: "britch clout," buckskin britches, scarlet cloth, silk handkerchiefs, stockings, leggings, gun locks, "riffle guns," pipe tomahawks, Jew's harps, "cags of rum," venison, bear meat, corn, milk, window glass, horse bells, sleeve buttons, "broaches," rugs, ear bobs, scalping knives, spurs, laced coats, black wampum, tea, butter, vermillion paint, pumps, Madeira wine.

necessary move, this complicated his defensive arrangements enormously; and he wrote Bouquet rather anxiously:

> We are so crowded in the fort that I fear disease; for in spite of every care, I cannot keep the place as clean as I should like. Besides, the smallpox is among us . . .

Captain Ecuyer, like his brilliant superior, Colonel Bouquet, was a professional Swiss soldier, resourceful, courageous, a fine leader who was proud of his motley force of red-coated Royal Americans, Pennsylvanians in their green hunting-shirts, and old Indian fighters in fringed buckskins. His garrison added up to 250 soldiers, half regulars, half militia—none too large a force to man the vast and complicated works of Fort Pitt.

Ecuyer waited for something to happen. All communication with the outside world had now been cut off. No expresses were arriving; no one knew what became of those sent off. To quiet the nerves of his people, Ecuyer distributed tomahawks and put everyone to work on the defenses. He set beaver traps in the ditch, hoping to catch a skulking Indian or two!

Hostilities opened, as usual, with the massacre of defenseless families in the vicinity of the fort. When a party of fourteen traders were lured into an ambush, and eleven of them killed, Ecuyer pretty well knew how matters stood. He wrote to Bouquet, praying that his express rider would get through:

> I see that the affair is general. I tremble for our outposts. I believe, from what I hear, that I am surrounded by Indians. I neglect nothing to give them a good reception; and I expect to be attacked tomorrow morning. Please God I may be. I am passably well prepared. Everybody is at work, and I do not sleep; but I tremble lest my messenger should be cut off.

A general attack did not, however, come at once. After mopping up the surrounding country, the Indians began a desultory fire on the fort, driving the sentries to cover, and making any venture beyond the ramparts an almost certainly fatal one. The number of Indians in the woods had grown to more than 400 Shawnee and Delaware. Still no word from outside. The tension in the fort increased daily and every man, like Ecuyer himself, longed for the attack to come.

On the afternoon of June 22, it did come. Suddenly a general fire erupted, and rifle balls thudded into the parapets from every side. The garrison gleefully replied with its howitzers, exploding shells in the midst of the startled Indians. The big guns kept the attackers at a prudent distance; and when, after a night of continuous harassment, the casualties were counted, only two of Fort Pitt's defenders were reported dead.

Next morning, several Indians approached the fort and, with the bland effrontery often displayed by the red men, offered Ecuyer a deal. The leader of the envoys, a Delaware named Turtle's Heart, stood at the edge of the ditch and proclaimed:

> My Brothers, we that stand here are your friends; but we have bad news to tell you. Six great nations have taken up the hatchet, and cut off all the English garrisons, excepting yours. They are now on their way to destroy you also.
>
> My Brothers, we are your friends, and we wish to save your lives. What we desire you to do is this: You must leave this fort, with your women and children, and go down to the English settlements, where you will be safe. There are many Indians already here; but we will protect you from them. You must go at once, because if you wait until the six great nations arrive here, you will all be killed, and we can do nothing to protect you.

To this generous offer, Ecuyer, who did not lack a grim sense of humor, replied:

> My Brothers, as you have shown yourselves such true friends, we feel bound in gratitude to inform you that an army of six thousand English will shortly arrive here, and that another army of three thousand is gone up the lakes to punish the Ottawas and Ojibways . . . Therefore take pity on your women and children and get out of the way as soon as possible. We have told you this in confidence, out of our great solicitude lest any of you should be hurt; and we hope you will not tell any of the other Indians, lest they escape from our vengeance.

This kind of double-talk was always a part of Indian warfare; and Ecuyer's impromptu invention of two powerful English

armies had its intended effect. Turtle's Heart and his followers
were so disconcerted that many of them struck their lodges and
started for their homes in the West.

While the defenders of Fort Pitt were still celebrating this
minor triumph of diplomacy, a soldier named Gray arrived with
news of Presqu' Isle's destruction and (Gray reported errone-
ously) the massacre of its garrison. Only a few hours later,
Ensign Price and seven haggard survivors of Fort Le Boeuf
appeared on the bank of the Allegheny. These two contacts with
"the outside" did not do much to reassure Ecuyer and his people.
Despite a sudden lull in the attacks, it was obvious that Fort
Pitt must eventually face an assault in force. Ecuyer, therefore,
kept his men busy preparing for the inevitable. The ramparts,
which had been badly damaged by the spring floods, were
repaired. The women's and children's barracks were bullet-
proofed. A crude fire engine was built to extinguish any blazes the
Indians might start with their fire-arrows. A hospital was installed
under the drawbridge.

Fort Pitt's elaborate outworks, as it turned out, were rather
more of a handicap than an advantage in fighting Indians—
particularly with so small a garrison. But Ecuyer made the most
of his resources, and awaited the hourly-expected attack with
confidence. "I am determined to hold my post," he wrote Bouquet, "spare my men, and never expose them without necessity.
This, I think, is what you require of me."

It was not until late in July that the savages made their move.
On the 26th, another party of chiefs strode up to the fort under
a flag of truce. With dogged unoriginality, they repeated about
what they had said on their previous visit: the fierce Ottawa
were on their way; wouldn't the English please take their women
and children and go home, while there was still time? But now
Ecuyer lost patience. After berating the Indians soundly, he
concluded:

"I tell you that if any of you appear again about this fort,
I will throw bombshells, which will burst and blow you to atoms,
and fire cannon among you loaded with whole bags full of
bullets. Therefore take care, for I don't want to hurt you."

This brought matters to a head. That same night, great numbers of Indians slithered up to the walls, completely surrounding

them, and began digging in with their knives. Under cover of
darkness, they ringed the whole perimeter of the fort with foxholes, and from them opened a hot fire at dawn. The attack threw
Fort Pitt's women and children into a panic; but the men on the
ramparts were keenly enjoying their release from weeks of ennui
and waiting. Experienced Indian fighters, many of them, they
swapped shots happily with the attackers; and, although seven
of them were wounded, they felt certain of having accounted for
at least 20 Indians. Ecuyer himself took a zestful part in the
defense, and was pinked in the leg by an arrow—a matter he dis-
missed with a few picturesque phrases in his broken English.

In contrast to the bitter complaints of many other commanders,
Ecuyer was eminently satisfied with the battle conduct of his
Provincial troops. "Our men are doing admirably," he wrote
Bouquet, "regulars and the rest. All they ask is to go out and
fight. I am fortunate to have the honor of commanding such
brave men."

The attack on Fort Pitt continued without interruption for
five days and nights. Then, on the morning of August 1, the sun
came up to reveal the foxholes along the river banks empty. In
the early dawn a strange silence filled the open spaces around the
fort. As the light grew stronger, sentinels on the ramparts saw
the Indians beyond the river, and far down the Point, striking
their lodges and making off. The exodus continued all day, and at
nightfall the weary garrison of Fort Pitt could turn in for their
first good sleep in weeks.

What, they must have wondered, could have come over the
Indians to cause such an abrupt leave-taking? Still cut off from
the world, they had no way of knowing what great and bloody
events were in the making—events that would help to decide
not only Fort Pitt's fate, but the outcome of Pontiac's whole
desperate gamble and, in fact, the red man's sorry destiny.

• 6 •

Sir Jeffrey Amherst was annoyed. He had just won a big war
with the French and deserved a rest. But here he was, apparently,
facing a nasty little war with the Indians. He tried to persuade

himself that it was all a flash in the pan—really nothing to take seriously.

The western frontiers were aflame, to be sure, with hundreds of terrified settlers recounting hoarse tales of horror in the border towns. But this Sir Jeffrey shrugged off as something to be expected, something that would pass. The important thing was that the frontier forts—the larger ones, at any rate—were beyond danger.

"The post of Fort Pitt," he assured Bouquet, "or any others commanded by officers, can certainly never be in danger from such a wretched enemy."

Then came the news from the West: bad news and lots of it. Under Pontiac's personal direction, Fort Detroit was closely invested, in imminent peril. A relief convoy led by Lieutenant Cuyler was ambushed by the Wyandot and 60 of its men killed or captured. A sortie under Captain Dalzel suffered 59 slain or wounded. Two fine British officers, Sir Robert Davers and Captain Robertson, were waylaid on Lake St. Clair; and Davers, it was said, was boiled and eaten. To cap a long list of massacres and atrocities, Captain Campbell, a brave and honorable officer, was treacherously killed on a peace mission, his body horribly mutilated, and his heart eaten by the Ottawa.

However indifferent he might be to the plight of the border settlers, Sir Jeffrey could not overlook these indignities to English officers and soldiers. Boiling with rage, he now demanded ruthless suppression of what he must admit, at last, was a formidable uprising. "I wish to hear of *no prisoners,*" he roared at Bouquet. "We must use every stratagem in our power to reduce them." He even urged Bouquet to spread smallpox among the Indians by means of infected blankets. Sir Jeffrey, indeed, was thoroughly upset by the rude behavior of Pontiac's braves; he was not much used to the realities of Indian warfare.

Colonel Bouquet, on the other hand, was. With seven years of bush fighting behind him, he was the most experienced of all the King's officers in America. Nobody could match his skill as a wilderness campaigner. And, on top of everything else, he was a superb tactician, leader of troops, and military organizer.

So it was to Bouquet that Sir Jeffrey, in his rage and impatience, now turned. Placing him in command of all the troops he could scrape together, he ordered Bouquet to relieve Fort Pitt, then to proceed to the relief of Venango, Le Boeuf, and Presqu' Isle; and after that to visit vengeance on the Ottawa, Ojibway, and other western tribes.

Most of Amherst's army had been disbanded at the end of the war with France, so it was with difficulty that he raised even 500 troops: about 350 Highlanders of the 44th and 77th regiments, and the rest Bouquet's own Royal Americans. Bouquet wished mightily for a company of rangers, to serve as scouts and flankers; but the frontiersmen were singularly uninterested. Carlisle, where the little relief army was mobilizing, was jammed with panic-stricken refugees—widows, orphans, scattered families in a state of terror bordering on hysteria. "The list of the people known to be killed," Bouquet wrote Amherst, "increases every hour." For the year, in fact, the total would reach some 2,000.[9] Yet the frontier refused to raise even a single rifleman for its own defense. "I find myself utterly abandoned," Bouquet wrote in bewilderment, "by the very people I am ordered to protect."

In Philadelphia matters were even worse. The Assembly, indeed, issued direct orders that Bouquet was not to be reinforced, no offensive moves were to be made against the Indians. On the seaboard, it was still hoped that if the savages were unmolested they would not carry their ravages too far eastward. As for the back settlements . . . they would have to look out for themselves.

What was back of this callous indifference to catastrophe on the border—this seeming hatred, indeed, of city dwellers for the frontier people? Bouquet gave up trying to find out. He had too many other problems pressing him. On July 3, an express rider galloped into Carlisle with news of Presqu' Isle, Le Boeuf, and Venango. "The Indians will soon be here, too," he assured the crowd that gathered while he watered his horse. "Any day, now."

So the word spread, and new hordes of quaking farmers tried to force their way into the already overcrowded little town; and on Bouquet's shoulders fell the added responsibility of feeding and housing them. Yet, disgusted as he had a right to be with their abduracy, he was deeply moved by their misery. He wrote

[9] This was George Croghan's estimate. See Parkman, *Pontiac's Conspiracy,* II, p. 115.

Amherst: "The despair of those who have lost their parents, relatives, and friends, with the cries of distracted women and children who fill the streets, form a scene painful to humanity and impossible to describe."

He was delayed for eighteen days by the haggard refugees who besieged his tents, begging for food. But on July 18 his kilted pipers struck up the Grenadiers' March, and a silent, hollow-eyed crowd in the streets of Carlisle watched his little army march out to the relief of Fort Pitt, 200 miles away.

• 7 •

The road to Fort Pitt was the old, familiar one that Bouquet himself had hacked through the wilderness and over the mountains. Some scattered settlements lay along it now. Then the farms grew fewer, and all were abandoned, with crops still standing. Soon the road plunged into long stretches of forest—deep, dark, as mysterious and menacing as ever. Lacking Indians or frontiersmen, Bouquet sent out his Highlanders as scouts; but they promptly lost themselves in the woods, and he had to call them in.

Groping its way thus through hostile country, the little army of worn-out veterans—many of whom had to be carried in wagons—crawled blindly westward.[10] It came to Shippensburg, on the eastern base of the Alleghenies, where almost 1,500 terror-stricken settlers were crowded into barns, stables, cellars, and leaky old sheds. It passed through Fort Loudon, Fort Littleton, and the Juniata post, all deserted. On July 25 it reached the true frontier at Bedford.

Here Bouquet, although it was "highly irregular," signed up 30 frontiersmen to serve as scouts. It is hard to see how he could have marched farther without them. For he had now reached a point where communication with all forward stations was completely cut off. Every express rider sent back by Capt. Archibald Blane from Fort Ligonier had been killed. For all that

[10] Scores of the Highlanders were still suffering from the after effects of tropical diseases contracted in Cuba the previous year; some 60 of the 77th were, indeed, too weak to march when the army left Carlisle.

Bouquet knew, Ligonier was in Indian hands. Even Fort Pitt
may have fallen to the savages.

All was uncertain—except for one thing. Sooner, or later, before he reached Fort Pitt, he would be attacked. The only question was: where? Bouquet had no possible way of knowing. He
could only wait, and march ahead, and do his best to avoid an
ambush. With his 30 frontiersmen now out ahead and on his
flanks, that danger, at any rate, had been greatly reduced. When
the attack came, his scouts would know about it in advance. They
would buy a little time in which he could improvise a defense.
He would see how things went, then he would know what to do.
It was how you fought Indians.

Bouquet reached Fort Ligonier on August 2—the same day
that some 400 Delaware and Shawnee had suddenly pulled out
from the vicinity of Fort Pitt. But Bouquet did not know that
these Indians were on their way to stop him. There had been
no word from Fort Pitt for weeks.

· 8 ·

At Ligonier, Bouquet left behind his wagons, oxen, and artillery. He was about two days' march from Fort Pitt now. The
danger of attack would increase every hour; and Fort Ligonier,
which he himself had built, was in such a state of disrepair that
it was useless as a place of refuge in case of disaster. Everything
—the relief of Fort Pitt, the fate of the frontier, the very survival of his own army—depended on his meeting and crushing
the savages somewhere on the next 40 miles of treacherous
mountain road. There could be no thought of retreat; there could
be only battle—and, God willing, victory.

So Bouquet stripped his little army for immediate action. He
had already left his invalids at Bedford. Now he pushed ahead
with 350 packhorses and only a few cattle for food. On August 4
he made camp less than a day's march from Turtle Creek. Ahead
lay the rough, dangerous tangle of defiles—ideal for ambush—
that Braddock had taken such pains to by-pass. But, instead of
avoiding this trap, Bouquet decided to march to a small stream
called Bushy Run, rest his troops there until night, then make a

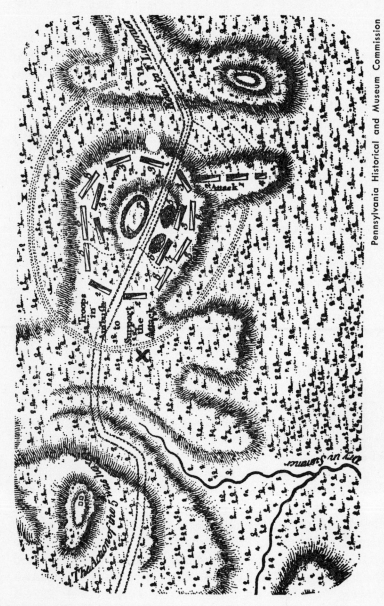

This plan of the Battle of Bushy Run, by Thomas Hutchins, shows Colonel Bouquet's troops formed in a defensive circle on the top of a hill. In the center of the circle is the "flour bag fort" protecting the wounded (7). The X marks the spot from which the Indians attacked.

237

forced march across Turtle Creek under cover of darkness. It was a bold, desperate move—the kind Bouquet was accustomed to make.

But the Indians did not wait for darkness to fall. At one o'clock in the afternoon, just as the tired troops came in sight of the proposed Bushy Run camp ground, they attacked.

The country had leveled off beyond Laurel Hill. It now presented a series of hummocks and valleys, covered with stands of fine lofty timber, mostly oak and chestnut. The forest floor was smooth and free from undergrowth. When the Indians struck, the column was fortunately on high ground, with a clear but limited field of fire on all sides. If a fight had to be made, this was probably as good a place as any to make it.

The first sign of trouble came from the van—scattered firing up ahead, perhaps the point in a brush with Indian scouts. Bouquet's weary troops—they had marched 17 miles since daybreak—grounded arms and waited for the advance patrols to clear the road. But, instead of slackening off, the fire stepped up to the sharp, nervous chatter of a close engagement. At the same time, the forest began to echo with the war cries of the Indians— certain evidence that this was not just a skirmish. Bouquet sent two companies to the support of the advance guard. The confused din of a pitched battle rolled back to the stalled column; bullets began to whine and ricochet through the timber. The shrill, excited cries of the savages began to curve back, toward the convoy, in the familiar pattern of encirclement.

The way the action was developing—not as a wild, disorganized rush but as a disciplined, apparently well-led attack—warned Bouquet that he was in for serious trouble. He deployed two light infantry companies of the 42nd, and ordered a bayonet charge. The Indians, who had no taste for cold steel, scattered and vanished.

It was no victory, not even a temporary one; but it gave Bouquet a little time to size up the situation. Very little, however. Almost immediately, firing broke out on both flanks, then in the rear. The terrified horses in the convoy began to rear and plunge. For a moment, panic hung over the column. It was not unlike the situation Braddock had blundered into on the Monongahela. But with this difference: Bouquet's troops, as raw as Braddock's when it came to Indian fighting, had a rocklike confidence in their commander. As soon as the first shock of uncertainty had passed, they quietly awaited orders—then obeyed them without a moment's hesitation.

They were complicated orders, calling for the formation of a modified hollow square—a circle, actually—protected by a barricade of pack-saddles, fallen trees, anything that would afford shelter.[11] For Bouquet allowed his men, once they were deployed, to fight the Indians from behind cover, in their own fashion.

And so, at midday, Colonel Bouquet found himself and his 400 men surrounded by perhaps an equal number of Indians, on the top of a hill about half a mile long and 200 to 300 yards wide. He had no place to go, and there was not much he could do but fight off recurring waves of attack, and hope for a break.

Seven hours later, with darkness coming on, his circle of Highlanders and Royal Americans was still intact; but reeling from exhaustion. During those seven hours, the savages had hurled themselves time after time against their thin line; and each time had been thrown back by steady volleys of musketry, often followed by a bayonet charge. But it had been discouraging work for Bouquet's bone-weary troops. The Indians, firing as they attacked, never waited for the counterattack. They simply faded into the forest, as was their style, suffering a few casualties themselves, but always leaving some dead or wounded English behind them.

When dusk thickened into darkness and the Indians withdrew

[11] Bouquet's Orderly Book for the expedition against the Ohio Indians in 1764 gives one an idea of the complicated nature of this manoeuvre: "If on the Army's being attack'd or otherwise the Square is ordered to form— on the March the Signal for that Maneuvre will be the Drums beating to Arms—the front Column will thereupon immediately form the front face of the Square—The left and right Faces marching in a Single file and covering the Convoy will continue moving in the same direction and in open Order till the front of each arrives at the rear of the face already formed: They will then face to the right and left outwards and move briskly in line abreast till the left of the right face and the right of the left face reach the right and left extremes of the front Face, by which they are Immediately to dress and stand fast. The Officers taking particular care that the Men of their respective Plattoons & Divisions do not crowd but divide their Ground Equally as already directed at the distance of two paces from each other. Etc., etc."

at last, Bouquet's battle-dazed troops dressed their lines and dropped to sleep on their arms. During the first seven hours of fighting, over 60 of their number had been killed or wounded. The seriously hurt had been placed in the center of the circle, surrounded by bags of flour, as a makeshift protection against bullets. They were without water, not a drop having been found on the hilltop. Worse, they were without much hope. Whatever the next day brought, the outlook for them could hardly have been bleaker. In case of defeat, of course, it was too gruesome to think about. But even if the Indians were driven off, how could the survivors carry away so many wounded? And to be left behind . . . So, through the night, Bouquet's wounded waited in an agony of thirst and pain and unbearable thoughts of what another day would bring.

As for Bouquet himself, time was too short for all that he must do. First he stationed pickets and outposts to guard against a night attack. He saw that the wounded were made as comfortable as possible, and sent some volunteers off to search for a spring or run of water. He made a tour of the lines, encouraging the men who were awake, chatting briefly with his officers. Then, in the darkened camp—for no fires could be built—he dictated a letter to General Amherst. He had not, in fact, much hope for the morrow; but he thought that some report should be sent back— provided an express rider could get through—of what was happening at Bushy Run. After describing the day's events, he closed with:

> The action has lasted from one o'clock till night, and we expect to begin at daybreak.
>
> Whatever our fate may be, I thought it necessary to give Your Excellency this early information, that you may at all events take such measures as you think proper with the Provinces, for their safety and the effectual relief of Fort Pitt, as in case of another engagement, I fear insurmountable difficulties in protecting and transporting our provisions, being already so much weakened by the losses of this day in men and horses, besides the additional necessity of carrying the wounded, whose situation is truly deplorable.
>
> I cannot sufficiently acknowledge the assistance I have received from Major Campbell during this long action, nor express my

admiration of the cool and steady behavior of the troops, who did not fire a shot without orders, and drove the enemy from their posts with fixed bayonets. The conduct of the officers is much above my praises.

I have the honor to be, with great respect,

Sir, &c.,

HENRY BOUQUET

That done, Bouquet could give thought to how he might extricate himself from what, on the face of it, was a completely hopeless situation. To remain where he was, exposed to the continuous fire of an invisible enemy, could end only in his obliteration. He must invent some ruse, some tactic that would draw the Indians out of the woods, provoke a mass attack . . . so that he could strike them in the open . . . man against man . . .

If Colonel Henry Bouquet slept at all that night, it was surely with this thought turning over and over and over in his weary mind.

◆ 9 ◆

The Indians greeted the new day with terrifying yells and a steady fire of musketry at extreme range. Then, drawing closer, they launched a series of brief, stabbing attacks, always falling back immediately when counterattacked, always striking again from another quarter.

Bouquet, studying the pattern of the Indians' offense, could see that his enemy was fighting a careful battle, according to plan, and under leaders who were making the most of every advantage they possessed. His own case, in the meantime, was growing more desperate by the hour. His men, staggering from fatigue, harassed by incessant rifle fire, maddened by thirst, wept with the frustration of fighting men denied the right to fight back. His losses were mounting. At ten o'clock more than a quarter of his troops were out of action, either killed or wounded; and those on their feet were holding on by sheer power of will. The ring around the convoy and the huddle of wounded behind their flour sacks was still unbroken; but inside the circle, all was despair and confusion. Bouquet's own estimate of the situation was expressed in a few tired words:

> Tied to our convoy, we could not lose sight of it without exposing it and our wounded to fall prey to the savages, who pressed us on every side, and to move it was impracticable, having lost many horses, and most of the drivers, stupified by fear, hid themselves in the bushes or were incapable of hearing or obeying orders.

It all added up to no freedom of maneuver, no possibility of withdrawal, no hope of rescue: the certainty, in short, of annihilation unless some miracle intervened. There was only one grim note of hope. The Highlanders and the Royal Americans were making the steady, methodical fight of brave and disciplined troops. Neither the agonies of thirst, the blood-chilling yells of the savages, nor the unremitting fire from a phantom foe had yet broken their spirit. Without hope, they did not lose courage; the circle thinned, but it remained intact.

This was little enough, perhaps; but to a leader of Bouquet's calibre it was the important thing. Like all great captains, Henry Bouquet valued men above strategies; and now, as the intensity of the attack stepped up, and the savages, eager for the kill, grew more audacious, he found a sudden gleam of hope—not in the tactical situation, which remained impossible, but in the increasing recklessness of the Indians and the disciplined steadiness of his own troops.

Balancing these two profoundly human tangibilities, one against the other, he evolved a plan, a strategy of desperation, to be sure, but still a possible way out of annihilation. Basically, it was the same plan that Hannibal had used to destroy the Romans at Cannae; that many another commander had employed—not always successfully—in other battles, large and small. Bouquet's genius lay in his application of a familiar tactic to a special situation, and in the precision with which he put it to use under extremely difficult conditions.

The stratagem was nothing more complicated than a feigned retreat, followed by an attack on the enemy's flanks and rear. By this means the already over-confident Indians might be lured into a mass assault and made to stand their ground when counterattacked. The difficulty would lie in performing so complicated and delicate a manoeuvre on rough, heavily-wooded ground, in the midst of deafening din and confusion, and under heavy fire. And it is to the infinite credit of the Highlanders and Royal Americans that it was carried out with perfect timing and precision.

At command, two companies of Highlanders began to fall back, as if unable to maintain their front. To fill the gap thus created in the defense perimeter, troops on the right and left opened their files and moved into the empty space. The circle, of necessity, contracted so as to tighten up the weakened segment. To the Indians, this unexpected movement had all the appearances of an incipient stampede. What they saw was two companies of British troops deserting their posts, their comrades wavering, the whole British defense at the point of disintegration.

This, of course, was exactly what Bouquet wished—and expected—them to see. And the Indians' reaction was exactly what he had hoped for.

Suddenly sure that their moment had come, the savages broke from cover and rushed in a solid body against the weakened segment of the British circle. Firing as they came on, yelling like demons straight out of hell, they hurled themselves against the thin line of Highlanders in a reckless frenzy. It was the proper way to effect a break-through, to turn a retreat into a rout; and at first it seemed likely to succeed. The Highlanders fired steadily at the oncoming wave of howling, paint-bedaubed Indians; but it quickly became clear that the question was simply one of how long—how many minutes longer—the attack could be held off.

Long enough, as it turned out. It was a near thing, a hair-line decision; but the Highlanders stood firm for the time Bouquet needed to complete the second phase of his manoeuvre. During the mass-attack against his weakened front, he had sent the two companies that had "abandoned" their positions on a secret detour through the woods. Now they suddenly emerged from the concealment of a ravine on the right flank of the attacking Indians.

No mean howlers themselves, the Highlanders charged with blood-curdling yells and poured a devastating volley of musketry into the closely-packed attackers. Surprise was complete, the effect of the Highlanders' massed fire overwhelming; but to the credit of the bewildered Indians, it must be recorded that they faced about and fought back. Until the Highlanders fell on them with the bayonet. Then they broke and fled—straight into the second trap that Bouquet had set for them.

Two other companies had also been withdrawn, from a less vulnerable segment of the circle, with orders to support the counterattack at the proper moment. This reserve now leaped from ambush and poured a second volley, even heavier than the first, into the flank of the fleeing Indians. That crashing discharge of musketry all but ended the battle of Bushy Run. The Highlanders gave the savages no time to reload or take cover. They were on top of them with bayonet and claymore, scattering them in all directions, until the woods were suddenly empty.

The Indians, brave fighters when the odds were in their favor, or at least even, had no fondness for desperate last stands. The remainder of their force, witnessing the slaughter of so many of their comrades, discreetly followed their instinct of survival and took off through the timber. The forest was once more quiet. The winded Highlanders plodded back from their pursuit and butchery. Slowly, Bouquet's badly-mauled little army pulled itself together and resumed its march. Camp was made that night at Bushy Run, and from it Bouquet wrote to Amherst:

> The woods now being cleared and the pursuit over, the four companies took possession of a hill on our front, and as soon as litters could be made for the wounded, and the flour and everything destroyed, which, for want of horses, could not be carried, we marched without molestation to this camp . . . I hope we shall not be more distrubed, for, if we have another action, we shall be hardly able to carry our wounded.

But, except for a few light skirmishes, there was no other action; and a few days later, Col. Henry Bouquet and his victorious army were welcomed by the joyful people at Fort Pitt.

Once again, a valiant and successful defense of a fortress at the Forks had been made, not by its garrison fighting from behind walls, but by a small army of resolute men engaging the enemy in the field. It was a defense that had become something of a tradition at the Forks. Contrecoeur, Beaujeu, Dumas, and de Ligneris would have approved.

EPILOGUE

• 1 •

When a fort loses its warlike usefulness, it dies. It falls into ruin, or it is "restored" and becomes a tourist attraction, or it vanishes completely beneath city streets or some farmer's plowed field.

Fort Pitt did not—like Fort Duquesne—die a quick, heroic death. It lingered on for a while—not really a fort any more, but still the focus of important events and movements, including that vast and peculiarly American phenomenon known as the advancing frontier.

After the battle of Bushy Run, the Delaware and Shawnee moved their women and children to the western side of the Muskingum River, then returned and fell on the English settlements with redoubled ferocity. Early in October, 1764, Colonel Bouquet left Fort Pitt with 1,000 Pennsylvania troops "to chastise the savages." In ten days he reached the Muskingum, and so overawed the Indians that the chiefs not only sued for peace but humbly returned more than 200 captives they had taken in the border raids. The finality of Bouquet's conquest may be judged from his speech to the assembled chieftains:

You are all in our power, and, if we choose, we can exterminate you from the earth . . . I give you twelve days from this date to deliver into my hands all the prisoners in your possession, without exception: Englishmen, Frenchmen, women, and children; whether adopted into your tribes, married, or living among you under any other denomination or pretense whatsoever. And

247

you are to furnish these prisoners with clothing, provisions, and horses to carry them to Fort Pitt. When you have fully complied with these conditions, you shall then know on what terms you may obtain the peace you sue for.

With the completion of Bouquet's spectacularly successful expedition to the Ohio, Fort Pitt ceased to have any real reason for existence. By the Treaty of Paris, New France had disappeared forever from the continent of North America, thus removing the need for a bastion against enemy attacks in the West. And now Bouquet had ended—seemingly for all time—the threat of massive Indian raids on the frontier.

Bouquet himself recommended in 1765 that Fort Pitt be converted into a "trading place." A single blockhouse, he suggested would thenceforth serve all defensive needs.

At this time the fort still boasted a rather formidable armament: six 12-pound guns, ten 6-pounders, two 8-inch and two 5½-inch howitzers, besides a variety of mortars. But the works themselves, badly damaged by flood waters and human neglect, were hardly in a defensible condition, even against Indian attack. And matters were swiftly going from bad to worse.

The town surrounding the fort was, however, increasing rapidly in population and, to judge from the acid remarks of visiting clergymen, in moral obliquity. Quite typical were the observations of the Rev. David McClure in 1772:

> They [the inhabitants of Pittsburgh] seem to feel themselves beyond the arm of the government, and freed from the restraining influence of religion. It is the resort of the Indian traders; and many here have escaped from justice and from creditors, in the old settlements. The greater part of the Indian traders keep a squaw, and some of them a white woman, as a temporary wife.

George Washington, who revisited the Point in 1770, was noncommittal about the village, but he noted that Fort Pitt was still standing and garrisoned by two companies of the Royal Irish. Two years later, according to the Reverend McClure, orders arrived from General Gage, then commander-in-chief of the British forces in America, to destroy the fort, and its demolition was immediately begun. "This," McClure notes, "was a matter of surprise and grief to the people around."

The frontier people, in fact, were still uneasy about future Indian uprisings; and the presence of the Irish troops and Fort Pitt's massive though dilapidated walls was a reassurance they did not wish to lose. Why, indeed, did the British government order the destruction of a fortress built and maintained at the cost of so much money and labor, and not a little blood?[1] Perhaps, it was conjectured, to pacify the Indians, who were restless in the shadow of a powerful military post so near their western preserves. Or, others suspected, because the storm of revolt was gathering east of the mountains; and it were just as well that a fort of such strength be removed from the grasp of disloyal Colonials.

Whatever the reason, in October, 1772, Maj. Charles Edmonstone, then commander at Fort Pitt, sold the buildings and materials for £50 New York currency to William Thompson and Alexander Ross. At the same time, demolition of the works was suspended.

· 2 ·

By an odd quirk of history, Maj. Edward Ward, who now took possession of Fort Pitt—perhaps as agent of Thompson and Ross—was no other than the same Ensign Edward Ward who had built Fort Prince George at the Forks, then surrendered it to the French forces under Captain Contrecoeur.

Ward almost immediately found himself in trouble with one Dr. John Connolly, who appeared at Fort Pitt as a representative of Lord Dunmore, Governor of Virginia. The Old Dominion had never got over the idea that the Ohio Country really belonged to Virginia, rather than to Pennsylvania. Connolly now posted a bombastic proclamation to that effect in the village of Pittsburgh. Then he knocked the head out of a cask of rum and called for volunteers with whom to back up his claim. Arrested,

[1] It has been estimated that to reproduce Fort Pitt by modern building methods would cost not less than $1,400,000.

then released, he went back to Virginia and raised a body of militia. With these he returned and took possession of Fort Pitt, changing the name of both fort and village to Fort Dunmore.

There now followed a period of intense confusion at the Forks. The Indians were again on the rampage, and the whites—a new breed of hard-bitten Scotch-Irish frontiersmen—were exacting horrible reprisals. Lord Dunmore collected a force of 1,200 men at Pittsburgh and descended the Ohio to devastate the Indian towns. Before he could do any damage, however, Gen. Andrew Lewis put an end to "Lord Dunmore's War" with a crushing defeat of the red men at Point Pleasant.

For a short time the Virginia Governor maintained his rule at the Forks, transfering the county court of Augusta County, Va. to Fort Dunmore, and setting up a ducking stool as a symbol of his authority. But the shots heard round the world had now been fired, the Revolution was under way, and Lord Dunmore fled with his family to the safety of a British man-of-war. Connolly left Pittsburgh in a similar hurry, and never returned.

At the outbreak of the war, a company of Virginians still garrisoned Fort Pitt; but in 1777 it was the standard of a Pennsylvania battalion that flew above the ramparts—a crimson flag bearing the cross of St. George, a rattlesnake with thirteen rattles, and the motto, "Don't Tread on Me." The private boundary was between Virginia and Pennsylvania continued throughout the Revolution, and it was not until the year 1786, indeed, that the dispute was finally settled.

◆ 3 ◆

During the Revolution, Fort Pitt was held continuously by the Americans. The war raging along the eastern seaboard did not spill over the mountains, and the post was unmolested by redcoats. At one point the British projected an attack from Canada, and a force of 300 soldiers and 500 Indians, with 12 pieces of artillery, marched as far as Lake Chautauqua; but there —on news that Fort Pitt had been strengthened—the leaders thought better of the invasion scheme and returned to Montreal.

It was from the Indians, rather than the British, that the West was seriously threatened at this time. Stirred up and armed by British agents, scalping parties once again "visited" the settlements, spreading death and destruction along the frontier and syphoning off troops badly needed in the main conflict.

Fort Pitt was the natural base for counter-operations against the savages, and several impressive expeditions were launched against the marauders. All were fiascos. Brig.-Gen. Edward Hand made several fruitless forays against the raiders, with no result but to spur them to more ferocious depredations. Brig.-Gen. Lachlan McIntosh built some forts on the Ohio, but brought no Indians to battle. Col. Daniel Brodhead, who succeeded him, made great plans but accomplished little, and was finally ousted by Washington.

With final victory over the British, Americans hoped that the Indians would at last bury the hatchet and peace would come to the Ohio. They were, however, disappointed. Not only did the redmen continue their desperate resistance to the inexorable advance of the frontier, but they taught their white enemy a few lessons in the art of war. To Brig.-Gen. Josiah Harmar, with a force of 300 Federal troops and 1,133 militia, the Miami administered a drubbing that dimmed considerably the legend of the Kentucky frontiersman's fighting ability. Then the same Indians defeated Maj.-Gen. Arthur St. Clair in a disaster even more overwhelming and humiliating than Braddock's. Out of 1,500 troops, St. Clair lost 900 killed, captured, or wounded; and the rest fled the field after abandoning cannon, equipment, and even their small arms. It was not until Gen. "Mad Anthony" Wayne marched out from Pittsburgh and decisively defeated the Miami at the great battle of Fallen Timbers that Indian power was shattered forever.

During these times of Indian trouble, a number of new forts, grouped around Fort Pitt as a base, were built in the West. Among them were Fort Armstrong at Kittanning and Fort McIntosh on the Ohio. Later on, posts were constructed on the sites of the old French forts at Venango and Le Boeuf, and two small blockhouses were located at Presqu' Isle.

As headquarters for the Western Department of the army, Fort Pitt was extensively repaired by Brig.-Gen. William Irvine, but soon fell into ruins again. The last years of the great fortress were, indeed, a depressing chronicle of crumbling walls, hungry and often mutinous garrisons, and squabbles between the military and civilian promoters over possession of the very land on which the fort stood. So ruinous was the condition of the once proud bastion of the Ohio in 1791 that, when a new Indian uprising threatened, another fort—a flimsy stockade called Fort Fayette—had to be built for protection of the town. On a dark night, a visitor to Pittsburgh remarked, a couple of grenadiers with a few bundles of dry wood could have burned down Fort Fayette and the garrison with it.

Aside from an attempted coup during the Whisky Rebellion, and service as a supply depot and lockup during the War of 1812, Fort Fayette made no ripple on the stream of history. In 1815 the ground was sold for building lots, the garrison was moved out, and Capt. Jacob Carmack, then commander of the fort, went into the saloon business.

Thus, once and for all, ended the sometimes heroic, sometimes sordid, but never uneventful story of the five forts at the Forks— Fort Prince George, Fort Duquesne, Mercer's Fort, Fort Pitt, and Fort Fayette.

• 4 •

While Fort Pitt was falling into ruin, and except for a short, somewhat ludicrous spell of fortification during the Civil War the Forks of the Ohio ceased to have any real military significance and the town of Pittsburgh continued to burgeon around the tumbled ramparts.

The decade following Wayne's victory and the close of the Indian War opened with Pittsburgh still a dirty, raucous, unruly village of Indian traders, suttlers, laborers, retired soldiers, and unsavory characters, male and female, of all descriptions. Then, after the dust of war had settled, came the scramble of land-hungry squatters, the "flood of mad people" that so perturbed the settled inhabitants. And, all at once, the explosive development of sprawling new industries.

All along the Allegheny, strong saline wells were discovered, and a vast number of salt works soon lined both banks. Down the Allegheny and Monongahela, and then down the Ohio, great rafts of timber began to float to the treeless, lumber-starved regions below—rafts 350 feet long and 40 wide, a million dollars worth of timber a year. Almost every day, new deposits of coal and iron were found. And travelers noted springs "on top of which floats an oil (known as Seneca oil in Pittsburgh), similar to that called Barbadoes Tar, and is found in such quantities that a person may gather several gallons a day."

Most spectacular of all, however, was the great rush of settlers to the newly-opened West, with Pittsburgh the funnel through which the "Kentucky Boats" poured to the Promised Land. Indians lay in wait for them downriver, and hundreds of hopeful emigrants never reached their destinations. But they formed their flatboats and keelboats into brigades at Pittsburgh—lashing as many as 16 together, with the women and children in the center —and made a run for it. And, despite all dangers and difficulties, traffic down the Ohio soon reached the astonishing volume of more than 1,000 boats a year leaving Pittsburgh, with 20,000 people and more than 12,000 head of stock, not to mention wagons, provisions, and household goods.

Except for a few months in the dry season, Pittsburgh swarmed with emigrants for the West, and the inns and taverns did a thriving business. The building of boats—pirogues, skiffs, bateaux, Kentucky broadhorns, barges, keelboats with masts and sails— became a flourishing industry. And Pittsburgh continued to grow as the natural distributing and reshipment point for supplies pouring into the Kentucky country. Schooners and brigs also sailed from the booming city for New Orleans, and even New York, with cargoes of flour, salt, whisky, deerskins, bear skins, peach and apple brandy, and cider royal.

Then the steamboat drove the keelboat and flatboat from the Ohio. The great National Road, linking East and West, was completed, and over it poured hundreds of thousands of people and a vast tonnage of freight into Pittsburgh.[2] Finally, in 1852, the Pennsylvania Railroad reached the city; and what had only yes-

[2] In 1848 a man counted 133 six-horse teams passing along the road in one day, and noted as many more teams of a lesser number of horses. "It looked," he said, "as if the whole earth was on the road, wagons, stages, horses, cattle, hogs, sheep, and turkeys being there without number."

terday been a huddle of bark huts around a feeble little fort called
Duquesne was on its way to civic greatness.

• 5 •

The transition, however, was a long and painful one. Pittsburgh, to be sure, grew steadily to a great metropolis of some
2,000,000 souls, a vast complex of blast furnaces, railroad yards,
factories, warehouses, docks, stockyards, office buildings, and
residential areas with the usual complement of schools, churches,
and cultural edifices. All of this was bound together by a be-
wildering maze of drives, bridges, tunnels, overpasses, and traffic
centers. And all of it was hidden under a never-lifting black
cloud through which the street lights glowed wanly at high noon.

The spot that Céloron had called "the finest place on the river,"
and Parkman described as "captivating to the eye of the artist,"
had become the "Smoky City," with a world-wide reputation for
dirt, ugliness, and barely-breathable air.

Then, quite suddenly in the scale of history, the miracle happened—"the Renaissance," they unabashedly call it in Pittsburgh.
In the 1940's, the confluence of the Allegheny and Monongahela
began to recapture the dramatic loveliness it had possessed in
the time of Washington and Contrecoeur. The hills became fresh
and green again; the sky blue; the rivers clear and sparkling in
the sun. At the same time, a new city, clean and beautiful,
emerged from the sooty pall that had so long hung over the Forks
of the Ohio. It was not just a "community improvement"; it was
the complete and spectacular transformation of the nation's
ugliest city into one of its most magnificent.

The instrument of this miracle was the Allegheny Conference
on Community Development, founded in 1943. It brought together the Mellon millions and the political genius of David
Lawrence, for 13 years mayor of Pittsburgh and later governor of
Pennsylvania. And it provided a channel through which the energies and financial resources of Pittsburgh's top industrial and
banking people could be directed toward the rescue of their city
from smoke-strangulation and chronic ugliness.

Beginning with smoke-control—which for the first time in a

hundred years washed the city's air and made it one of the cleanest towns in America—the Conference went on to urban redevelopment, slum clearance, housing, parks and landscaping, cultural centers. Typically, Pittsburgh's worst slum—95 acres of it—was bulldozed away and replaced by the Civic Arena, with its great retractable dome and facilities for sports, open-air musicals, community gatherings, and conventions. Still in the planning stage, under the energetic leadership of H. H. Heinz II, is an even more impressive Center of the Arts complex, to include a pillared Symphony Hall and an Art Museum with a sculpture garden on its roof.

On the Point itself—an area which in recent times has become known as the Golden Triangle—a $115,000,000 urban redevelopment project called the Gateway Center has been carried out under the aegis of the Equitable Life Assurance Society. Twenty three acres of grimy warehouses, flophouses, and shabby business structures were cleared with the monkey-ball and replaced with gleaming office buildings and the elegant Hilton Hotel. Nearby, Mellon Square Park, the $4,000,000 gift of the Mellon family, has opened up a pleasant oasis of trees and grassy walks in the heart of the business district.

But most interesting of all, in some ways, is a project that has just been started at the very tip of the Point—where, in the old days, Fort Duquesne and then Fort Pitt guarded the approaches to a continent.

• 6 •

In 1945 the Allegheny Conference began to plan Point State Park. At the request of Governor Edward Martin, the Point Park Committee was set up under the chairmanship of Arthur B. Van Buskirk to carry on the work; and Charles M. Stotz and Ralph E. Griswold were authorized by the Pittsburgh Planning Commission to draw up definitive plans for the park.

Late in 1963, it was announced that actual work on the project would begin shortly. It will not be a simple undertaking. To conform to the incredibly complicated traffic needs of Pittsburgh in its rivers-and-mountains setting, two large bridges—the Point and Manchester spans—will have to be removed and replaced by a new one, with the proper approaches upstream. Thirty six acres of land in the heart of the city will then be turned into a magnificent park commemorating the frontier fortresses that once stood on this historic ground.

Of the original fortifications, nothing now remains but the red brick Blockhouse—the oldest building in Western Pennsylvania —that Bouquet erected in 1764 as a redoubt to protect the flood-weakened defenses of Fort Pitt. It will stand unchanged on its original site.

The so-called Flag Bastion of Fort Pitt, restored about five years ago, will remain a feature of the Park; and the Monongahela Bastion will be restored as a museum, to contain a large-scale model of Fort Pitt, dioramas, historical exhibits, and offices. The Music Bastion will be excavated, so as to expose the original foundations of Fort Pitt.

Fort Duquesne—the most interesting and historically the most important of the five forts at the Forks—will be commemorated by its outline traced in stone paths on the lawn, and by a bronze marker showing its plan.

Surrounding these reminders of the past will extend 36 acres of lawns and trees; and then the gleaming elegance of Gateway Center and the broad waters of the Allegheny and Monongahela, merging to send the Ohio on her thousand-mile course to the Mississippi; and beyond all this, the rugged heights above the Monongahela and the rolling hills across the Allegheny—surely one of the loveliest natural settings ever vouchsafed any city in the world.

At the very tip of the Point, a fountain will rise from a circular pool, 150 feet into the air. The plash of its falling waters will be the only sound in the quiet and peaceful environs of Point Park. It will always be serene and restful here—a place to stroll on shady walks, and look about, and reflect on events that, after all, happened only yesterday: Contrecoeur, with his 500 Frenchmen, descending on Ensign Ward and his little band of sweating fort builders; Contrecoeur desperately raising the walls of Fort Duquesne against British guns; Villiers setting out from here to avenge his brother's death at Fort Necessity; Beaujeu leading his handful of French and Indians against Braddock's host; Grant suffering his humiliating disaster; the dying Forbes gazing here at the smoking ruins of Fort Duquesne; Ecuyer gaily defending Fort Pitt against Pontiac's painted devils—and Bouquet destroying them and the great Ottawa's threat forever . . . It all happened here.

If, on a busman's holiday, the shade of Contrecoeur should ever visit this spot on a quiet, moonlit night, he would be a little bewildered, perhaps, by what he saw: by a column of water, soaring higher than any pine tree, from the very spot on which his little fort had stood; by the great mass of the Hilton, not far from the bark-covered sheds in which his troops had lived; by the clean, uncluttered expanses of the Point, where the campfires of the Indians had once glowed like fireflies in a meadow . . .

But if, turning his back on all this, he should gaze westward, the feeling of strangeness would pass, perhaps. The broad sweep of waters from right and left would be just as he had known them, and their meeting at his feet; so would the mysterious presence of the hills beyond the darkness; and the sense of continental distances stretching away in all directions . . . Everything else changes, but the great, simple facts of geography remain the same. And the shade of Capt. Claude-Pierre Pécaudy, Sieur de Contrecoeur, looking down the night-shrouded reaches of the Beautiful River, could feel at home.

BIBLIOGRAPHY

Amherst Papers. (Transcripts.) Public Archives of Canada, Ottawa.

Anderson, Niles. "The General Chooses a Road." *Western Pennsylvania Historical Magazine,* Vol. 42, Nos. 1, 2 & 3.

Bailey, Kenneth P. *The Ohio Company of Virginia.*

Bolton, Herbert E. *The Spanish Borderlands.*

Bouquet, Col. Henry. *Papers of Henry Bouquet, Vol. 2, The Forbes Expedition.* Ed. by S. K. Stevens, Donald H. Kent, and Autumn L. Leonard.

Bouquet. "The Orderly Book of Colonel Henry Bouquet's Expedition against the Ohio Indians, 1764." Ed. by Edward G. Williams. *Western Pennsylvania Historical Magazine,* Vol. 42, No. 1.

Brady, Cyrus Townsend. *Colonial Fights and Fighters.*

Brackenridge, Hugh. *Indian Atrocities.*

Brodhead, Col. Daniel. "Correspondence," in *The Olden Time,* Vol. 2.

Bryce, George. *The Remarkable History of the Hudson's Bay Company.*

Buck, Solon J. and Elizabeth H. *The Planting of Civilization in Western Pennsylvania.*

Burpee, Lawrence J. *The Search for the Western Sea.* 2 vols.

Canadian Archives Reports (1905). Public Archives of Canada, Ottawa.

Chatham Papers. (Transcripts.) Public Archives of Canada, Ottawa.

Charlevoix, Pierre F. X. *Journal.* Louise P. Kellogg, ed.

Cowan, John P. "George Washington at Fort Necessity." *Western Pennsylvania Historical Magazine,* Vol. 37, Nos. 3 & 4.

Craig, Neville B. Ed. of *The Olden Time,* 2 vols.

Creighton, Donald. *The Story of Canada.*

Cribbs, George Arthur. "The Frontier Policy of Pennsylvania." *Western Pennsylvania Historical Magazine,* Vol. 2, No. 1.

Croghan, George. *Journals,* in *Early Western Travels,* Vol. 1. Reuben G. Thwaites, ed.

Dahlinger, Charles W. "The Marquis Duquesne." *Western Pennsylvania Historical Magazine,* Vol. 15, Nos. 1, 2, & 3.

Dinwiddie, Gov. Robert. *The Official Papers of Robert Dinwiddie.* R. A. Brock, ed.

Doddridge, Joseph. *Notes on the Settlement and Indian Wars of Virginia and Pennsylvania.*

Downes, Randolph C. *Council Fires on the Upper Ohio.*

Eavenson, Howard N. "Pattin's Map of the Road to Shannopintown." *Western Pennsylvania Historical Magazine,* Vol. 27, Nos. 1 & 2.

Fernow, Berthold. *The Ohio Valley in Colonial Days.*

Forbes, Thomas. (Description of Fort Duquesne after its destruction.) *Maryland Historical Magazine.* Vol. 4.

Fort Frontenac. *Royal Fort Frontenac,* Richard A. Preston and Leopold Lamontagne, eds. and translators. Champlain Society, Toronto.

Fort Duquesne and Fort Pitt. Fort Pitt Soc. of D.A.R., Allegheny County, Pa.

Franklin, Benjamin. *Autobiography.*

Freeman, Douglas Southall. *George Washington,* Vols. 1 & 2.

Frontier Forts of Pennsylvania. (Report of the commission to locate sites of.) 2 vols. George Dallas Albert, ed. Harrisburg, 1896.

Gipson, Lawrence Henry. *The British Empire before the American Revolution: The Great War for the Empire,* Vols. 4, 5 & 6.

Gist, Christopher. *Journals.* William H. Darlington, ed.

Gordon, Harry. *Journal,* in *Military Affairs in North America,* Stanley M. Pargellis.

Halkett's Orderly Book, in *Braddock's Defeat,* Charles Hamilton, ed.

Hamilton, Charles. Ed. of *Braddock's Defeat,* containing "Journal of a British Officer," "Captain Robert Cholmley's Batsman's Journal," and "Halkett's Orderly Book."

Hamilton, Edward P. *The French and Indian Wars.*

Hanna, Charles A. *The Wilderness Trail.* Vols. 1 & 2.

Harrington, J. C. *New Light on Washington's Fort Necessity.* Pub. by Eastern National Park and Monument Ass'n, Richmond, Va.

Heckenwelder, Rev. John. *History, Manners, and Customs of the Indian Nations.*

Henry, Alexander. *Travels and Adventures.*

Hodge, Frederick Webb. *Handbook of the American Indian,* 2 vols.

Hughes, Rupert. *George Washington,* Vol. 1.

Hunter, William A. *Forts on the Pennsylvania Frontier.* Pennsylvania Historical and Museum Commission.

J. C. B. *Travels in New France.* Ed. by Sylvester K. Stevens, Donald H. Kent, and Emma Edith Woods.

James, Alfred Proctor. *Drums in the Forest: Decision at the Forks.* Historical Society of Western Pennsylvania.

Jillson, Willard Rouse. *Pioneer Kentucky.*

Kent, Donald H. "The French Advance into the Ohio Country." *Western Pennsylvania Historical Magazine,* Vol. 37, Nos. 3 & 4.

Kent, Donald H. *The French Invasion of Western Pennsylvania,* Pennsylvania Historical and Museum Commission.

Kenny, James. *Diary. Pennsylvania Magazine of History and Biography.* Vol. 6.

Lahontan, Louis-Armand. *New Voyages to North America.*

Lambing, A. A. Ed. of *The Baptismal Record of Fort Duquesne.*

Lévis Papers. (Transcripts.) Public Archives of Canada, Ottawa.

Long, John. *Voyages and Travels, Early Western Travels,* Vol. 2. Reuben G. Thwaites, ed.

Lowdermilk, W. H. *History of Cumberland Maryland.*

Macleod, William Christie. *The American Indian Frontier.*

McKinney, John. (Description of Fort Duquesne.) *Pennsylvania Archives.* First series, Vol. 12.

Maryland. *Archives of Maryland,* Vol. 1.

Massachusetts. *Collections of the Massachusetts Historical Society,* Vol. 7.

Mercer, George. *Papers Relating to the Ohio Company.* Lois Mulkearn, ed.

Mitchell, John. *Map of the British Colonies, 1775.*

Mulkearn, Lois. "Half King, Seneca Diplomat." *Western Pennsylvania Historical Magazine,* Vol. 37, No. 2.

New York. *Documents Relating to Colonial History,* Vols. 6 & 10. E. B. O'Callaghan, ed.

Northcliffe Collection. Public Archives of Canada, Ottawa.

Orme, Captain Robert. *Journal,* in Sargent's *History of an Expedition against Fort Duquesne.*

Papiers Contrecoeur. Edits par Fernand Grenier. Les Presses Universitaires Laval.

Pargellis, Stanley M. *Military Affairs in North America.*

Pargellis, Stanley M. "Braddock's Defeat," in *American Historical Review,* Vol. 41, No. 2.

Parkman, Francis. *The Conspiracy of Pontiac.*

Parkman, Francis. *The Old Regime in Canada.*

Parkman, Francis. *Wolfe and Montcalm.*

Pennsylvania. *Archives.* First Series, Vol. 12; Second Series, Vol. 6.

Phillips, Paul Chrisler. *The Fur Trade.*

Post, Christian Fredrich. *Journal,* in *Early Western Travels,* Vol. 1. Reuben G. Thwaites, ed.

Pouchot, Captain François. *Memoir of the State of War in North America.* Franklin B. Hough, trans.

Roosevelt, Theodore. *The Winning of the West.*

Sargent, Winthrop. *The History of an Expedition against Fort Duquesne.*

Schlarman, J. H. *From Quebec to New Orleans.*

Seaman, Narrative of. In Sargent's *History of an Expedition against Fort Duquesne.*

Severance, Frank H. *An Old Frontier of France.* Vol. 2.

Shea, John Gilmore. *Daniel H. M. L. de Beaujeu.*

Shepherd, William R. *Historical Atlas.*

Shippen Papers. *"Letters and Papers Relating Chiefly to Pennsylvania."* Joseph Balch, ed.

Sloan, William Milligan. *The French War and the Revolution.*

Stevens, Sylvester K. Ed. of *Wilderness Chronicles of Northwestern Pennsylvania,* with Donald H. Kent.

Stevens, Sylvester K. Ed. of *J.C.B. Travels in New France,* with Donald H. Kent and Emma Edith Woods.

Stobo, Major Robert. *Memoirs,* ed. by Neville B. Craig.

Stotz, Charles Morse. *Drums in the Forest: Defense in the Wilderness.* Historical Society of Western Pennsylvania.

Stotz, Charles Morse. *The Story of Fort Ligonier.* Fort Ligonier Memorial Foundation, Ligonier, Pa.

Thwaites, Reuben Gold. Ed. of *Early Western Travels,* 32 vols.

Turner, Frederick Jackson. *The Frontier in American History.*

Van Every, Dale. *Forth to the Wilderness.*

Villiers, Coulon de. *Journal,* in *The Olden Time,* Neville B. Craig, ed.

Walker, Dr. Thomas. *Journal.*

Wallace, Paul A. W. *Indians in Pennsylvania.* Pennsylvania Historical and Museum Commission.

Wallace, Paul A. W. *Historic Indian Paths in Pennsylvania.* Pennsylvania Historical and Museum Commission.

Washington, George. *The Diaries of George Washington,* John C. Fitzpatrick, ed.

Washington, George. *Washington's Diaries,* Joseph M. Toner, ed.

Washington, George. *Writings,* Jared Sparks, ed.

Weiser, Conrad. *Journal,* in *Early Western Travels,* Vol. 1. Reuben G. Thwaites, ed.

Wessler, Clark. *Indians of the United States.*

Wilderness Chronicles of Northwestern Pennsylvania, Ed. by Sylvester K. Stevens and Donald H. Kent.

Williamson, Peter. *French and Indian Cruelty.*

Winsor, Justin. *The Mississippi Basin.*

Wisconsin Historical Collections, Vol. XVII, "The French Regime in Wisconsin."

INDEX

Six Nations of the Iroquois (*cont.*):
  Duquesne and, 114, 136
  English and, 9n
  neutrality of, 27, 114, 136
  treaty with, 47
  vassal tribes and, 27
"Speech belts," 5
"Spendlowe's Road," 126
Spotswood, Capt. Robert, 175
Stanwix, Brig.-Gen. John, 215, 218
Stephen, Col. Adam, 103, 195, 216
Stotz, Charles Morse, 66, 221, 255
Strobo, Maj. Robert, 66, 103
  map by, 126
Swivel guns, 92n

Tanaghrisson, *see* Half King
Tecaughretango, 201n
Terrorization by French and Indians, 157–61, 172
Thompson, David, 124n
Thompson, William, 248
Treaty of Aix-la-Chapelle, 8
Treaty of Paris, 248
Treaty of Utrecht, 9n
Trent, Capt. William
  in building of Ft. Prince George, 40, 41–42
  recruiting by, 48–49, 77–78
  in Washington's expedition, 80–82
Turner, John, 174
Turtle's Heart, 230–31

Uniforms, 126n

Van Braam, Jacob, 3, 79
  at Ft. Necessity, 101–3
Van Buskirk, Arthur B., 255
Varin, Commissary, 104, 113–14
Vauban, Sebastiian le Prestre de, 21, 61, 69–70
Vaudreuil, Marquis de, 18
  on Dumas' raids, 173
  on Ft. Cumberland, 160–61
  on Ft. Duquesne, 156, 158, 210
  as Governor General, 115, 116, 117
  yields New France, 224

Venango, 5, 14, 43–45, 192, 251
  Braddock's strategy and, 110
  French reinforce, 44, 215
  new fort built, 116
  Pontiac's uprising and, 227, 233
  Washington's mission to, 3–6
  See also Ft. Machault
Vérendrye, Pierre Gaultier de La, 9
Verrazano, Giovanni di, 9
Villiers, Capt. Coulon de, 72, 93–104
  at Ft. Granville, 174
  revenge of, 93
Villiers, François, 93
Vilmonde, Beajeu de, 162n

Walker, Capt., 178
Walpole, Horace, 110
War of 1812, 252
Ward, Maj. Edward
  as ensign, 49–50, 58, 81
  at Ft. Pitt, 249
Washington, George, 87, 159, 171
  in Braddock's expedition, 127, 131, 140
  deserters and, 176
  as Dinwiddie's envoy, 3–8, 31–39
  in Forbes' campaign, 186, 189, 193, 196, 207–8
  on Ft. Duquesne, 59
  at Ft. Pitt, 248
  frontier defenses and, 167–68, 170–71, 175–77
  illness of, 134, 135n
  Joncaire and, 3–5
  journals of, 45, 87–88, 131
  in "Jumonville affair," 86–88, 103–4
  on McKees Rocks, 40
  map by, 32
  at Monongahela battle, 145, 147, 148
  recruiting by, 48, 77
  resigns commission, 109
  Saint-Pierre and, 6–7, 31–34
Wayne, Gen. "Mad Anthony," 251
Webb, Gen., 183
Weiser, Conrad, 26
Whiskey Rebellion, 252
Wolfe, Gen. James, 185

ABOUT THE AUTHOR

WALTER O'MEARA, a native of Minnesota, has for many years divided his time between Connecticut and Arizona. He was graduated from the University of Wisconsin School of Journalism, from which he received a citation for distinguished services in the field of journalism in 1957. He has been a newspaper reporter, advertising man, and author of ten previous books. In World War II he was Chief of the Planning Staff in The Office of Strategic Services (OSS).

Mr. O'Meara, having grown up on the St. Louis River, ancient highway of the *voyageurs,* has long been a student of the fur trade frontier. His first novel dealing with this phase of North American history, *The Grand Portage,* was a national best seller and won an award from The American Association for State and Local History.

The background of Mr. O'Meara's novels and historical writing has since ranged from the 18th Century Canadian fur trade and horse-logging era in Minnesota to the Spanish Colonial Regime in the Southwest and now the Anglo-French struggle for mastery of North America. He has thoroughly covered the ground of each of his books, traveling the old war roads with the Indians (he is a Courtes Oreilles Chippewa by adoption), living a *voyageur's* life on many Canadian canoe trips, retracing the routes of early Spanish military expeditions across the Great Plains, and exploring the sites of Fort Duquesne and Fort Necessity. "That, and recourse to the sources," he says, "is the only way to get *inside* your subject."

What happened at the forks of the Ohio between 1750 and 1760 profoundly affected the course of world history. It sparked a terrible global conflict. It helped decide the fate of empires.

Typogra

This first volume in the AMERICAN FORTS SERIES tells the story of two frontier forts, Fort Duquesne and Fort Pitt, and their part in the epic struggle between England and France for mastery of North America during the French and Indian Wars.

Young George Washington was one of the principal actors in this dramatic struggle. It was Washington, then a 21-year-old major, who delivered the ultimatum, sent by Governor Dinwiddie of the Virginia Colony, instructing the French to withdraw from the Ohio country. The French answer was to build Fort Duquesne where the city of Pittsburgh now stands. In the wilderness war that followed, Washington twice met the French on the battlefield, once in victory, once in defeat. O'Meara describes Washington as a man who had a "strong sense of public duty and an unlimited capacity for punishment."

Following Washington's unsuccessful attempt to capture Fort Duquesne, Gen Edward Braddock was ordered to march on the French fort with 1400 British regulars, accompanied by Lt. Col. George Washington, in command of 750 Colonials. With his regimental colors flying and his drums beating, Braddock was suddenly surrounded by a mixed force of French and Indian and was soundly defeated at the banks of the Monongahela, just a stone's throw from the fort.

The *fleur-de-lis* was now riding high in the Ohio country. The fierce Indian allies of the French had done much to thwart English military efforts by savagely attacking military expeditions and brutally massacring colonial frontier families. It was not until 1758 that Gen. Forbes and Col. Henry Bouquet finally engineered the crushing defeat of the French at Fort Duquesne.

In later years the fort lost its military importance and the city of Pittsburgh grew up around it.

An epilogue describes the city of Pittsburgh and brings the book up-to-date with an account of the city's remarkable renaissance in recent years.

Guns At The Forks represents a major contribution to the literature of early American history. Walter O'Meara, a master storyteller, thoroughly familiarized himself with the actual terrain on which the French and English fought and researched contemporary documents to make this narrative as complete and authentic as possible.

Illustrated with portraits, plans of Fort Duquesne and Fort Pitt, battle plans and historical maps, this volume combines firs rate scholarship with all the color and citement of a great historical novel.